EXERCISE SCIENCE

An Introduction to Health and Physical Education

Student Workbook/Lab Manual

Revised Edition

DEVELOPMENT TEAM FOR EXERCISE SCIENCE

Workbook/Lab Manual

Ted Temertzoglou, *Toronto District School Board*
Paul Challen, *Hamilton Author*
Jamie Nunn, *Hamilton-Wentworth District School Board*
Kim Parkes, *Hamilton-Wentworth District School Board*
Carolyn Temertzoglou, *Conference of Independent Schools*

The textbook *Exercise Science: An Introduction to Health and Physical Education* represents a long-term commitment to the teaching of physical education in Canada. To this end, we have provided this Student Workbook/Lab Manual, as well as a Teacher's Manual, and a set of PowerPoint slides. We have made every effort to ensure that these materials integrate closely with the textbook and we would welcome suggestions as to how to make these materials even better in subsequent editions.

Ontario Physical and Health Education Association

The writing and publishing team would like to thank the management and staff at Ophea (the Ontario Physical and Health Education Association) for their support at every stage of this project—from our early discussions about developing a textbook to match the PSE4U curriculum, to their input during the writing and reviewing process, to their endorsement and widespread promotion of the text. Without Ophea's support and assistance, the completion of the textbook and its supporting materials would not have been possible.

EXERCISE SCIENCE

An Introduction to Health and Physical Education
Student Workbook/Lab Manual
Revised Edition

Ted Temertzoglou

Paul Challen

Jamie Nunn

Kim Parkes

Carolyn Temertzoglou

THOMPSON EDUCATIONAL PUBLISHING, INC.
Toronto, Ontario

Information on how to obtain copies of this book may be obtained from:
Website: www.thompsonbooks.com
E-mail: publisher@thompsonbooks.com
Telephone: (416) 766-2763
Fax: (416) 766-0398

ISBN 978-1-55077-180-0

Credits:

Cover Photo: Donovan Bailey, 2000. The Canadian Press/Kevin Frayer
All text and photo references and credits are provided on the appropriate page in the text.

Illustrations not otherwise acknowledged have been provided by Bart Vallecoccia, B.Sc. AAM, Medical Illustrator (Toronto) and are copyrighted by him. Illustrations of bones, muscles, and joints were redrawn from illustrations provided courtesy of Bartleby, Inc. from *Henry Gray's Anatomy of the Human Body*. Philadelphia: Lea & Febiger, 1918; © 2000 copyright Bartleby. com, Inc.

The publisher and authors wish to thank David J. Sanderson Ph.D. for his assistance in developing the biomechanics exercises in Section 15. Professor Sanderson is with the UBC Biomechanics Laboratory in the School of Human Kinetics at University of British Columbia.

The publisher and authors also wish to thank the following individuals: Rowan Thompson, Jeff Claydon, and Kimberlee French. Their photos and video stills appear in the sections on Biomechanics and Motor Learning and Skills Development.

Publisher: Keith Thompson
Cover design: Elan Designs
Page design, graphic art, and special effects: Tibor Choleva
Production editor: Crystal J. Hall
Production coordinator: Christine Kwan
Copyeditor: Katy Bartlett

Every reasonable effort has been made to acquire permission for copyrighted materials used in this book and to acknowledge such permissions accurately. Any errors or omissions called to the publisher's attention will be corrected in future printings.

We acknowledge the support of the Government of Canada through the Book Publishing Industry Development Program for our publishing activities. We acknowledge the support of the Government of Ontario through the Ontario Media Development Corporation Book Initiative.

Printed in Canada.
5 6 7 8   16 15 14 13

Table of Contents

Introduction

Exercise Science: An Introduction to Health and Physical Education covers an extremely wide range of topics—from anatomy and physiology, to human movement and biomechanics, to social and ethical issues in sport. At first glance, all this may appear daunting. However, much that is presented in the textbook is in the form of an overview of key concepts and issues. Indeed, as you go through the course, you will likely want to consult other sources in order to deepen your knowledge of particular subjects. Later on, at college or university, you will find that many of these topics are academic sub-disciplines in themselves, with large numbers of research-level books and articles devoted to them.

Much like an athlete training to become better at his or her sport or skill, it is possible for you to develop a deeper understanding of the concepts presented in the textbook by engaging in "workouts" that test your knowledge and require you to do further research. You may be asked by your teacher to use the questions and exercises in this workbook as "practice sessions" leading up to the actual "competitions"—the essays and examinations that will be used to calculate your final mark for the course.

With that approach in mind, this Student Workbook/Lab Manual has been divided into sections that correspond to the sections of the textbook. Each section contains the following components designed to test and further your knowledge of the material presented in the text:

- **Learning Objectives**, which outline what you covered in the textbook;

- **Section Quizzes,** which are divided into multiple-choice, short-answer, and essay questions. These questions are designed to test your understanding of the central concepts in each section and demand further reflection and assimilation of key principles;

- **Terminology Review**, which will allow you to review the important words, phrases, and concepts presented in each section; and

- **Exercises and Lab Activities**, which encourage you to go beyond what you have learned in your *Exercise Science* textbook and to examine key topics in greater depth by conducting research, engaging in observation sessions, and applying what you have learned.

What's New in This Revised Edition:

This edition of the Student Workbook/Lab Manual includes several new features that will help you gain a deeper understanding of the exciting field of Exercise Science. Here are the main updates:

- **Textbook Preview**, which is a "scavenger hunt" that provides you with an overview of your *Exercise Science* textbook.

- **"Look in the Book" Feature**, which guides you to the page (or pages) in your *Exercise Science* textbook that pertains to the exercise at hand.

- **All-New Muscle Drawings** that leave lots of room for you to use a coloured pencil crayon to colour-code muscle names with the illustration of these muscles.

- **New CPAFLA Fitness Appraisals (3rd Edition)**, which were developed by the Canadian Physical Activity, Fitness & Lifestyle Approach (CPAFLA), and released by the Canadian Society of Exercise Physiologists (CSEP).

- **Biomechanical Analysis**. A new worksheet/ lab exercise designed to give you a working knowledge of the Seven Principles of Biomechanics.

- **Laminated Illustrations** that are included at the back of this workbook for your continued use. Keep these illustrations for future reference, especially if you are thinking of going into the health sciences field at college or university.

- **Looking for a Great Career?** At the back of this workbook you will find a chart that summarizes the range of exciting careers available to you in Kinesiology, Physical Education, Recreation & Leisure, and Health Education.

- **Student Website.** In addition to the revised workbook, we have created a new student website. Here you will find quizzes, tests (multiple choice and bell ringers), crossword puzzles, and PowerPoint slides for every section of your *Exercise Science* textbook. Ask your teacher how to access this website as a study aid and as a review.

Have fun with your Exercise Science course. There is no course quite like it, anywhere.

Previewing Your *Exercise Science* Textbook

Name:

Date:

You will need to return to your *Exercise Science* textbook time and time again during this course, so it is a good idea to know your way around it. This exercise will help you preview your textbook.

Mission: With your textbook close at hand, answer the following questions.

1. Which half of the *Exercise Science* textbook focuses more on anatomy/physiology?

2. Which half of the *Exercise Science* textbook focuses more on the social and historical aspects of Canadian sport?

3. The best way to view the overall contents of your *Exercise Science* textbook is to go to the "Table of Contents." Where will you find the Table of Contents?

4. The "Skeletal System" and the "Muscular System" are covered in which sections of the *Exercise Science* textbook?

5. "The Cardiovasular and Respiratory Systems" are covered in which section of the *Exercise Science* textbook?

6. "The Principles of Biomechanics" are covered in which section of the *Exercise Science* textbook?

7. "The Psychology of Sport" is covered in which section of the *Exercise Science* textbook?

8. "Women and Sport" is covered in which section of the *Exercise Science* textbook?

9. The "Key Terms" are singled out twice in each section of the *Exercise Science* textbook. First, they are highlighted in a list at the beginning of each section. How are the Key Terms made prominent again in each section?

10. There are five "Careers in *Exercise Science*" sections throughout the *Exercise Science* textbook. At what point in the textbook do these career exercises appear?

11. The definitions of all the Key Terms in the *Exercise Science* textbook can be found in the "Glossary." Where will you find the Glossary?

12. If a particular *Exercise Science* topic interests you and you want to know more, you will probably find a page reference to the topic in the "Index"? Where will you find the Index?

UNIT 1

INTRODUCTION TO ANATOMY AND PHYSIOLOGY

Simon Whitfield, 2000. THE CANADIAN PRESS/AP/David Guttenfelder

1

Introduction to Anatomy and Physiology: Principles & Terminology

Learning Objectives

The exercises in this section of the workbook will help to reinforce your knowledge of the following topics covered in the *Exercise Science* textbook:

- Basic terminology of anatomy and physiology
- The anatomical position
- Anatomical planes
- Anatomical axes
- Basic movements involving joints
- The ten biological systems of the human body

Section Quiz

Name: _Rose_   Date: _Sept. 13. 2015_

Multiple-Choice Questions

Mission: Circle the letter beside the answer that you believe to be correct.

1. The sagittal plane

    (a) is perpendicular to the longitudinal axis

    (b) is the only plane that does not form a 90-degree relationship with either axis

    (c) segments the body into a distinct right and left side

    (d) is also known as the "frontal plane"

2. The frontal plane

    (a) is perpendicular to the longitudinal axis

    (b) is also known as the "coronal plane"

    (c) segments the body into a distinct right and left side

    (d) can only be seen from the anatomical position

3. The transverse plane

    (a) is perpendicular to the longitudinal axis

    (b) is also known as the "antero-posterior plane"

    (c) bisects the body into front and back segments

    (d) involves movements of adduction

4. From the anatomical position, flexion occurs in the

    (a) horizontal axis and sagittal plane

    (b) longitudinal axis and transverse plane

    (c) antero-posterior axis and frontal plane

    (d) none of the above

5. From the anatomical position, extension occurs in the

    (a) horizontal axis and sagittal plane

    (b) longitudinal axis and transverse plane

    (c) antero-posterior axis and frontal plane

    (d) none of the above

6. The movement of medial rotation involves

    (a) the thumb coming into contact with a finger

    (b) moving in a posterior (backward) direction

    (c) inwardly moving the anterior surface of a limb

    (d) pointing your feet out to the side

7. The movement of supination involves

    (a) raising the lateral border of the foot

    (b) a combination of flexion, extension, abduction, and adduction

    (c) movement away from the median plane, occurring in the frontal plane

    (d) lateral rotation of the hand and forearm such that the palm faces forward

Short-Answer Questions

Mission: Briefly answer the following questions in the space provided:

1. What is the distinction between the fields of anatomy and physiology?

    Anatomy – study of structure of body parts
    Physiology – study of functions and relationships
    of body parts.

2. On what do exercise physiologists concentrate their research?

    Focus on the application of bodily movements.

3. How is the body positioned in the anatomical position?

    ① Body in an upright standing position
    ② Face and feet pointing forward
    ③ Arms at side and forearms fully supinated.

4. What is the position of the axis of rotation in relation to the plane of movement?

    The position of axis is perpendicular
    to the plane of movement.

5. Around which axis and through which plane does rotation of extremities and axial rotation of the spine occur?

    Transverse plane – longitudinal axis

6. What movement are you performing and which joint are you using when you stand on your "tip-toes"?

    Plantar flexion – Calcaneus

Essay Questions

Mission: On a separate piece of paper, develop a 100-word response to the following questions.

1. Explain why it is important for an athlete to have a basic understanding of all anatomical terminology.

2. State the opposite actions of all of the following movements and give an example of where they occur: flexion, abduction, external rotation, pronation, retraction, plantar flexion, and depression.

3. Choose any four of the ten biological systems described in the *Exercise Science* textbook and summarize their importance to the human body.

Terminology Review

Defining Key Terms

Mission: Briefly explain the meaning of the following key terms:

Name:
Rose

Date:
Sept. 13. 2015

Key Term	Definition
Anatomy	- study of structure of body parts.
Physiology	- study of functions and relationships of body parts.
Exercise physiology	- study of physiological systems and how they apply to wellness and health.
Anatomical position	- the standard standing point of the human body. ↳ body in an upright standing position ↳ face and feet pointing forward. ↳ arms at side and forearms fully supinated.
Anatomical planes/axes	ANATOMICAL PLANES - relate to positions in space and are at right angles to one another ↳ Transverse ↳ Sagittal ↳ Frontal ANATOMICAL AXES - describe the direction of movement at joints ↳ Longitudinal ↳ Horizontal ↳ Antero-posterior
Flexion/extension	FLEXION - decreasing the angle between the two bones EXTENSION - increasing the angle between the two bones.
Abduction/adduction	ABDUCTION - moving away from the midline ADDUCTION - moving towards the midline
Internal/external rotation	INTERNAL ROTATION - rotating inward towards the midline EXTERNAL ROTATION - rotating outward away from the midline
Circumduction	- circular motion combining flexion, extension, abduction and adduction.

Supination/pronation	SUPINATION - lateral rotation of hand and forearm PRONATION - medial rotation of the hand and forearm
Protraction/retraction	PROTRACTION - moving in a forward (anterior) position RETRACTION - moving in a backward (posterior) position
Dorsiflexion/ plantar flexion	DORSIFLEXION - pointing the foot upward (decreasing angle) PLANTAR FLEXION - pointing the foot downward (increasing angle)
Eversion/inversion	EVERSION - sole of the foot is turned outward (pinky toe goes out) INVERSION - sole of the foot is turned inward (big toe goes out)
Elevation/depression	ELEVATION - raising up to a more superior position DEPRESSION - pulling down to a more inferior position
Opposition/reposition	OPPOSITION - when the thumb comes into contact with one of the other fingers. REPOSITION - when thumb is returned to anatomical position.

Anatomical Planes and Anatomical Axes

Mission: Describe the anatomical plane and axis of rotation involved in the actions listed below.

Movement of the body during the swinging of a bat for a line drive in baseball	Plane: Transverse Axis: Longitudinal
Movement of the body during the back flip of a gymnast	Plane: Sagittal Axis: Horizontal
Movement of the body during a quadruple jump in ice skating	Plane: Transverse Axis: Longitudinal
Movement of the body when bending over to touch the toes	Plane: Sagittal Axis: Horizontal
Movement of the body when performing a cartwheel	Plane: Frontal Axis: Antero-posterior

The Anatomical Position

The "anatomical position" is the universally accepted starting point for anatomical description and analysis.

Mission: To gain familiarity with the features of the anatomical position, axes, and planes, label the four illustrations below.

Name: _Rose_

Date: _Sept. 13. 2015_

Look in the Book! Page: 3

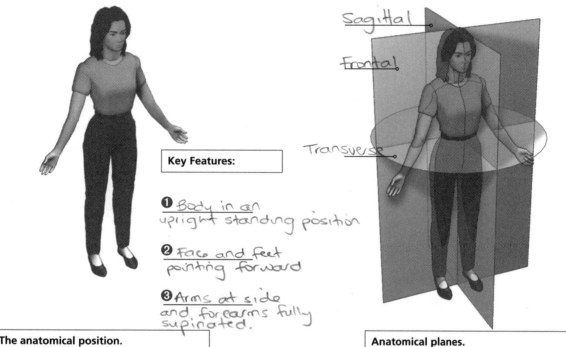

Key Features:

❶ _Body in an upright standing position_

❷ _Face and feet pointing forward_

❸ _Arms at side and forearms fully supinated._

The anatomical position.

Sagittal

Frontal

Transverse

Anatomical planes.

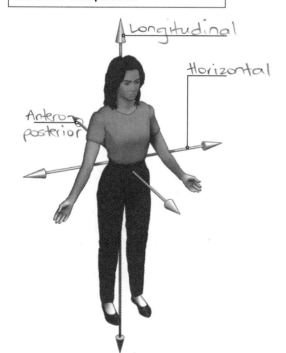

Longitudinal

Horizontal

Anterior posterior

Anatomical axes.

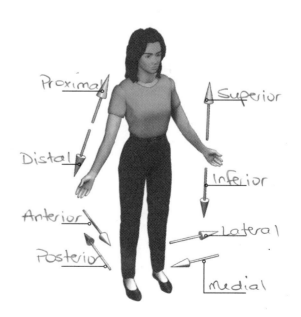

Proximal

Distal

Anterior

Posterior

Superior

Inferior

Lateral

Medial

Terms of direction and body position.

Movements Involving a Joint

The basic types of movement that occur at joints can be described by using the appropriate terminology.

Mission: Use the appropriate terms to label the movements that occur at each joint featured in the illustrations below.

Name:
Rose

Date:
Sept. 13. 2015

Look in the Book! Page: 5

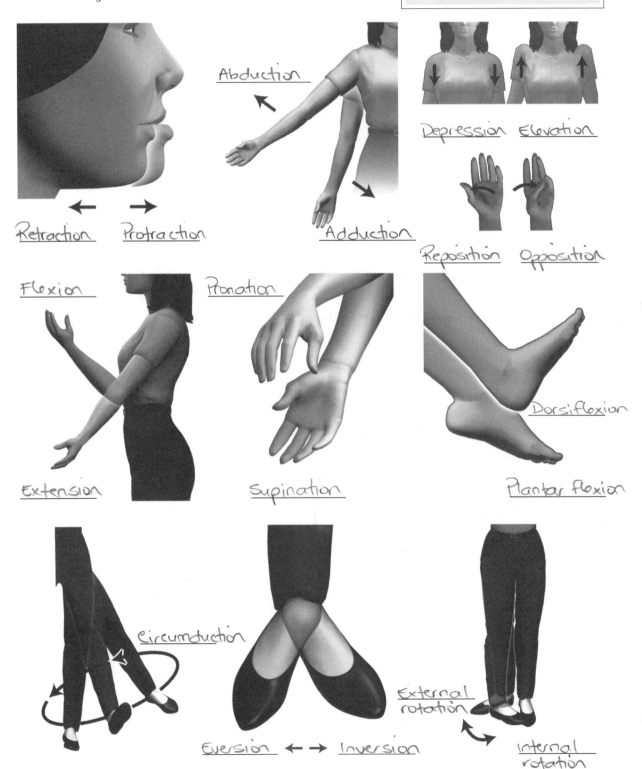

Abduction

Retraction   Protraction

Adduction

Depression   Elevation

Reposition   Opposition

Flexion

Pronation

Extension

Supination

Dorsiflexion

Plantar flexion

Circumduction

Eversion ← → Inversion

External rotation

Internal rotation

2

The Skeletal System

Tammy Sutton-Brown, 2000. THE CANADIAN PRESS/AP/Rick Havner

Learning Objectives

The exercises in this section of the workbook will help to reinforce your knowledge of the following topics covered in the *Exercise Science* textbook:

- The role and functions of the skeleton in the human body
- The human skeleton's basic structure and composition
- The five types of human bones
- The names and locations of the body's key bones and bone structures
- The concepts of bone landmarks and insertions, and key landmark/insertion sites throughout the body
- The process of ossification and bone formation
- Epiphyseal or growth plates of bones
- The main types of bone fractures
- How bones heal
- Bone disease, stress fractures, and the effects of aging

Section Quiz

Name: _____ Date: _____

Multiple-Choice Questions

Mission: Circle the letter beside the answer that you believe to be correct.

1. The appendicular skeleton
   (a) features the sternum as its central aspect
   (b) is the division of the skeleton from which all muscles originate
   (c) can only be seen from the anterior view
   (d) includes the limbs and plays a key role in allowing us to move

2. The structure found on the ends of long bones is
   (a) periosteum
   (b) diaphysis
   (c) articulating cartilage
   (d) bone marrow

3. Tendons usually unite and attach to
   (a) periosteum
   (b) diaphysis
   (c) articulating cartilage
   (d) bone marrow

4. Which of these muscles originate on the ischial tuberosity?
   (a) semitendinosus, semifemoris, and biceps femoris
   (b) vastus lateralis, vastus medialis, and rectus femoris
   (c) semitendinosus, semimembranosus, and biceps femoris
   (d) gracilis, pectineus, and adductor brevis

5. This muscle originates on the anterior inferior iliac spine.
   (a) iliopsoas
   (b) sartorius
   (c) rectus femoris
   (d) psoas minor

6. This muscle inserts on the radial tuberosity.
   (a) coracobrachialis
   (b) brachioradialis
   (c) triceps brachii
   (d) biceps brachii

7. The os coxae consists of the
   (a) ilium, pubis, and ischium
   (b) symphysis pubis, obturator foramen, and acetabulum
   (c) anterior superior iliac spine, anterior inferior iliac spine. and sacrum
   (d) Ilium, pubis, and sacrum

Short-Answer Questions

Mission: Briefly answer the following questions in the space provided:

1. List the five functions of the skeletal system.

   _____

2. Why is the axial skeleton so important to body movement?

   _____

3. Name the five types of bones and give an example of each.

   _____

4. What are the functions of the periosteum, medullary cavity, and bone marrow?

   _____

5. Describe the role played by osteoblasts in the formation of compact bone.

   _____

6. When is the process known as bone remodelling most active? Why?

   _____

7. Name and describe the three kinds of fractures?

   _____

8. Who is particularly vulnerable to the condition known as osteoporosis and why?

   _____

Essay Questions

Mission: On a separate piece of paper, develop a 100-word response to the following questions.

1. What are some habits and behaviours that can help us to maintain and strengthen our skeletal systems?

2. Explain the processes of bone formation and bone remodelling in the human body.

3. Explain the significance of the presence of an epiphyseal line and epiphyseal plate.

Terminology Review

Defining Key Terms

Name:
Date:

Mission: Briefly explain the meaning of the following key terms:

Key Term	Definition
Skeleton	
Axial skeleton	
Appendicular skeleton	
Articulating cartilage	
Periosteum	
Medullary cavity	
Compact bone	
Diaphysis/epiphysis	

Cancellous bone	
Cortex	
Trabeculae	
Ossification	
Bone remodelling	
Epiphyseal plates/lines	
Simple, compound, and comminuted fractures	
Stress fracture	
Osteoporosis	

Anatomy of a Long Bone

The long bone is the most familiar of the five basic bone types. Examples of long bones are the femur, fibula, and tibia.

Mission: To gain familiarity of the composition of the long bone, label the main parts on the illustration below (some labels may be used twice) by using the terms on the left-hand side of this page.

Name: Rose

Date: Oct. 2 2015

Look in the Book! Page: 12

Labels

- ☑ Cartilage
- ☑ Cancellous bone
- ☑ Diaphysis
- ☑ Epiphysis
- ☑ Medullary cavity
- ☑ Periosteum
- ☑ Compact bone

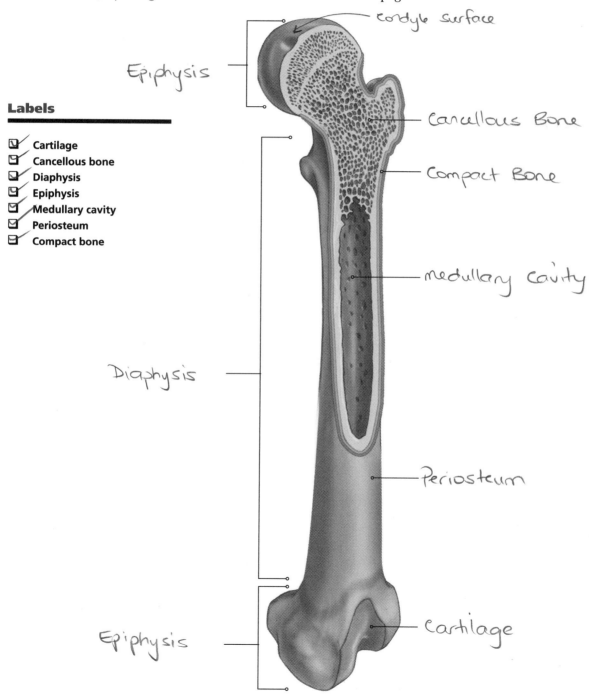

Handwritten labels on illustration: condyle surface, Epiphysis, Cancellous Bone, Compact Bone, medullary cavity, Diaphysis, Periosteum, Epiphysis, Cartilage

The composition of a long bone.

The Body's Key Bones

There are several different types of bone, usually classified with respect to their shape and size.

Mission: Label the illustrations on the following three pages using the list of labels provided on each page. Some labels may need to be used more than once.

Name:

Rose

Date:

Sept. 15. 2015

Look in the Book!
Pages: 11, 14–15

- ☑ **Irregular**
- ☑ **Flat**
- ☑ **Long**
- ☑ **Short**
- ☑ **Sesamoid**

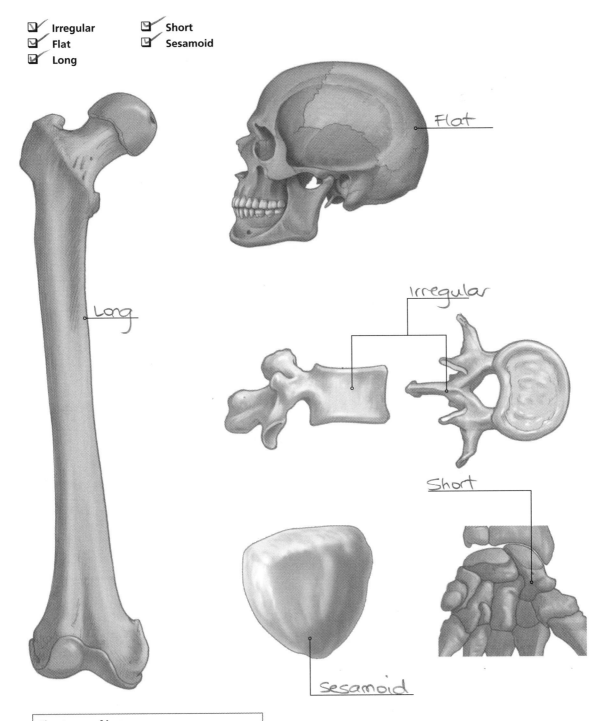

Flat

Long

Irregular

Short

Sesamoid

Five types of bones.

Sept. 14. 2015

Labels

The human skeleton (anterior view).

☑ 12 Ribs
  (7 True; 3 False; 2 Floating)
☑ Carpals
☑ Clavicle
☑ Costal Cartilage
☑ Femur
☑ Fibula
☑ Frontal Bone
☑ Humerus

☑ Ilium
☑ Mandible
☑ Manubrium
☑ Metatarsals
☑ Maxilla
☑ Metacarpals
☑ Patella
☑ Phalanges (digits)
☑ Radius

☑ Sacrum
☑ Sternum
☑ Symphysis Pubis
☑ Talus
☑ Temporal Bone
☑ Tibia
☑ Ulna
☑ Xiphoid Process
☑ Zygomatic Bone

1 Frontal Bone
2 Temporal Bone
3 Zygomatic Bone
4 Xiphoid Process
5 12 Ribs
6 Sacrum
7 Carpals
8 Metacarpals
9 Phalanges (digits)
10 Fibula
11 Tibia
12 Maxilla
13 Mandible
14 Clavicle
15 Manubrium
16 Sternum
17 Costal Cartilage
18 Humerus
19 Radius (thumb side)
20 Ilium
21 Ulna
22 Symphysis Pubis
23 Femur
24 Patella
25 Talus
26 Metatarsals
27 Phalanges (digits)

The human skeleton (posterior view).

Labels

- ☑ Calcaneus
- ☑ Cervical Spine (C1–C7)
- ☑ Coccyx
- ☑ Femur
- ☑ Fibula

- ☑ Humerus
- ☑ Ilium
- ☑ Lumbar (L1–L5)
- ☑ Occipital Bone
- ☑ Parietal Bones

- ☑ Sacrum
- ☑ Sagittal Suture
- ☑ Scapula
- ☑ Thoracic Spine (T1–T12)
- ☑ Tibia

1 Sagittal Suture

2 Cervical Spine (C1-C7)

3 Thoracic Spine (T1-T12)

4 Lumbar (L1-L5)

5 Sacrum

6 Parietal Bones

7 Occipital Bone

8 Scapula

9 Humerus

10 Ilium

11 Coccyx

12 Femur

13 Tibia

14 Fibula

15 Calcaneus

Bone Landmarks

The specific locations at which major muscles, ligaments, or other connective tissue attach to bone are known as "landmarks."

Mission: To strengthen your understanding of the body's key bones and bone landmarks, label the illustrations on the following pages using the list of labels provided on each page. Some labels may need to be used more than once.

Name: Rose

Date: Sept. 15. 2015

Look in the Book! Pages: 16–28

Labels

- ☑ External auditory meatus
- ☑ Frontal bone
- ☑ Mandible
- ☑ Mastoid process
- ☑ Maxilla
- ☑ Nasal bone
- ☑ Nuchal line
- ☑ Occipital bone
- ☑ Parietal bone
- ☑ Temporal bone
- ☑ Zygomatic bone

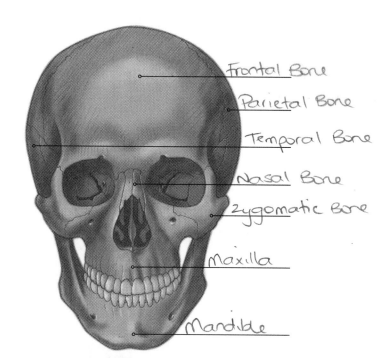

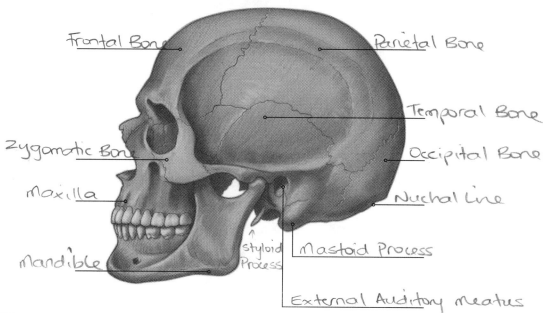

Bones of the skull, anterior and lateral views.

The vertebral column, lateral view.

Labels

☑ Atlas
☑ Axis
☑ Cervical region
☑ Coccyx
☑ Fifth lumbar vertebra

☑ First lumbar vertebra
☑ Intervertebral disk
☑ Lumbar region
☑ Sacral and coccygeal region
☑ Sacrum

☑ Seventh cervical vertebra
☑ Thoracic region
☑ Twelfth thoracic vertebra

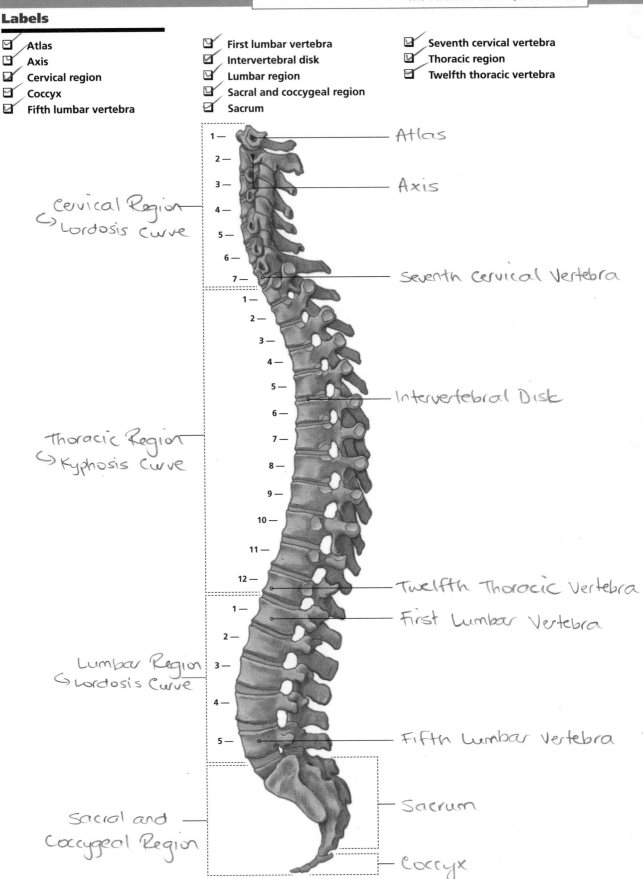

Cervical Region
↳ Lordosis Curve

Thoracic Region
↳ Kyphosis Curve

Lumbar Region
↳ Lordosis Curve

Sacral and
Coccygeal Region

1 — Atlas

3 — Axis

7 — Seventh Cervical Vertebra

5 — Intervertebral Disk

12 — Twelfth Thoracic Vertebra

1 — First Lumbar Vertebra

5 — Fifth Lumbar Vertebra

Sacrum

Coccyx

Sept 18, 2015

Labels

- [x] Body
- [x] Clavicle
- [x] First thoracic vertebra
- [x] Manubrium
- [x] Scapula
- [x] Seven true ribs
- [x] Sternum
- [x] Three false ribs
- [x] Two floating ribs
- [x] Xiphoid process

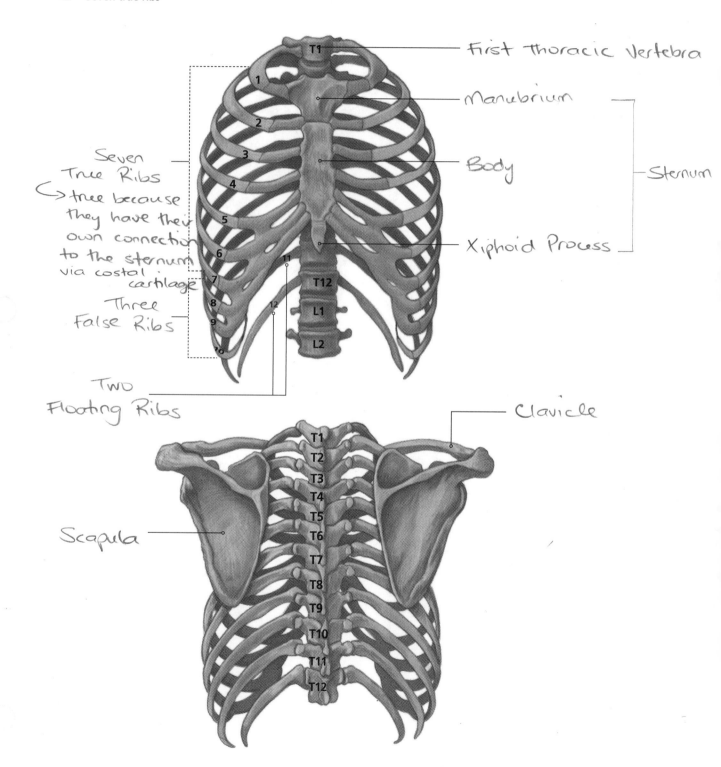

First Thoracic Vertebra

Manubrium

Body

Sternum

Xiphoid Process

Seven True Ribs
↳ true because they have their own connection to the sternum via costal cartilage

Three False Ribs

Two Floating Ribs

Clavicle

Scapula

Labels

☑ **Acromion process**
☑ **Acromion**
☑ **Coracoid process**
☑ **Glenoid cavity**
☑ **Glenoid fossa**
☑ **Inferior angle**

☑ **Infraglenoid tubercle**
☑ **Infraspinous fossa**
☑ **Lateral border**
☑ **Medial border**
☑ **Scapular notch**
☑ **Scapular spine**

☑ **Subscapular fossa**
☑ **Superior angle**
☑ **Supraglenoid tubercle**
☑ **Supraspinous fossa**

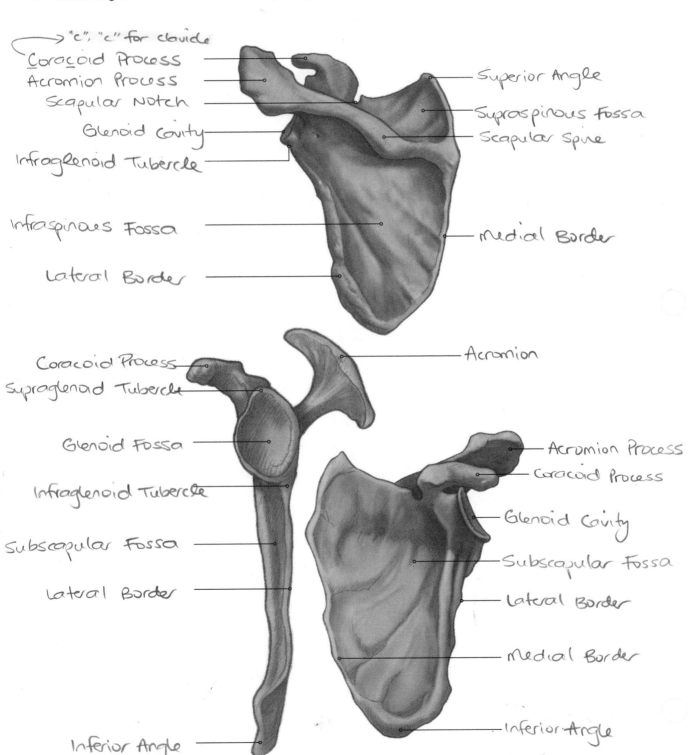

"c", "c" for clavicle
Coracoid Process
Acromion Process
Scapular Notch
Glenoid Cavity
Infraglenoid Tubercle
Infraspinous Fossa
Lateral Border

Superior Angle
Supraspinous Fossa
Scapular Spine
Medial Border

Coracoid Process
Supraglenoid Tubercle
Glenoid Fossa
Infraglenoid Tubercle
Subscapular Fossa
Lateral Border
Inferior Angle

Acromion
Acromion Process
Coracoid Process
Glenoid Cavity
Subscapular Fossa
Lateral Border
Medial Border
Inferior Angle

Labels

☑ Capitulum
☑ Coronoid fossa
☑ Deltoid tuberosity
☑ Greater tubercle
☑ Head

☑ Intertubercular (bicipital groove)
☑ Lateral epicondyle
☑ Lesser tubercle
☑ Medial epicondyle

☑ Olecranon fossa
☑ Radial fossa
☑ Shaft
☑ Trochlea

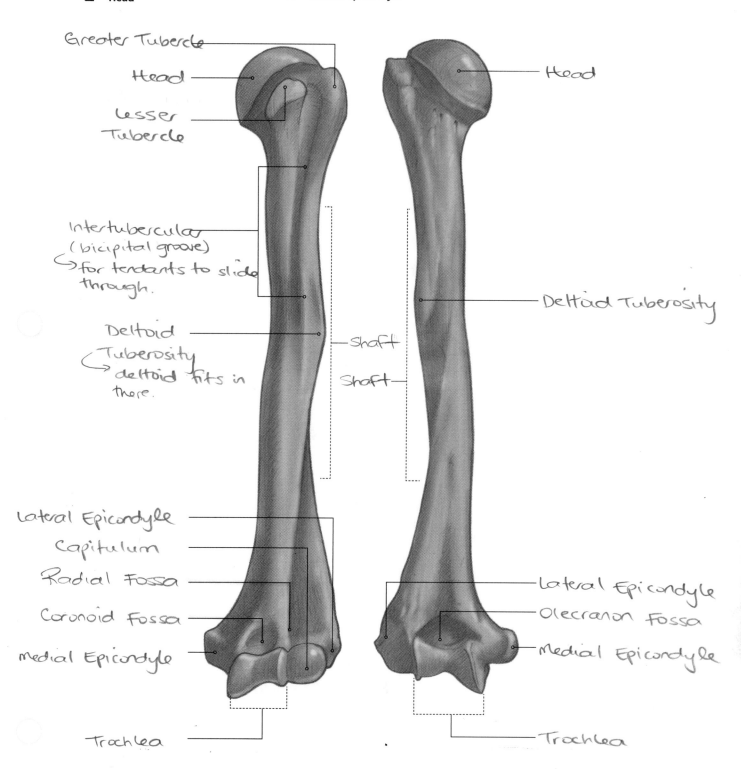

Greater Tubercle

Head

Lesser Tubercle

Intertubercular (bicipital groove)
↳ for tendonts to slide through.

Deltoid Tuberosity
↳ deltoid fits in there.

Shaft

Shaft

Head

Deltiod Tuberosity

Lateral Epicondyle
Capitulum
Radial Fossa
Coronoid Fossa
medial Epicondyle

Trochlea

Lateral Epicondyle
Olecranon Fossa
Medial Epicondyle

Trochlea

2. The Skeletal System ▷ **29**

Left ulna and radius, anterior view.

Labels

- ☑ Coronoid process
- ☑ Head
- ☑ Olecranon
- ☑ Olecranon process

- ☐ Radial notch of ulna
- ☑ Radial tuberosity
- ☐ Radius
- ☑ Styloid process of radius

- ☑ Styloid process of ulna
- ☑ Trochlear (semilunar) notch
- ☐ Ulna
- ☑ Ulna tuberosity

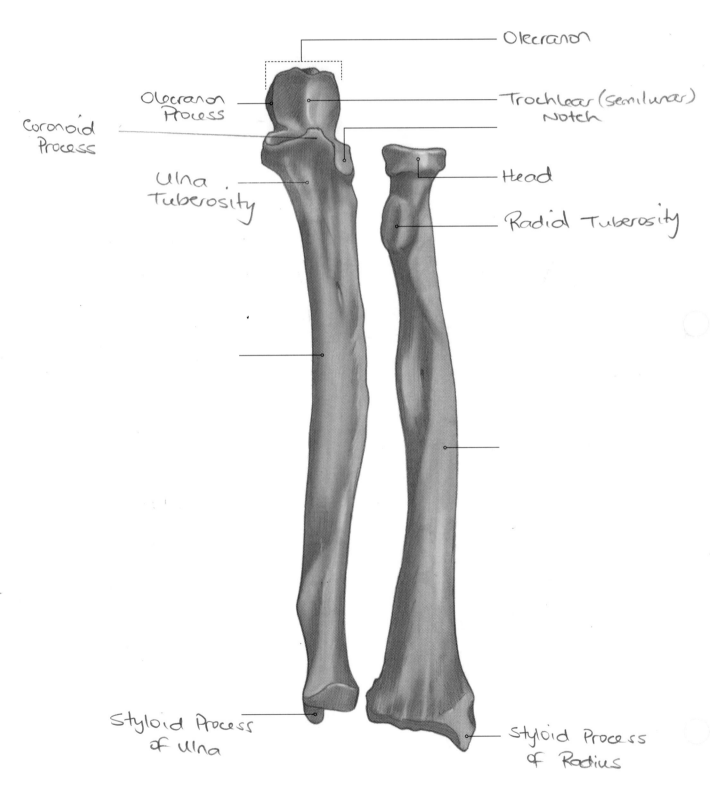

Olecranon

Olecranon Process

Coronoid Process

Trochlear (semilunar) Notch

Ulna Tuberosity

Head

Radial Tuberosity

Styloid Process of Ulna

Styloid Process of Radius

Labels

- ❑ Capite bone
- ❑ Carpals (distal)
- ❑ Carpals (proximal)
- ❑ Distal phalanx (of finger)
- ❑ Distal phalanx (of thumb)
- ❑ Hamate bone
- ❑ Lunate bone

- ❑ Metacarpals
- ❑ Middle phalanx (of finger)
- ❑ Phalanges (Digits)
- ❑ Pisiform bone
- ❑ Proximal phalanx (of finger)
- ❑ Proximal phalanx (of thumb)
- ❑ Radius

- ❑ Scaphoid bone
- ❑ Sesamoid bone
- ❑ Trapezium bone
- ❑ Trapezoid bone
- ❑ Triquetrum bone
- ❑ Ulna

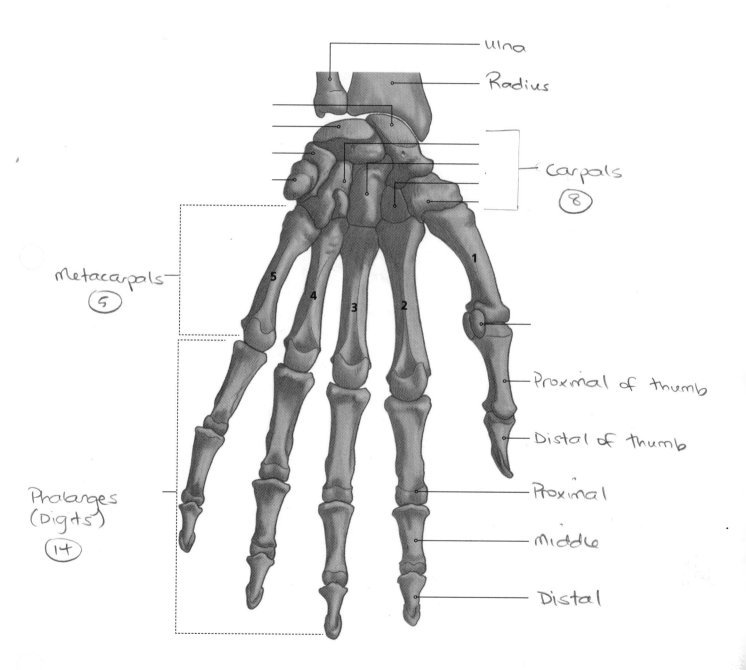

Ulna
Radius
Carpals (8)
Metacarpals (5)
Phalanges (Digts) (14)
Proximal of thumb
Distal of thumb
Proximal
Middle
Distal

Labels

- ☑ Acetabulum
- ☑ Anterior inferior iliac spine
- ☑ Anterior superior iliac spine
- ☑ Coccyx
- ☑ Crest of ilium
- ☑ Fifth lumbar verterbra
- ☑ Ilium
- ☑ Inferior ramis of pubis
- ☑ Ischial spine
- ☑ Ischial tuberosity
- ☑ Ischium
- ☑ Obturator foramen
- ☐ Os coxae
- ☑ Posterior superior iliac spine
- ☑ Pubis
- ☑ Sacroiliac joint
- ☑ Sacrum
- ☑ Superior ramis of pubis
- ☑ Symphysis pubis
- ☑ Posterior inferior iliac spine

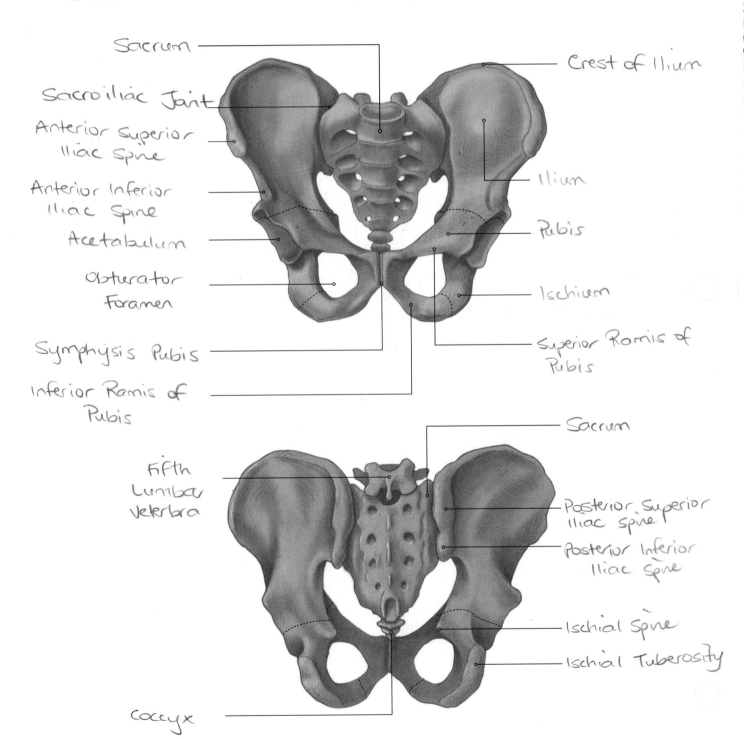

Sacrum
Sacroiliac Joint
Anterior Superior Iliac Spine
Anterior Inferior Iliac Spine
Acetabulum
Obturator Foramen
Symphysis Pubis
Inferior Ramis of Pubis
Fifth Lumbar Veterbra
Coccyx

Crest of Ilium
Ilium
Pubis
Ischium
Superior Ramis of Pubis
Sacrum
Posterior Superior Iliac Spine
Posterior Inferior Iliac Spine
Ischial Spine
Ischial Tuberosity

Right femur, anterior and posterior views.

Labels

- ☑ Adductor tubercle
- ☐ Gluteal tuberosity
- ☑ Greater trochanter
- ☑ Head
- ☐ Intercondylar fossa
- ☐ Intertrochanteric crest

- ☐ Intertrochanteric line
- ☑ Lateral condyle
- ☑ Lateral epicondyle
- ☑ Lesser trochanter
- ☑ Linea aspera
- ☑ Medial condyle

- ☑ Medial epicondyle
- ☑ Neck
- ☐ Patellar groove
- ☐ Pectineal line
- ☑ Shaft

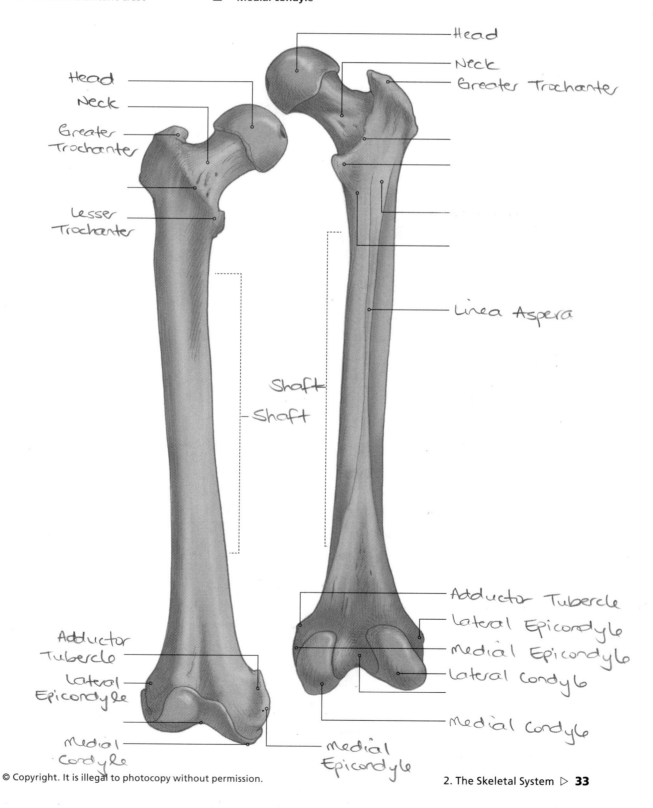

Head
Neck
Greater Trochanter
Lesser Trochanter
Shaft
Adductor Tubercle
Lateral Epicondyle
Medial Condyle

Head
Neck
Greater Trochanter
Linea Aspera
Shaft
Adductor Tubercle
Lateral Epicondyle
Medial Epicondyle
Lateral Condyle
Medial Condyle

Sept. 28. 2015

Labels

- ☑ Anterior crest
- ☑ Fibula
- ☑ Head
- ☐ Intercondylar eminence
- ☑ Lateral condyle
- ☑ Lateral condyle of tibia
- ☑ Lateral malleolus
- ☑ Medial condyle
- ☑ Medial condyle of tibia
- ☑ Medial malleolus
- ☑ Tibia
- ☑ Tibial tuberosity

Lateral condyle

Medial condyle

Tibial Tuberosity

Lateral Epicondyle of Tibia

Head

Medial Epicondyle of Tibia

Tibial Tuberosity

Anterior Crest

Fibula

Tibia

Lateral Malleolus

Medial Malleolus

Labels

- ☑ Calcaneus
- ☐ Cuboid
- ☑ Distal phalanx
- ☑ Distal phalanx (of great toe)
- ☐ Intermediate cuneiform
- ☐ Lateral cuneiform
- ☐ Medial cuneiform
- ☑ Metatarsals
- ☑ Middle phalanx
- ☑ Navicular
- ☑ Phalanges (Digits)
- ☑ Promixal phalanx
- ☑ Proximal phalanx (of great toe)
- ☑ Talus
- ☑ Tarsals

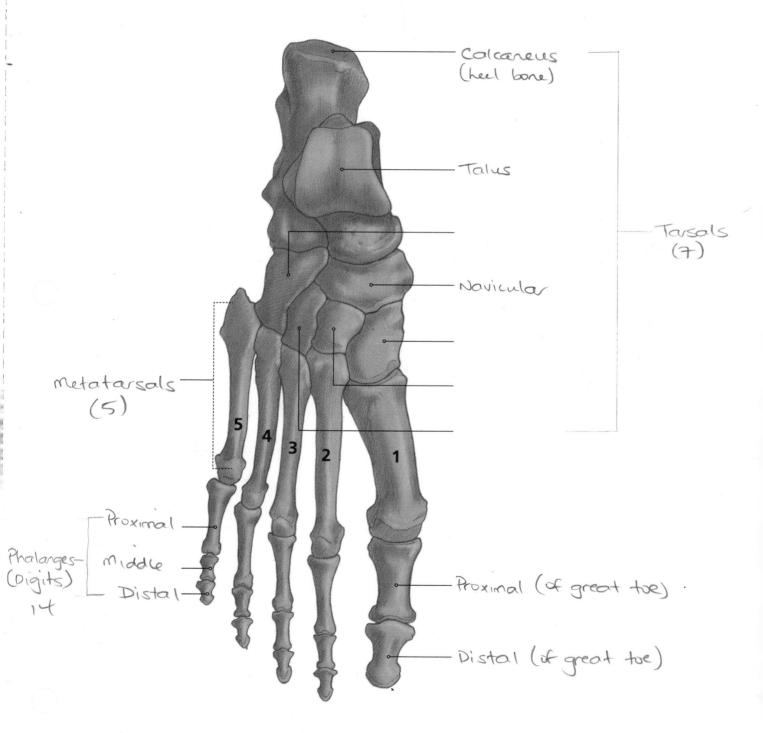

Calcaneus (heel bone)

Talus

Navicular

Tarsals (7)

Metatarsals (5)

5 4 3 2 1

Phalanges (Digits) 14

Proximal
Middle
Distal

Proximal (of great toe)

Distal (of great toe)

Crossword on the Skeletal System

Across

1. The correct anatomical name for the longest bone in the body
3. This type of bone fracture results from a major blow
7. Skeletal division central to human movement
8. As well as protecting vital organs, the skeleton provides this for the body
10. Cells produced in the marrow of bones
11. Girdle connecting the trunk and legs
14. Bone-forming cells
17. The seven bones that make up the ankle
18. Correct anatomical term for the bone that protects the knee
19. Anatomical term for upper arm bone
20. The sphenoid is classified as this type of bone
21. This bone disease affects mainly women
23. Skeletal division composed of the spine, much of the skull, and the rib cage
24. What some of the body's 300-plus bones do over time

Down

2. Disease characterized by defective bone growth
4. Bottom bone of the skull
5. Another name for "growth" plates
6. Muscle that inserts above the styloid process of the radius
8. The Greek word meaning "dried up"
9. Muscles that are centrally located and provide stability and support
12. View of skeleton from the rear
13. Division of the skeleton comprising the lower jaw and branchial arches
15. Bone that has a landmark called the coracoid process
16. The mineral of which bones are primarily composed
22. Key bone that consists of four fused vertebra

Bone Landmarks—Review Exercise

Name:

Date:

This exercise will further your understanding of bones and bone landmarks.

Mission: Review the illustrations on the previous pages and locate the landmarks listed below and on the next page. Place a check mark in the box once you have found it, and colour-code the box as well as the area of the bone.

Bone	Important Landmarks
Skull	❏ mastoid process
	❏ nuchal line
Vertebral column	❏ cervical
	❏ thoracic
	❏ lumbar
Sternum	❏ manubrium
	❏ body
	❏ xiphoid process
Clavicle	❏ body
Rib cage	❏ ribs 1–12
Scapula	❏ coracoid process
	❏ acromion process
	❏ supraglenoid tubercle
	❏ infraglenoid tubercle
	❏ spine of scapula
	❏ lateral border
	❏ inferior angle
	❏ superior angle
	❏ medial border
	❏ supraspinous fossa
	❏ infraspinous fossa
	❏ subscapular fossa

Humerus	☐ greater tubercle
	☐ lesser tubercle
	☐ intertubercular groove
	☐ deltoid tuberosity
	☐ surface
	☐ medial epicondyle
	☐ lateral epicondyle
Radius	☐ radial tuberosity
	☐ styloid process
	☐ surface
Wrist and hand	☐ surface
	☐ metacarpals
Ulna	☐ surface
	☐ olecranon
	☐ coronoid process
Pelvic girdle	☐ iliac crest
	☐ sacrum
	☐ anterior superior iliac spine
	☐ anterior inferior iliac spine
	☐ pubic crest
	☐ pubis
	☐ ilium
	☐ ischial tuberosity
Femur	☐ surface
	☐ greater trochanter
	☐ lesser trochanter
	☐ medial condyle
	☐ lateral condyle
	☐ adductor tubercle
	☐ linea aspera
Tibia	☐ surface
	☐ medial condyle
	☐ lateral condyle
	☐ tibial tuberosity
Fibula	☐ body
	☐ head
Calcaneus/tarsals	☐ posterior side

Daniel Igali, 2000. *THE CANADIAN PRESS/COA*

3

The Muscular System

Learning Objectives

The exercises in this section of the workbook will help to reinforce your knowledge of the following topics covered in the *Exercise Science* textbook:

- The number of muscles in the human body
- The three types of muscles (skeletal, cardiac, and smooth) and their unique roles in the muscular system
- Muscle-fibre types
- The neuromuscular system and the relationship between the muscles and the nervous system
- The motor unit and the concept of muscle twitch
- The all-or-none principle
- How muscles are named, and the basic naming groups within the muscular system
- The ways in which muscles attach to bones
- The concept of agonist and antagonist muscles
- The origin and insertion of muscles throughout the skeletal system
- Muscular contraction, and the three basic kinds of contraction
- The sliding filament theory of muscle contraction
- How muscle fibre responds to physical training
- The process of excitation-contraction coupling
- The location of key muscles and muscle groups throughout the body
- Ways in which the body's major muscle groups can be exercised, and the role of resistance training as a way of exercising muscles

Section Quiz

Name: _____ Date: _____

Multiple-Choice Questions

Mission: Circle the letter beside the answer that you believe to be correct.

1. Which of the following muscles dorsiflexes the ankle?

   (a) gastrocnemius
   (b) soleus
   (c) gluteus maximus
   (d) tibialis anterior

2. Which of the following muscles flex the knee?

   (a) semitendinosus, semimembranosus, and rectus femoris
   (b) vastus lateralis, vastus intermedius, vastus medialis, and rectus femoris
   (c) supraspinatus, infraspinatus, teres minor, and subscapularis
   (d) none of the above

3. Which of the following muscles originates on the coracoid process?

   (a) pronator teres
   (b) brachioradialis
   (c) coracobrachialis
   (d) triceps brachii

4. Which of these muscles insert on the tibial tuberosity?

   (a) semitendinosus, semifemoris, and biceps femoris
   (b) vastus lateralis, vastus medialis, vastus intermedius, and rectus femoris
   (c) semitendinosus, semimembranosus, and biceps femoris
   (d) gracilis, pectineus, and adductor brevis

5. Which muscles make up the rotator cuff?

   (a) trapezius, deltoid, and latissimus dorsi
   (b) biceps brachii, triceps brachii, and rectus abdominis
   (c) supraspinatus, infraspinatus, teres minor, and subscapularis
   (d) iliopsoas, psoas major, and biceps brachii

6. The primary function of rectus abdominis is

   (a) trunk elevation
   (b) trunk depression
   (c) trunk extension
   (d) trunk flexion

7. The anterior muscles of the forearm serve primarily as

   (a) wrist flexors
   (b) wrist extensors
   (c) elbow extensors
   (d) pronators

Short-Answer Questions

Mission: Briefly answer the following questions in the space provided:

1. Which two types of muscle tissue are referred to as being "striated" and why?

   _____

2. Which parts of the body are surrounded by smooth muscles?

   _____

3. Explain the "all-or-none" principle in relation to muscle contraction.

   _____

4. What lies beneath the endomysium of skeletal muscle and what does it contain?

   _____

5. What role do myosin and actin play in muscle contraction? What happens to the sarcomere in this process?

   _____

6. List and describe the five properties of muscle fibres.

   _____

   _____

   _____

   _____

   _____

Essay Questions

Mission: On a separate piece of paper, develop a 100-word response to the following questions.

1. Describe the sliding filament theory of muscle contraction.

2. Describe the response of muscle fibres to training and detraining.

3. Describe the differences between isotonic, isometric, and isokinetic exercises.

Terminology Review

Defining Key Terms

Name:
Date:

Mission: Briefly explain the meaning of the following key terms:

Key Term	Definition
Muscle tissue	
Tendons	
Skeletal muscles	
Cardiac muscles	
Smooth muscles	
Neuromuscular system	
Muscle twitch	
Motor unit	
Neuromuscular junctions	
All-or-none principle	
Perimysium	

Epimysium	
Endomysium	
Sarcolemma	
Sarcoplasm	
Myofibrils	
Sarcomere	
Adductor muscles	
Abductor muscles	
Extensor muscles	
Flexor muscles	
Agonist muscle	
Antagonist muscle	

Origin and insertion	
Isotonic exercise	
Isometric exercise	
Isokinetic exercise	
Sliding filament theory	
Myosin crossbridges	
Adenosine triphosphate	
Transient/chronic hypertrophy	
Muscle atrophy	
Hyperplasia	
Excitation-contraction coupling	
Transverse tubulae system	
Troponin and tropomyosin	

Agonist and Antagonist Muscle Pairs

In a muscle pair, the agonist muscle is primarily responsible for the movement of a body part; the antagonist muscle counteracts, and lengthens when the agonist muscle contracts.

Name: Rose

Date: Oct. 14. 2015

Look in the Book! Pages: 38

Mission: Indicate the opposing muscle or muscle group in the table below.

Agonist	Antagonist
Triceps (elbow extension)	Biceps Brachii
Pectoralis major (flexion of arm)	Latissimus Dorsal
Hamstrings (flexion of knee)	Quadriceps (extension of knee)
Trapezius (retraction of the scapula)	Serratus anterior / Pectoralis minor
Gluteus maximus (hip extension)	Iliopsoas, sartorius, TFL, Rectus femoris
Erector spinae group (trunk extension)	Rectus abdominus
Gastrocnemius	Tibialis Anterior
Wrist flexors	Wrist extensors
Supinator	Pronator teres
Tibialis anterior	
Anterior deltoid	
Latissimus dorsi	
Iliacus	
Adductor magnus (hip adduction)	Glutes med. and min., TFL (hip abductors)
External obliques (flex + rotate trunk)	Quadratus lumborum (extend and laterally bend)
Infraspinatus (laterally rotates arm)	Subscapularis (medially rotates arm)
Rhomboids (retraction of scapula)	Serratus anterior (protraction of scapula)
Sternocleidomastoid (flexion of neck and lateral flexion)	Semispinalis capitis (extends neck), SCM on opposite side

The Structure of Skeletal Muscle

Skeletal muscles attach to bones by tendons and other tissue and are the most prevalent muscles in the human body.

Name:

Date:

Look in the Book! Pages: 36–37

Mission: To gain familiarity with how skeletal muscle is constructed, label the key parts of the muscle and muscle fibre on the diagram below. Some labels may need to be used more than once.

Labels

- ❏ Tendon
- ❏ Perimysium
- ❏ Epimysium
- ❏ Endomysium
- ❏ Sarcomere (partially contracted)
- ❏ Actin

- ❏ Muscle fibre
- ❏ Myofibril
- ❏ Myosin
- ❏ Sarcolemma (muscle membrane)
- ❏ Sarcoplasmic reticulum (web-like)
- ❏ Z-line

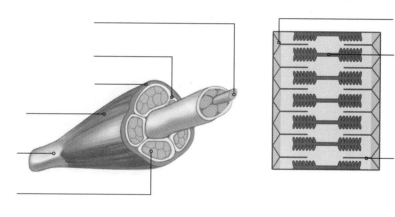

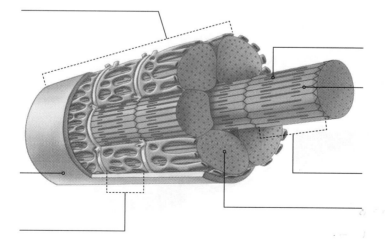

The structure of skeletal muscle.

The Neuromuscular System

The neuromuscular system is a general term used when referring to the complex linkage between the muscular system and the nervous system.

Mission: To gain familiarity with the components of the neuromuscular system and neuromuscular junction, label the illustrations below.

Name:

Date:
Oct. 30. 2015

Look in the Book! Pages: 34–35

Labels

☐ Direction of action potential
☑ Axon
☑ Axon terminal
☑ Dendrites
☐ Motor neuron
☐ Muscle fibres
☑ Neuron cell body

☐ Neuromuscular junction
☐ Receptor
☑ Neurotransmitter acelytcholine (ACh)
☐ Sarcolemma
☑ Synaptic cleft

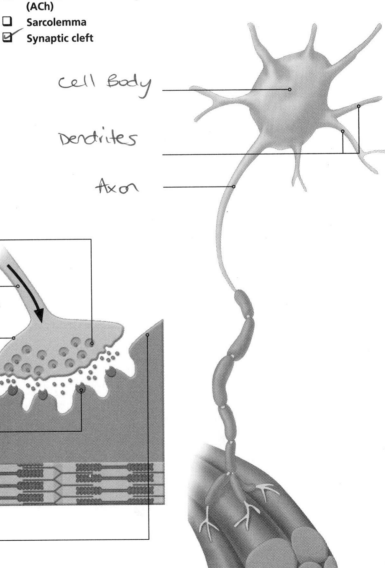

Cell Body

Dendrites

Axon

Neurotransmitter acelytcholine (ACH)

Axon of motor neuron

Axon Terminal/ Snaptic Knob

Synaptic cleft

Receptor for Arch

Sarcolemma

Muscle Fibres

Major Muscles of the Human Body

Major Muscles And Muscle Groups

Mission: Using the table provided, label the anterior and posterior muscles shown on the illustrations below.

Name:
Date:
Look in the Book! Pages: 44–45

1		9		16	
2		9		16	
3		10		17	
4		11		18	
5		12		19	
6		13		20	
7		14		21	
8		15		22	

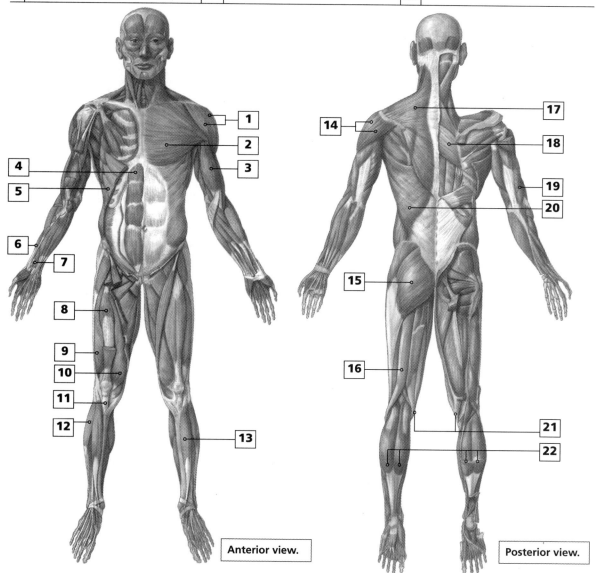

Anterior view.

Posterior view.

Using pencil crayons, colour the muscle names in the table on the right, and use the same colour to shade in the muscle on the illustrations below.

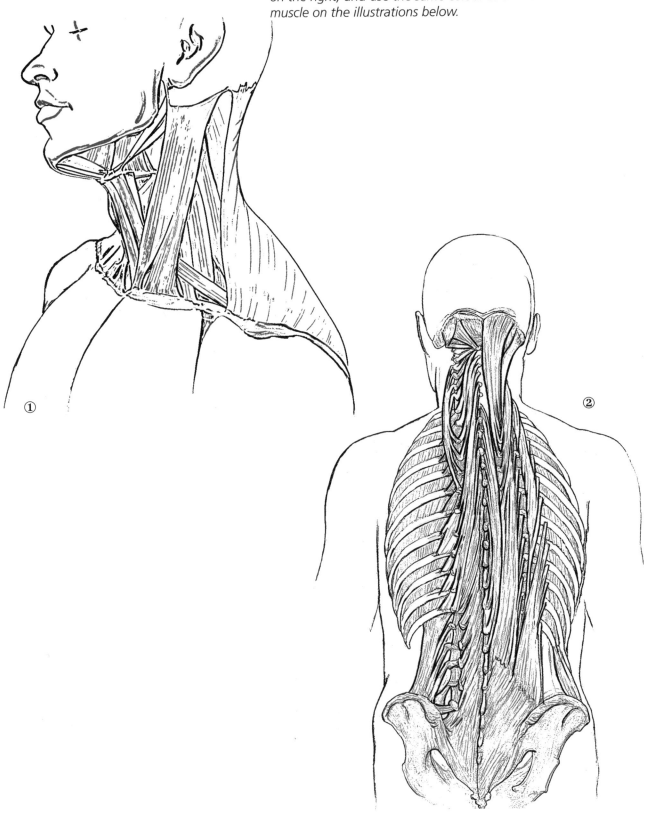

①

②

Origin, Insertion, and Function

Mission: For each of the next nine exercises complete the following tasks: (1) fill in the chart providing the name of the muscle, its origin, insertion, and function; (2) label the illustrations on the adjacent page; (3) colour-code each muscle name in the chart with the muscle in the illustration.

Name:

Date:

Look in the Book! Pages: 46–63

EXERCISE 3.7: Muscles of the Neck and Vertebral Column

	Origin	Insertion	Function
Muscles of the Neck			
❑ STERNOCLEIDOMASTOID Sternocleidomastoid is the broad, superficial muscle running upward at each side of the neck.			
❑ SPLENIUS Splenius runs along the posterior side of the neck and joins the skull with the spine.			
❑ SCALENUS ANTERIOR One of three scalene muscles on the side of the neck.			
❑ SCALENUS MEDIUS One of three scalene muscles on the side of the neck.			
❑ SEMISPINALIS CAPITIS Semispinalis capitis is a deep muscle on the back of the neck that lies below trapezius.			
Deep Muscles of the Vertebral Column			
❑ SPINALIS Spinalis is the most medial of the erector spinae group and is comprised of capitis, cervicis, and thoracis parts.			
❑ LONGISSIMUS Longissimus is lateral to spinalis, and it also has capitis, cervicis, and thoracis attachments.			
❑ ILIOCOSTALIS Iliocostalis the most lateral of the erector spinae group.			

Top: Muscles of the anterior thoracic wall, (1) posterior view.
Bottom: Muscles of the abdominal wall, (2) lateral superficial view.

Using pencil crayons, colour the muscle names in the table on the right, and use the same colour to shade in the muscle on the illustrations below.

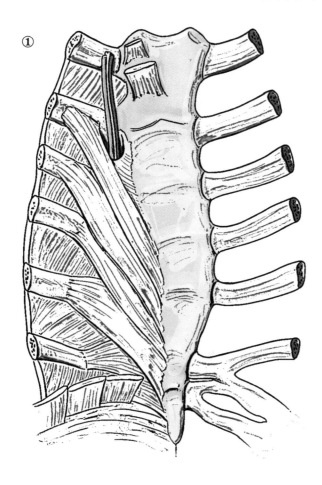

①

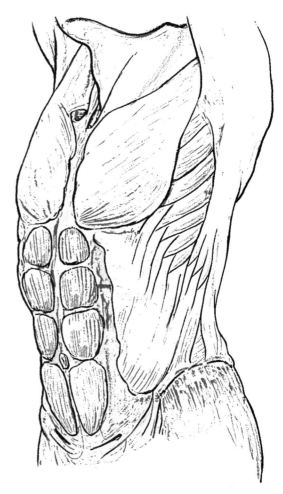

②

EXERCISE 3.8: Muscles of Respiration and the Abdomen

The muscles of the thoracic cage are mainly involved with breathing; those of the abdominal wall, with flexion and rotation of the vertebral column. When included with the back muscles, these groups represent the major muscles of the trunk.

	Origin	Insertion	Function
Muscles of the Thoracic Cage			
❑ THE DIAPHRAGM The diaphragm acts as an anatomical border, separating the thoracic and abdominal cavities. Think of it as a plate, in the middle of the thorax held together by a central tendon.			
❑ INTERCOSTAL MUSCLES The intercostal muscles (external, internal, and the innermost intercostals) are arranged in layers. They are located between each rib, and are often referred to as the breathing muscles.			
❑ TRANSVERSUS THORACIS Transversus thoracis is a triangular muscle acting on the abdominal wall.			
Muscles of the Abdomen			
❑ RECTUS ABDOMINIS Rectus abdominis is located on each side of a tendinous line (the linea alba) extending from the xiphoid process of the sternum to the pubis. It is also transected horizontally by three "tendinous intersections," giving the abs the classic "washboard" appearance.			
❑ EXTERNAL OBLIQUE AND TRANSVERSUS ABDOMINIS External oblique is the most external of the abdominal oblique muscles.			
❑ QUADRATUS LUMBORUM Quadratus lumborum, as its name suggests, has a quadrilateral shape, and it has an attachment site on the lumbar region of the body.			

Using pencil crayons, colour the muscle names in the table on the right, and use the same colour to shade in the muscle on the illustrations below.

①

②

③

④

EXERCISE 3.9: Muscles of the Shoulder

The muscles that affect the shoulder joint can be grouped into four categories. Two large muscles serve mainly to act on the upper limb of the axial skeleton, and four rotator cuff muscles act directly to stabilize and rotate the joint itself. The other two sets of shoulder muscles (those more directly associated with the scapula) are considered in the following section.

	Origin	Insertion	Function
Muscles Acting on the Upper Limb			
These superficial muscles act on the upper limb.			
❏ PECTORALIS MAJOR Pectoralis major is the thick muscle covering most of the front of the chest. It is comprised of two sub-regions – the clavicular and sternocostal heads.			
❏ LATISSIMUS DORSI Latissimus dorsi makes up about a quarter of the back area and is commonly referred to as "lats" or "wings."			

Muscles of the Rotator Cuff

The rotator cuff (musculotendinous cuff) consists of four muscles that extend from the scapula to the humerus and wrap around the shoulder joint, essentially holding it in place. The group is commonly referred to as the S.I.T.S. or S.S.I.T. muscles (an acronym of the muscle names) because they "sit" on the shoulder girdle. In addition to stabilizing the shoulder joint, the rotator cuff helps to decelerate arm movements (e.g., during a throwing action). If any of the rotator cuff muscles is damaged, due to strain or bad mechanics, the consequences are serious for actions that involve the shoulder and arm.

	Origin	Insertion	Function
❏ SUPRASPINATUS Supraspinatus is located above (hence, "supra") the spine of the scapula.			
❏ INFRASPINATUS Infraspinatus is located below (hence, "infra") the spine of the scapula.			
❏ TERES MINOR A rotator cuff muscle located below the spine of the scapula.			
❏ SUBSCAPULARIS Subscapularis is a large triangular muscle, and the only S.I.T.S. muscle located on the anterior surface of the scapula.			

Muscles on the scapula, (1) posterior view, (2) posterior deep view, (3) anterior deep view, (4) anterior superficial view.

Using pencil crayons, colour the muscle names in the table on the right, and use the same colour to shade in the muscle on the illustrations below.

①

②

③

④

EXERCISE 3.10: Muscles that Act on the Scapula

The scapula facilitates a wide range of movement at the shoulder. Apart from the rotator cuff muscles, the scapular muscles can be grouped into two categories: (1) those anchoring it to the axial skeleton, and (2) those muscles directly acting on the humerus.

	Origin	Insertion	Function
Muscles that Position the Scapula			
❑ TRAPEZIUS Trapezius is the large muscle of the upper back that gets its name from its trapezoid-like shape.			
❑ RHOMBOID MAJOR AND MINOR Rhomboid major and minor lie underneath trapezius. Rhomboid minor is superior to rhomboid major.			
❑ LEVATOR SCAPULAE Levator scapulae lies along the back and side of the neck and, as its name suggests, raises the scapula.			
❑ SERRATUS ANTERIOR Serratus anterior is a large muscle that runs along the rib cage, also known as the "boxer's muscle."			
❑ PECTORALIS MINOR Pectoralis minor is generally classified as a muscle of respiration during sub-maximal and maximal work.			
Scapular Muscles that Move the Humerus			
❑ DELTOID The deltoid gets its name from its resemblance to the Greek letter delta (hence, it is referred to as the "delts"). It has three heads — anterior, lateral, and posterior.			
❑ CORACOBRACHIALIS Coracobrachialis is a small muscle that gets its name from its attachments sites.			
❑ TERES MAJOR Teres major is often confused as one of the rotator cuff muscles.			

Using pencil crayons, colour the muscle names in the table on the right, and use the same colour to shade in the muscle on the illustrations below.

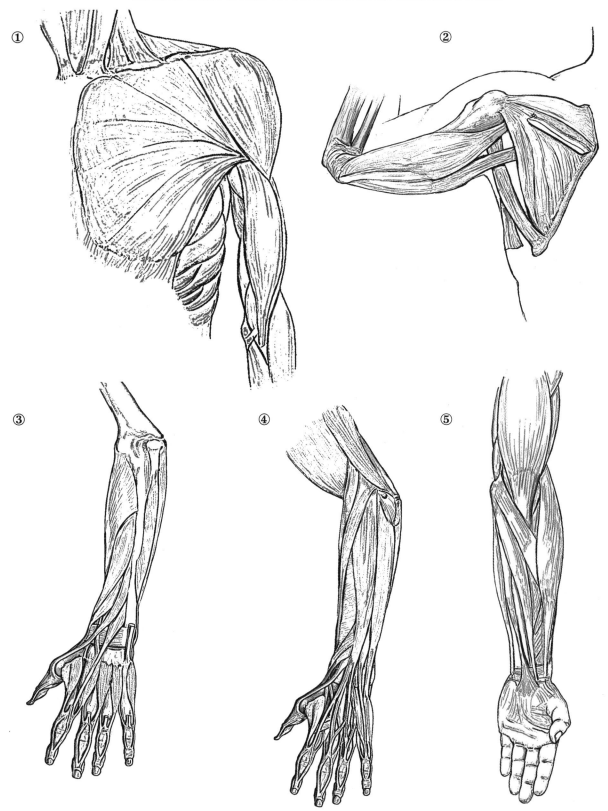

① ② ③ ④ ⑤

EXERCISE 3.11: Muscles of the Arm

The muscles of the arm control the movement of the forearm. Two major groups can be distinguished—those muscles that flex and extend the elbow (the elbow flexors and extensors) and those responsible for pronation and supination of the forearm.

	Origin	Insertion	Function
Elbow Flexors and Extensors			
❑ BICEPS BRACHII ("BICEPS") Biceps brachii is the prominent muscle on the front side of the upper arm. Its long head tendon passes within the intertubercular groove.			
❑ BRACHIALIS Brachialis is sometimes referred to as the lower biceps.			
❑ TRICEPS BRACHII Triceps brachii has three heads – short, long, and medial. As with the term "biceps" (two heads), "triceps" describes any muscle with three heads or points of origin.			
❑ BRACHIORADIALIS Brachioradialis gets its name from its attachment to the upper arm (brachium) and the radius (radialis).			
❑ ANCONEUS Anconeus is a triangular muscle.			
Supination and Pronation of the Forearm			
❑ PRONATOR QUADRATUS Pronator quadratus gets its name from its function and shape.			
❑ PRONATOR TERES Pronator teres gets its name from its function.			
❑ SUPINATOR Supinator derives it name from its function.			

Top: **Extrinsic hand muscles, (1) anterior view, (2) posterior view.**
Bottom: **Intrinsic hand muscles, (3) anterior view.**

Using pencil crayons, colour the muscle names in the table on the right, and use the same colour to shade in the muscle on the illustrations below.

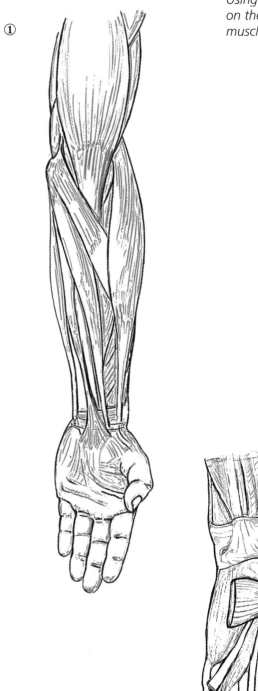

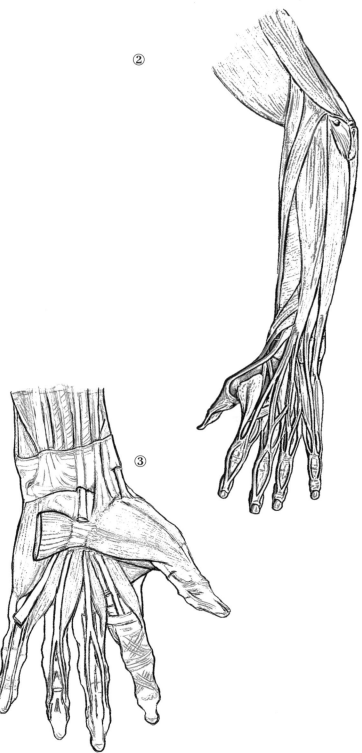

① ② ③

EXERCISE 3.12: Muscles of the Forearm and Hand

The muscles of the forearm (extrinsic hand muscles) are responsible for flexion, extension, abduction, and adduction of the wrist. The intrinsic hand muscles are those contained within the hand itself.

	Origin	Insertion	Function
Extrinsic Hand Muscles			
❑ FLEXOR CARPI RADIALIS			
❑ PALMARIS LONGUS			
❑ FLEXOR CARPI ULNARIS			
❑ FLEXOR DIGITORUM SUPERFICIALIS			
❑ EXTENSOR CARPI RADIALIS LONGUS			
❑ EXTENSOR CARPI RADIALIS BREVIS			
❑ EXTENSOR CARPI ULNARIS			
❑ EXTENSOR DIGITORUM			
❑ EXTENSOR DIGIT MINIMI			
Intrinsic Hand Muscles			
❑ THENAR EMINENCE Flexor pollicis brevis / Abductor polliicis brevis / Opponens pollicis			
❑ HYPOTHENAR EMINENCE Abductor digiti minimi / Flexor digiti minimi brevis / Opponens digiti minimi			

Using pencil crayons, colour the muscle names in the table on the right, and use the same colour to shade in the muscle on the illustrations below.

① ② ③

EXERCISE 3.13: Muscles of the Hip

	Origin	Insertion	Function
Hip Flexors and Extensors			
Posterior Hip Muscles			
❏ GLUTEUS MAXIMUS Gluteus maximus is the largest, strongest, and most superficial muscle of this group.			
❏ GLUTEUS MEDIUS Gluteus medius lies on top of gluteus minimus.			
❏ GLUTEUS MINIMUS Gluteus minimus is the deepest of this group.			
❏ TENSOR FASCIAE LATAE This muscle lies on the lateral side of the thigh and is enclosed between two layers of the fascia lata (its sheath).			
❏ SARTORIUS Sartorius is a superficial anterior muscle of the thigh. It derives its name from the Latin word sartor meaning "to mend."			
Anterior Hip Muscles			
❏ ILIOPSOAS Iliopsoas is a coming together of iliacus and psoas major. • Iliacus • Psoas major			
❏ PSOAS MINOR Psoas minor is present in approximately 40 percent of the human population.			
Hip Adductors			
❏ ADDUCTOR LONGUS			
❏ ADDUCTOR MAGNUS			
❏ ADDUCTOR BREVIS			
❏ PECTINEUS			
❏ GRACILIS			

Quadriceps and hamstring muscle groups, (1) anterior view, (2) posterior view.

Using pencil crayons, colour the muscle names in the table on the right, and use the same colour to shade in the muscle on the illustrations below.

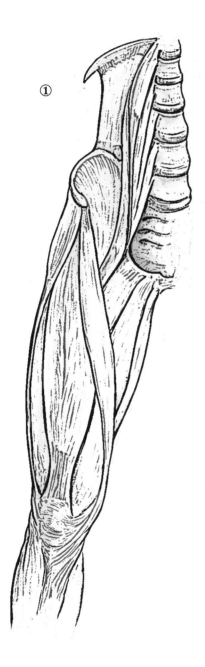

①

②

EXERCISE 3.14: Muscles of the Thigh

	Origin	Insertion	Function
Anterior Thigh—Quadriceps Group			
The muscles of the anterior thigh include the quadriceps femoris group. Quadriceps femoris is the large muscle group that covers the front and sides of the thigh. In this group, there are four separate muscles (hence the "quad"): rectus femoris, vastus lateralis, vastus medialis, and vastus intermedius.			
❑ RECTUS FEMORIS	- AIIS	- common tendon - which blends with the patellar ligament and inserts on the tibial tuberosity	- knee extension - steadies the hip joint - aids in hip flexion.
❑ VASTUS LATERALIS	- greater trochanter and lateral lip of linea aspera.	↓	↓
❑ VASTUS INTERMEDIUS	- intertrochanter line/medial lip of linea aspera.	↓	↓
❑ VASTUS MEDIALIS	- anterior/ lateral surface of femur.	↓	↓
Posterior Thigh—Hamstring Group			
There are three muscles of the posterior thigh. They are referred to collectively as "the hamstrings." They are: the biceps femoris, the semimembranosus, and semitendinosus.			
❑ BICEPS FEMORIS	- long head: ischial tuberosity - short head: linea aspera	- lateral side of head of fibula	- knee flexor - hip flexor
❑ SEMIMEMBRANOSUS	- ischial tuberosity	- posterior part of medial condyle of tibia	- knee flexor
❑ SEMITENDINOSUS	- ischial tuberosity	- medial surface of superior part of tibia.	- knee flexor

Extrinsic foot muscles, (1) posterior deeper view, (2) anterior view, (3) posterior deep view. Intrinsic foot muscles, plantar views, (4) superficial, (5) deep, (6) intermediate.

Using pencil crayons, colour the muscle names in the table on the right, and use the same colour to shade in the muscle on the illustrations below.

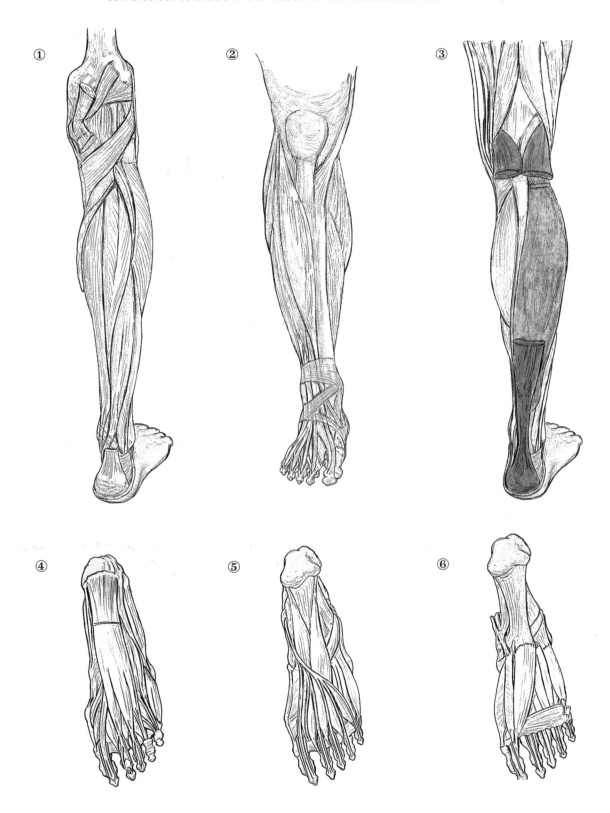

① ② ③

④ ⑤ ⑥

EXERCISE 3.15: Muscles of the Leg and Foot

Anatomically speaking, the "leg" refers to the lower limb below the knee. The muscles of the leg can be categorized into two broad groups, the extrinsic foot muscles and the intrinsic foot muscles.

	Origin	Insertion	Function
Extrinsic Foot Muscles			
Anterior Compartment			
❑ EXTENSOR DIGITORUM LONGUS			
❑ EXTENSOR HALLUCIS LONGUS			
❑ TIBIALIS ANTERIOR	-superior half of lateral surface of tibia and interosseous membrane	-medial and inferior surfaces of cuneiform tarsal and base of 1st metatarsal	-dorsiflexes ankle and inverts foot
Posterior Compartment			
❑ GASTROCNEMIUS	-lateral and medial condyle of femur.	-inserts into the calcaneus via the calcaneal tendon.	-plantar flexes the ankle.
❑ SOLEUS	-posterior head of fibula, fibula soleal line 'medial border of tibia	-posterior surface of calcaneous via calcaneal tendon.	-plantarflexes the ankle.
❑ FLEXOR DIGITORUM LONGUS			
❑ FLEXOR HALLUCIS LONGUS			
❑ TIBIALIS POSTERIOR			-plantarflexes ankle and inverts foot.
❑ POPLITEUS			
Lateral Compartment			
❑ FIBULARIS BREVIS AND FIBULARIS LONGUS (peroneus brevis and peroneus longus)			-everts foot
Intrinsic Foot Muscles			
❑ FLEXOR DIGITORUM BREVIS			
❑ QUADRATUS PLANTAE			
❑ FLEXOR HALLUCIS BREVIS			

Excitation-Contraction Coupling

Muscles work essentially by converting chemical energy (ATP) into mechanical energy, a process often referred to as excitation-contraction coupling.

Name:

Date:

Look in the Book! Pages: 39, 42

Mission: To gain familiarity with the sequence of events that occur during muscle contraction, list in order of occurrence what happens when you abduct your arm.

1.	
2.	
3.	
4.	
5.	
6.	
7.	
8.	
9.	
10.	
11.	

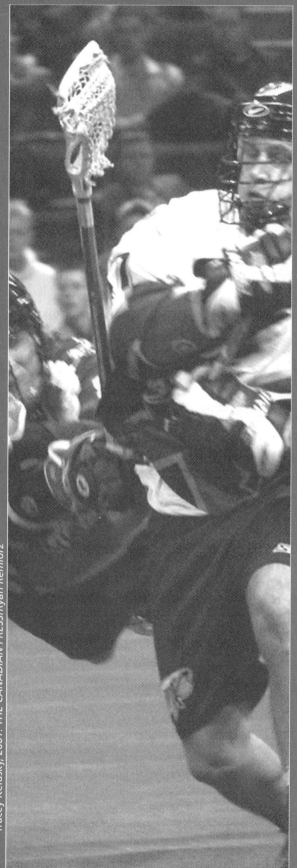

4

Joints Mechanics and Joint Injuries

Learning Objectives

The exercises in this section of the workbook will help to reinforce your knowledge of the following topics covered in the *Exercise Science* textbook:

- The role of joints within the human body
- The structural classification of joints (fibrous, cartilaginous, and synovial)
- Characteristics and types of synovial joints
- Joint tissue and its properties
- Tears, sprains, and pulls
- Tendinitis
- Dislocations and separations
- Cartilage and how it can be damaged
- Stress fractures
- Injury treatment
- The S.H.A.R.P. method of injury diagnosis
- The P.I.E.R. principle of injury treatment
- The properties of the shoulder joint and its common injuries
- The properties of the knee joint and its common injuries
- The properties of the ankle joint and its common injuries

Section Quiz

Name: _____ Date: _____

Multiple-Choice Questions

Mission: Circle the letter beside the answer that you believe to be correct.

1. Which of the following best describes a synovial joint?
   (a) hyaline cartilage is located on the ends of the bones
   (b) it features a joint cavity
   (c) synovial fluid is present
   (d) all of the above

2. Which of the following synovial joints is a ball and socket?
   (a) knee joint
   (b) metatarsal joints
   (c) hip joint
   (d) radioulnar joint

3. Which of the following joints is classified as uni-axial?
   (a) shoulder joint
   (b) elbow joint
   (c) carpal joints
   (d) thumb joint

4. Which of the following bone(s) make up the shoulder joint?
   (a) clavicle
   (b) scapula
   (c) humerus
   (d) all of the above

5. Which of the following muscles help to stabilize the knee joint on the anterior side?
   (a) hamstrings
   (b) quadriceps
   (c) gastrocnemius
   (d) gluteus maximus

6. Tough bands of white, fibrous tissue that allow a certain amount of stretch are called
   (a) bursae
   (b) ligaments
   (c) tendons
   (d) cartilage

7. Which of the following injuries is specific to the knee joint?
   (a) Pott's fracture
   (b) rotator cuff tears
   (c) patellofemoral syndrome
   (d) biceps tendonitis

Short-Answer Questions

Mission: Briefly answer the following questions in the space provided:

1. Joints are classified by structure and by function. Name them, giving an example of each type.

   _____

2. What are the six different types of synovial joints?

   _____

3. Identify and describe the three types of cartilage.

   _____

4. List the three common shoulder injuries.

   _____

5. Distinguish the difference between first-, second-, and third-degree tears, sprains, and pulls.

   _____

6. What are the three symptoms of a dislocation?

   _____

7. Why is the knee joint classified more precisely as a modified ellipsoid joint?

   _____

   _____

Essay Questions

Mission: On a separate piece of paper, develop a 100-word response to the following questions.

1. Describe the various properties of joint tissue with respect to the likelihood of injury.

2. Describe the proper and improper treatment of an injury to a joint.

3. Summarize which type of sports or activities tend to cause injury to the ankle and shoulder joints, and why.

Terminology Review

Defining Key Terms

Name:

Date:

Mission: Briefly explain the meaning of the following key terms:

Key Term	Definition
Articulations	
Fibrous joints	
Cartilaginous joints	
Synovial joints	
Gliding (or plane or arthrodial) joints	
Hinge (ginglymus) joints	
Pivot (or trochoid) joints	
Ellipsoid joints	
Saddle joints	
Ball-and-socket (spheroidal) joints	
Ligament	
Tendon	
Vascularity	
Strains, pulls, and tears	

Tendinitis	
Dislocation	
Separations	
Cartilage	
Arthroscopy	
Shin splints	
P.I.E.R. principle	
Biceps tendinitis	
Shoulder separation	
Shoulder dislocation	
Rotator cuff tears	
Knee ligament tears	
Q-angle	
Osgood-Schlatter syndrome	
Patellofemoral syndrome (PFS)	
Inversion sprains	
Eversion sprains	
Pott's Fracture	

The Characteristics of a Synovial Joint

Name:

Date:

Look in the Book! Page: 70

Synovial joints are one of the three major joint types. They permit movement between two or more bones.

Mission: To gain familiarity with the main aspects of the synovial joint, label the illustration below.

Labels

- ❑ Articular cartilage
- ❑ Blood vessel
- ❑ Bone
- ❑ Bursa
- ❑ Fibrous capsule

- ❑ Fibrous layer
- ❑ Joint capsule
- ❑ Joint cavity (filled with synovial fluid)
- ❑ Membranous layer

- ❑ Nerve
- ❑ Periosteum
- ❑ Synovial membrane
- ❑ Tendon
- ❑ Tendon sheath

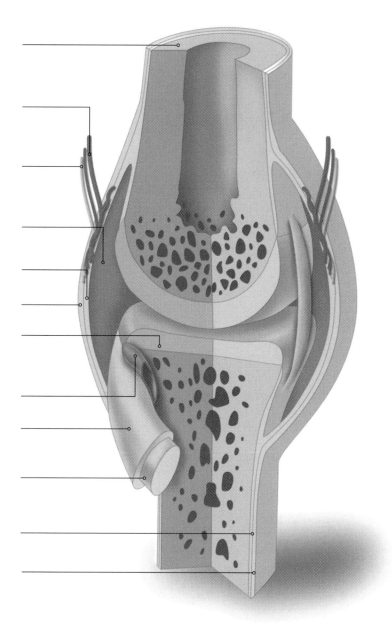

Shoulder and Knee Joints

Because of their size and composition, the shoulders and knees are key joints in the human body.

Mission: Label the main components of the shoulder joint illustrated below, as well as the four anatomical views of the knee joint on the following pages. Some labels may need to be used more than once.

Name:
Date:
Look in the Book! Pages: 74–77

Labels

- ❏ Acromioclavicular ligament
- ❏ Acromion
- ❏ Clavicle
- ❏ Coracoacromial ligament

- ❏ Coracoclavicular ligament
- ❏ Coracoid process
- ❏ Glenohumeral ligaments and joint capsule

- ❏ Humerus
- ❏ Scapula
- ❏ Tendon of biceps brachii (long head)

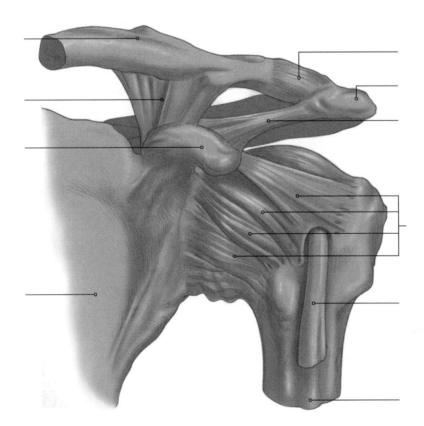

Left shoulder joint, anterior view.

Labels

- ☑ Anterior cruciate ligament
- ☑ Femur
- ☑ Fibula
- ☑ Lateral (Fibular) collateral ligament removed
- ☐ Lateral condyle
- ☑ Lateral meniscus

- ☐ Medial condyle
- ☑ Medial (Tibial) collateral ligament
- ☑ Medial (Tibial) collateral ligament removed
- ☑ Medial meniscus
- ☑ Patella (wrapped within a tendon—sesamoid bone)

- ☑ Patellar ligament
- ☑ Posterior cruciate ligament
- ☐ Quadriceps tendon (patellar tendon)
- ☑ Tibia
- ☑ Tibial tuberosity

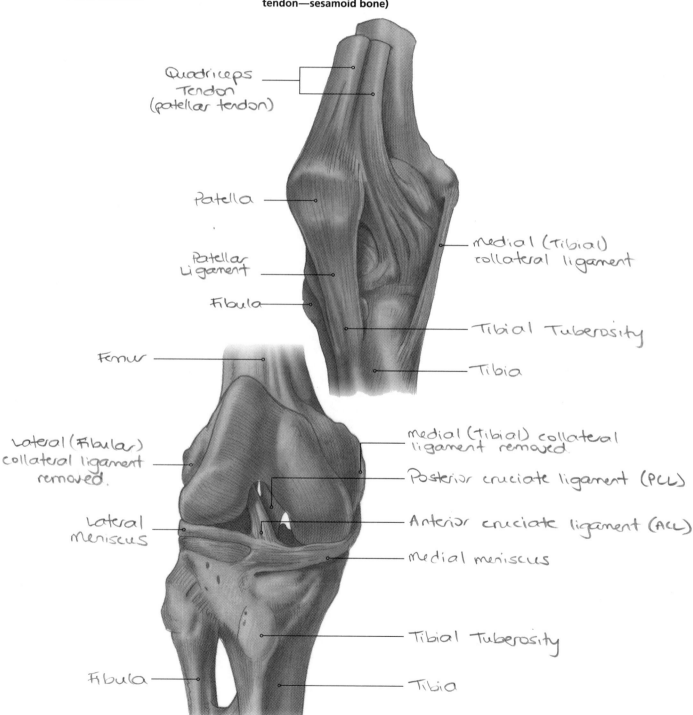

Quadriceps Tendon (patellar tendon)

Patella

Patellar Ligament

Fibula

Femur

medial (Tibial) collateral ligament

Tibial Tuberosity

Tibia

Lateral (Fibular) collateral ligament removed.

Lateral Meniscus

medial (Tibial) collateral ligament removed.

Posterior cruciate ligament (PCL)

Anterior cruciate ligament (ACL)

medial meniscus

Tibial Tuberosity

Fibula

Tibia

Labels

- ☑ **Adductor magnus tendon**
- ☑ **Anterior cruciate ligament**
- ☑ **Femur**
- ☑ **Fibula**
- ☑ **Fibular head**
- ☑ **Lateral (Fibular) collateral ligament**

- ☑ **Lateral head of gastrocnemius tendon**
- ☑ **Lateral meniscus**
- ☑ **Medial (Tibial) collateral ligament**
- ☑ **Medial head of gastocnemius tendon**
- ☑ **Medial meniscus**

- ☑ **Oblique popliteal ligament**
- ☑ **Popliteal tendon**
- ☑ **Posterior cruciate**
- ☑ **Posterior meniscofemoral ligament**
- ☑ **Sememembranosus tendon**
- ☑ **Tibia**

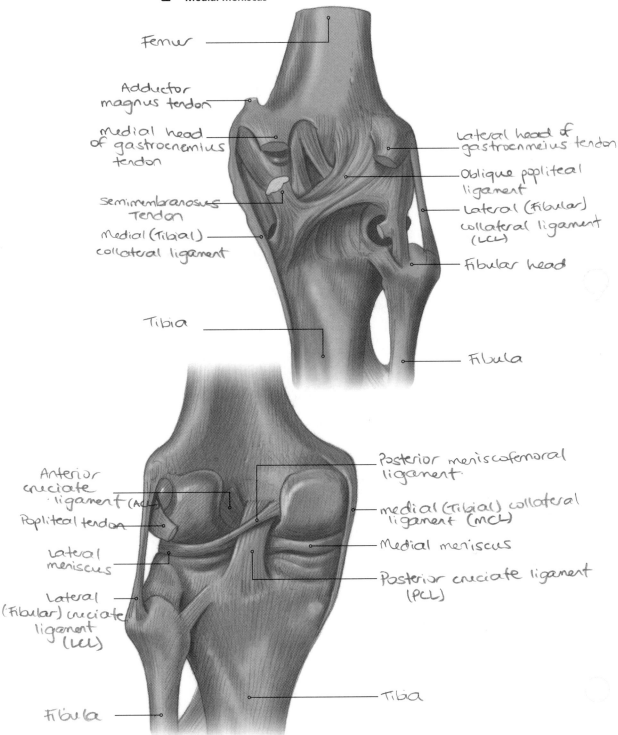

Constructing a Model of a Synovial Joint

<table>
<tr><td>Name:</td></tr>
<tr><td>Date:</td></tr>
<tr><td>Look in the Book! Pages: 70–71</td></tr>
</table>

Synovial joints are comprised of: cartilage, the joint capsule, synovia, the joint cavity, the bursae, and ligaments (intrinsic and extrinsic).

Mission: Use the table below to outline the components needed to construct a movable joint of your choice (remember, the joint must be able to articulate).

Name(s) of creator(s)	1. _____ 2. _____ 3. _____
Name of joint	
Due date and timelines	
Research sources (e.g., Internet, visit physiotherapy clinic, etc.)	

Materials Required to Construct the Joint

Bones (e.g., paper towel rolls)	
Cartilage (e.g., concave plastic lining from a water bottle)	
Ligaments (e.g., Velcro)	
Tendons (e.g., rubber bands)	
Muscles (e.g., balloons)	

Movement at Joints

Muscles and joints are affected by different types of exercises, depending on the type of muscle at work and the particular strains placed on it by each exercise.

Name:

Date:

Mission: In the worksheet below, indicate which are the agonist muscles (major muscles) in use, the joints involved, and the type of movement that is produced. A sample entry is provided below.

Machine	Major Muscles	Joints Involved	Movement Produced
Bench press	pectoralis major, anterior deltoid, and triceps brachii	elbow and shoulder	elbow extension and medial shoulder rotation and flexion
Dumbbell flies			
Lat pull downs			
Shoulder press			
Leg press			
Leg curls			
Military press			
Squats, lunges			
Seated row			
Shoulder shrug			
Triceps extension			
Push-ups			
Crunches			
Power clean			
Arm curls			

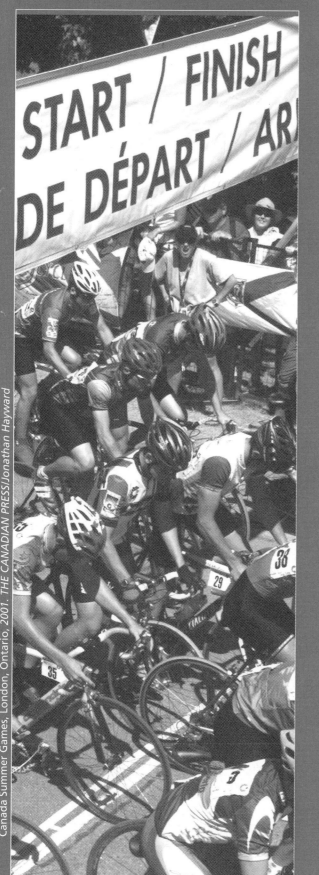

Canada Summer Games, London, Ontario, 2001. THE CANADIAN PRESS/Jonathan Hayward

5

Energy Systems and Muscle Fibre Types

Learning Objectives

The exercises in this section of the workbook will help to reinforce your knowledge of the following topics covered in the *Exercise Science* textbook:

- The three energy nutrients (proteins, fats, and carbohydrates) that the body needs
- The role of ATP in human energy
- The aerobic and anaerobic energy systems
- The body's three metabolic pathways (ATP-PC, glycolysis, and cellular respiration)
- The role of pyruvate and lactic acid
- The basic functions of the ATP-PC system, or anaerobic alactic system
- The basic functions of the glycolysis, or anaerobic lactic, system
- The basic functions of the aerobic system and the role of cellular respiration
- The Lactic Acid Threshold and the Cori cycle
- How the body derives energy from fats and proteins
- Slow-twitch and fast-twitch muscle fibre types and their roles in human muscular activity
- The function and distribution of Type I, IIA, and IIB muscle fibre types
- The relationship between muscle fibre types and athletic performance

Section Quiz

Name: *Rose Ramsaran*   Date: *Dec. 2. 2015*

Multiple-Choice Questions

Mission: Circle the letter beside the answer that you believe to be correct.

1. Cellular respiration involves which of the following energy pathways?
   - (a) glycolysis
   - (b) electron transport chain
   - (c) Krebs cycle
   - (d) all of the above

2. Which energy system uses fatty acids, glucose, and glycogen to make ATP?
   - (a) anaerobic alactic
   - (b) anaerobic lactic
   - (c) aerobic
   - (d) all of the above

3. Minimum levels of stored ATP and creatine phosphate are limiting factors for this energy system.
   - (a) anaerobic alactic
   - (b) anaerobic lactic
   - (c) aerobic
   - (d) glycolysis

4. Which of the following is the main product of glycolysis?
   - (a) acetyl CoA
   - (b) pyruvate
   - (c) ADP
   - (d) creatine phosphate

5. Which of the following sport activities primarily use the ATP-PC system?
   - (a) circuit training
   - (b) shot put
   - (c) 400-metre sprint
   - (d) all of the above

6. Which energy system does a marathon runner rely heavily upon?
   - (a) ATP-PC
   - (b) glycolysis
   - (c) cellular respiration
   - (d) none of the above

7. At which level of intensity does a trained individual generally meet their lactate threshold?
   - (a) 100% VO_2max
   - (b) 50-60% VO_2max
   - (c) 20-30% VO_2max
   - (d) 70-80% VO_2 max

Short-Answer Questions

Mission: Briefly answer the following questions in the space provided:

1. What is the role of carbohydrates as an energy source?
   —most abundant and easily accessible at any intensity.
   - stored within the liver as glycogen.
   - Glucose used as an energy source

2. What is the anaerobic threshold and how does it differ between untrained and trained individuals?

3. What is the role of myoglobin?
   -oxygen storage unit that delivers oxygen to working muscles.

4. What are the three metabolic pathways to create sufficient energy?
   - Anaerobic Alactic (ATP-PC)
   - Anaerobic Lactic (Glycolysis)
   - Aerobic (cellular Respiration)

5. Describe the importance of the Cori cycle with respect to lactic acid.

6. Describe the three separate pathways within cellular respiration.

   Glycolysis
   ↳ in the presence of O_2, pyruvic acid converts to acetyl CoA

   Krebs cycle
   ↳ 2 ATP produced

   Electron Transport chain
   ↳ large amounts of ATP produced
   ↳ CO_2 + H_2O = by products

Essay Questions

Mission: On a separate piece of paper, develop a 100-word response to the following questions.

1. Describe the three main energy systems and their limitations.

2. During which performance events does the anaerobic lactic system contribute little energy? Why is this so?

3. Describe the role of fats, protein, and carbohydrates in the production of ATP.

Terminology Review

Defining Key Terms

Mission: Briefly explain the meaning of the following key terms:

Name: Rose

Date: Dec. 2. 2015

Key Term	Definition
Bioenergetic conversion	- the food we take in is broken down into three nutrients in the course of digestion ① proteins ② fats ③ carbohydrates. - through conversion of these nutrients, our bodies are able to function and are able to carry out phy. activity
Carbohydrates	- the most abundant organic substances in nature. ↳ originate from plants; vegetables, fruits, and grain-based foods such as breads & pasta.
Glycogen	- glucose is the usual form in which carbs are assimilated by animals. - stored within skeletal muscle and within the liver as glycogen
Metabolism	- the highly complex by which energy is supplied throughout the body and by which energy-rich-material (fats and proteins and carbs) are assimilated by the body for the purposes of energy renewal
Adenosine triphosphate (ATP)	- is the common energy molecule for all living things. ↳ ATP captures the chemical energy resulting from the breaking down of food to fuel the various cellular processes.
Anaerobic system	- occurs relatively quickly in the cell fibre, utilizing chemicals and enzymes for powerful short-lived physical actions.
Aerobic system	- leads to the complete breakdown of glucose - fats and protein enter cycle at this stage. - takes place in the mitochondria.
ATP-PC (Anaerobic alactic)	- relies on the action of phosphocreatine (normally stored in muscle) ↳ high energy molecule where the phosphate can be broken off easily and used to convert ADP back to ATP.
Glycolysis (Anaerobic lactic)	↳ small amount of creatine phosphate can sustain the level of ATP required during the initial phase of short but intense activity - the ATP energy produced during this process will allow an athlete to engage in high level of performance for about an additional 90 seconds.
Lactic acid	- the main product of glycolysis is pyruvate (pyruvic acid) - in the absence of adequate oxygen, the process is halted at the glycolysis stage. ↳ pyruvic acid is converted to lactic acid and exhaustion or pain in the muscles begin to set in.

Cellular respiration (Aerobic)	– the process where the cells use O_2 to generate energy through the different metabolic pathways found in the mitochondria.
Krebs cycle	– occurs in the mitochondria and is the common pathway to completely oxidize fuel molecules. – through 8 reactions, 2 ATP molecules are produced, along with new compounds capable of storing high-energy electrons.
Electron Transport Chain	– large amounts of ATP are produced with CO_2 & H_2O as the only by products
Blood lactate threshold/ anaerobic threshold	– the point at which lactate levels in the blood increase beyond resting values.
Cori cycle	– process by which lactic acid is converted to pyruvate for future conversion to glucose and glycogen.
Fatty acids	– acids stored in the body as triglycerides. ↳ triglycerides are broken down and the resulting fatty acids become available as an energy source in a process called lipolysis.
Beta oxidization	– the process by which fatty acids are converted to acetyl-CoA before entering the energy supply chain.
Amino acids	– protein in the body consists of at least 20 different amino acids which are used by the body to form tissue. – 9 essential amino acids, which we must consume as food.
Myoglobin	– the protein that is the oxygen-storage unit that delivers oxygen to working muscles, thereby enabling energy-producing biochemical reactions to be sustained over a long period.
Type I fibre (SO)	– generate muscles slowly – are fatigue resistant – primarily depend on the aerobic process.
Type IIA fibre (FOG)	– these intermediate-type fibres allow for high speed energy release and glycolytic capacity.
Type IIB fibre (FG)	– store large amounts of glycogen and sufficiently high levels of enzymes for quick contraction without requiring oxygen.
Tonic muscles	– muscles that assist the body with maintaining posture or stability during activities such as standing, walking, and throwing. – characterized by a high percentage of Type I fibre (slow-twitch)
Phasic muscles	– muscles characterized by a higher percentage of Type IIA and Type IIB fibres. ex. biceps have a lower percentage of Type I fibres

Three Energy Pathways Compared

| Name: |
| Rose Ramsairan |
| Date: |
| Dec. 2. 2015 |
| Look in the Book! Pages: 82–87 |

ATP-PC (the anaerobic alactic system), glycolysis (the anaerobic lactic system), and the aerobic system (cellular respiration) are the three basic energy pathways.

Mission: Fill in the following table based on the criteria provided in the left-hand column.

Three Energy Pathways Compared

	ATP-PC (Anaerobic alactic system)	Glycolysis (Anaerobic lactic system)	Cellular respiration (Aerobic system)
Location of activity	sarcoplasm	Sarcoplasm	mitochondria
Energy source	phosphocreatine	glucose (glycogen)	glycogen, fats, proteins
Uses oxygen or not	NO	NO	yes
ATP produced	1	2	36
Duration	10-15 seconds	15 seconds - 3 mins.	120 seconds +
Number of chemical reactions	1-2	11	Glycolysis, Krebs cycle, electron transport chain (8)
By-products	None	Lactic acid	carbon dioxide water
Basic chemical reaction formula	PC + ADP ⟹ ATP + creatine	Glucose + 2ADP + 2Pi ⟹ Lactate + 2ATP + 2H_2O	Glucose + 6O_2 + 36ADP + 36Pi ⟹ 6CO_2 + 36ATP + 6H_2O
Type of activities	power surges speed events	intermediate activities, sprint finish	endurance - type events
Types of exercise that rely on this system	50- 100 metre dash weightlifting high jump	400 - 800 metre sprint shift in a hockey game	marathon entire soccer match
Advantages	very quick surge of power provides the highest rate of ATP synthesis in comp to other systems	- capable of producing ATP rapidly without need for oxygen. (quick surge of power)	long duration; complete breakdown of glucose
Limitation of energy system	short duration; muscles store small amounts of ATP and creatine phosphate	buildup of lactic acid eventually hampers breakdown of glucose + decreases ability for muscles to contract.	slow; requires large amount of oxygen
Muscle fibre type recruited	Type IIB (fast-twitch)	Type IIA (fast twitch)	Type I (slow twitch)

Energy Systems for Various Sports

Name: Rose

Date: Dec. 7. 2015

Look in the Book! Pages: 86–87

Every sport or activity involves the use of the three energy systems to varying degrees, based on the sport's unique requirements. Some sports or activities rely more heavily on one system while others utilize a combination of all three.

Mission: Complete the following chart by indicating the extent (expressed as a percentage or as "highly," "moderately," or "seldom used") to which the four activities listed below rely on each of the three energy systems. In the remaining spaces in the left-hand column, choose a sport and provide the same information.

Energy Systems For Various Sports			
Sport	**ATP-PC (Anaerobic Alactic System)**	**Glycolysis (Anaerobic Lactic System)**	**Cellular Respiration (Aerobic System)**
Weightlifting (8-10 reps)	Moderate	Highly	Seldom
Endurance running (at least 20 min)	Seldom	Moderate	Highly
100-metre sprint (11 seconds)	Highly	Moderate	seldom / Recovery
A 30-second shift in hockey (45 seconds)	Moderate / High	Highly	seldom / Recovery
weight Lifting (15-20 reps)	Seldom	Moderate	Highly
200-m Sprint (22 seconds)	Highly	Highly	Seldom
Power Lifter (1 repetition max)	Highly	Moderate	seldom / Recovery
800-m race (2:20 min)	Highly	Highly	Moderate
Dance Routine (intense for 2 min)	Moderate	Highly	Highly

Myriam Bedard, 1992. THE CANADIAN PRESS/COA/Ted Grant

6

The Nervous System and the Control of Movement

Learning Objectives

The exercises in this section of the workbook will help to reinforce your knowledge of the following topics covered in the *Exercise Science* textbook:

- How the nervous system controls human movement
- The two components of the human nervous system: the central nervous system and the peripheral nervous system
- The basic functions of the brain in coordinating human movement, and the key brain areas in which this activity occurs
- The role of the vertebral column and the spinal cord
- The basic functions of the peripheral nervous system, and its division into the autonomic and somatic nervous systems
- The concept of the "reflex arc" and its function in facilitating movement
- Proprioceptors and their function in controlling human movement
- The role of Golgi tendon organs and muscle spindles
- Polysynaptic reflexes and their role in human movement
- The importance of the spinal cord and the potential injuries to the spinal cord, including paraplegia and quadriplegia
- The significance and treatment of head injuries and concussions

Section Quiz

Name: _____ Date: _____

Multiple-Choice Questions

Mission: Circle the letter beside the answer that you believe to be correct.

1. Which part of the brain is responsible for coordinating muscle movement and balance?
   (a) brain stem
   (b) cerebellum
   (c) diencephalon
   (d) limbic system

2. Which of the following is not an autonomic response of the body to an emergency?
   (a) increased heart rate
   (b) release of adrenaline
   (c) widening of the blood vessels
   (d) skeletal muscle contraction

3. Proprioceptors are located in
   (a) tendons
   (b) muscles
   (c) joints
   (d) all of the above

4. Which bones are formed by the fusing of bones of the vertebral column?
   (a) sacrum and coccyx
   (b) thoracic and coccyx
   (c) sacrum and cervical
   (d) thoracic and lumbar

5. Which vertebrae take the burden of the weight placed on the back?
   (a) cervical
   (b) thoracic
   (c) lumbar
   (d) tail bone

6. Which of the following is a symptom of a concussion?
   (a) memory problems
   (b) fatigue
   (c) dizziness
   (d) all of the above

7. The somatic nervous system is responsible for
   (a) preparing the body for emergencies
   (b) muscle movement and balance
   (c) our awareness and adjustment to the external environment
   (d) various automatic functions

8. The most important function of Golgi tendon organs is
   (a) to detect changes in muscle length
   (b) to detect tension exerted on muscles
   (c) to house and protect motor neurons
   (d) to prevent the the "knee-jerk" reflex

Short-Answer Questions

Mission: Briefly answer the following questions in the space provided:

1. Describe the roles of the autonomic and somatic nervous system.

2. Explain the difference between a cerebral reflex and a spinal reflex.

3. Describe the difference between a monosynaptic reflex and a polysynaptic reflex.

4. What three types of reflex responses indicate problems with portions of the nervous system?

5. Identify the three different neurons and describe their different roles.

6. Define the terms paraplegic and quadriplegic.

7. Who comprises the "rehab team" for people undergoing spinal cord rehabilitation?

8. Define a concussion.

Essay Questions

Mission: On a separate piece of paper, develop a 100-word response to the following questions.

1. List the main parts of the brain and their function.

2. Why do some professional athletes continue to compete despite repeated head injuries?

3. Describe the different roles of the tendon organs and muscle spindles of the neuromuscular system.

Terminology Review

Defining Key Terms

Name:

Date:

Mission: Briefly explain the meaning of the following key terms:

Key Term	Definition
Central nervous system	
Peripheral nervous system	
Efferent nerves	
Afferent nerves	
Autonomic nervous system	
Sympathetic system	
Parasympathetic system	
Somatic nervous system	

Reflex arc	
Proprioceptors	
Golgi tendon organs	
Muscle spindles	
Stretch reflex	
Reciprocal inhibition	
Withdrawal reflex	
Crossed-extensor reflex	
Magnetic resonance imaging (MRI)	
Computerized axial tomography (CAT)	
Paraplegia	
Quadriplegia	
Concussion	

The Reflex Arc

Reflex actions are how the body responds rapidly to painful—or the threat of painful—situations, and the reflex arc is the mechanism by which the response occurs. It is the name given to the pathway within the nervous system along which an initial stimulus and a corresponding response message travel.

Name:
Date:
Look in the Book! Page: 99

Mission: Label the illustration below using the labels on the left, and briefly describe the five components of the reflex arc in the space provided below.

① _____

② _____

③ _____

④ _____

⑤ _____

Labels

- ☐ **Effector Organ**
- ☐ **Interneuron**
- ☐ **Motor Neuron (efferent)**
- ☐ **Sensory Receptor**
- ☐ **Sensory Neuron (afferent)**

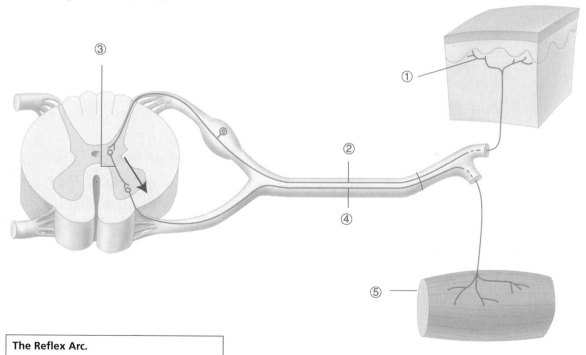

The Reflex Arc.

Golgi Tendon Organs at Work

Name:

Date:

Look in the Book! Page: 100

Golgi tendon organs are a highly specialized proprioceptor that detects increased tension on the tendon.

Mission: The illustration below shows a tension reflex action involving the Golgi tendon organs. Referring to the components already labelled in the illustration below, list and describe the various stages of this reflex action.

① _____

② _____

③ _____

④ _____

⑤ _____

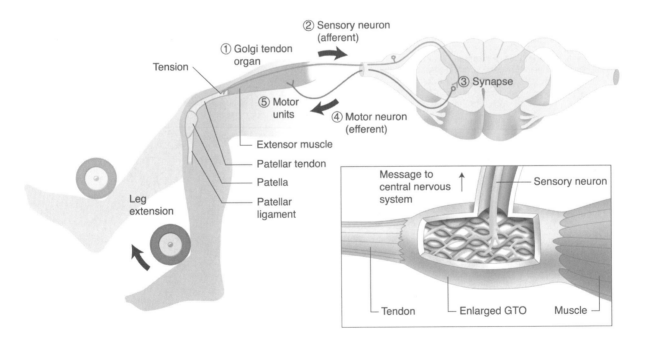

Golgi tendor organ (tension detector).

Polysynaptic Reflexes

In more complicated reflex actions—often called polysynaptic reflexes—one or more interneurons are involved. This type of reflex can also involve the presence of a compensation response in an opposing limb.

<table>
<tr><td>Name:</td></tr>
<tr><td>Date:</td></tr>
<tr><td>Look in the Book! Page: 103</td></tr>
</table>

Mission: The illustration below not only outlines the actions involved in the reflex-withdrawal from a painful object touching the skin but also shows the possibility of a compensation response in an opposing limb. Making reference to the components already labelled in the illustration, list and describe the various stages of this more complex reflex arc.

① _____

② _____

③ _____

④ _____

⑤ _____

⑥ _____

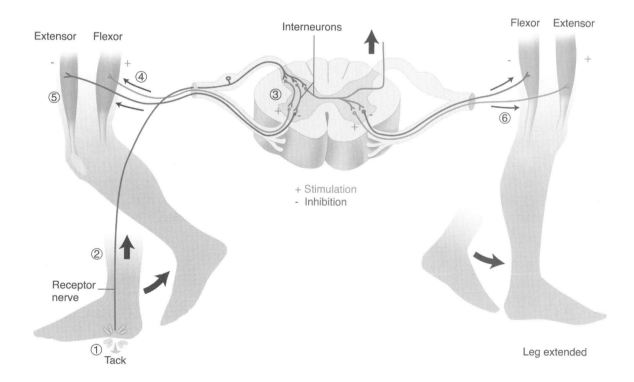

+ Stimulation
- Inhibition

The stretch reflex.

Athletes with Spinal Cord Injuries

Name:
Date:
Look in the Book! Page: 105

Many athletes who have sustained a spinal cord injury have learned to work with the physical limitations placed upon them, and continue to excel in sports and physical activity.

Mission: Research four athletes—Canadian or international—who have sustained a spinal cord injury but still compete successfully in sport. Try to include athletes from a variety of sports—both male and female—in your research, and, using your findings, complete the table. A sample entry is provided below

Athlete	Cause of Spinal Cord Injuries	Result of Injuries	Sport(s) Competed in After Injuries	Achievements
1. Rick Hansen	Motor vehicle accident	Paraplegia—loss of ability to walk	Track events Road races (e.g., marathons) Tennis Basketball Volleyball	Co-author of 2 books; Multiple marathon winner and world champion in track; Raised millions of dollars for spinal cord research with "Man in Motion" tour
2.				
3.				
4.				
5.				

Alison Sydor, 1996. THE CANADIAN PRESS/STF/Frank Gunn

7

The Cardiovascular and Respiratory Systems

Learning Objectives

The exercises in this section of the workbook will help to reinforce your knowledge of the following topics covered in the *Exercise Science* textbook:

- The basic function and structure of the cardiovascular system
- How blood flows through the heart
- The heart's contractions and electrical "excitations"
- The role of arteries, arterioles, capillaries, veins, and blood within the cardiovascular system
- The cardiovascular system's response to exercise, including the concepts of cardiac output, blood pressure, and blood flow distribution
- The effects of training on the cardiovascular system
- Cardiovascular disease, its causes, risks, and cures
- The basic function and structure of the respiratory system and its importance to the body's overall function
- The two basic zones (conductive and respiratory) of the respiratory system
- Ventilation and its controls within the respiratory system
- The body's system of oxygen transport, including carbon dioxide transport, ventilation, and the regulation of blood pH
- Respiratory dynamics, including pulmonary ventilation, external respiration, internal respiration, and adaptations to training
- Oxygen consumption and the concept of VO_2max
- Oxygen deficit and excess post-exercise oxygen consumption (EPOC)

Section Quiz

Name: _____ Date: _____

Multiple-Choice Questions

Mission: Circle the letter beside the answer that you believe to be correct.

1. Which of the following blood vessels drains the head, neck, and arms?
   (a) pulmonary artery
   (b) inferior vena cava
   (c) superior vena cava
   (d) aorta

2. Which mechanism is responsible for bringing blood back to the lungs and thorax?
   (a) respiratory pump
   (b) muscle pump
   (c) gravity
   (d) cardiac pump

3. Cardiac output is equal to which of the following?
   (a) heart rate x breathing rate
   (b) heart rate x stroke volume
   (c) resting heart rate
   (d) ventricular systole

4. Which of the following blood vessels carries deoxygenated blood?
   (a) pulmonary vein
   (b) coronary arteries
   (c) aorta
   (d) pulmonary artery

5. The mitral valve is located between the
   (a) right ventricle and pulmonary artery
   (b) left ventricle and aorta
   (c) left atrium and left ventricle
   (d) right atrium and right ventricle

6. The respiratory zone is composed of the
   (a) pharynx, trachea, and respiratory bronchioles
   (b) mouth, nose, bronchi, and alveolar sacs
   (c) trachea, bronchi, bronchioles, and alveolar ducts
   (d) respiratory bronchioles, alveolar ducts, and alveolar sacs

7. Which phase does the QRS complex represent on an electrocardiogram?
   (a) ventricular depolarization
   (b) atrial depolarization
   (c) ventricular repolarization
   (d) all of the above

8. Which of the following remains unaffected with respect to blood distribution during exercise?
   (a) the brain
   (b) the digestive system
   (c) skeletal muscle
   (d) skin

Short-Answer Questions

Mission: Briefly answer the following questions in the space provided:

1. What are the three mechanisms that assist in venous return?

2. Describe the difference between arteries and veins.

3. What are the main components of blood?

4. What is hypertension?

5. What are the distinguishing characteristics of an elite athlete's heart?

6. What does a-vO_2 diff represent?

7. Why are active recovery methods more beneficial with respect to anaerobic lactic training?

Essay Questions

Mission: On a separate piece of paper, develop a 100-word response to the following questions.

1. Describe the phenomenon known as cardiovascular drift that occurs during prolonged exercise.

2. Describe several risk factors that may lead to coronary heart disease.

3. Outline the pathway of an oxygen molecule from external respiration to a working quadriceps muscle and the pathway of a carbon dioxide molecule from the quadriceps to external respiration.

Terminology Review

Defining Key Terms

Mission: Briefly explain the meaning of the following key terms:

Name: Rose

Date: Dec. 9. 2015

Key Term	Definition
Pulmonary/systemic circulation	pulmonary circulation: the main function of the right heart is to pump deoxygenated blood, which has just returned from the body to the lungs. systematic circulation: the role of the left heart is to pump oxygenated blood, which has just returned from the lungs to the rest of the body.
Oxygenated/deoxygenated blood	oxygenated blood: blood that has returned from the lungs and is pumped by the left heart to the rest of the body. Systematic circulation (red in colour) deoxygenated blood: blood that has returned from the body and is pumped by the right heart to the lungs (pulmonary circulation) dark red in colour
Arteries/veins	- vessels that carry blood away from the heart. - in the systematic circulation, arteries carry oxygenated blood (red) from the left side of the heart towards body tissues - in the pulmonary circulation, arteries carry deoxygenated blood (blue) from the right side of the heart to the lungs.
Myocardium	- The muscle tissue that makes up the heart. - cardiac muscle cells are interconnected and allow the passage of electrical signals from cell to cell.
Sinoatrial node (SA node)	
Atrioventricular node (AV node)	
Atrioventricular bundle	
Purkinje fibres	
Electrocardiogram (ECG)	
Coronary arteries/veins	
Capillaries	- oxygen, carbon dioxide and nutrients are exchanged between the blood and cells in the capillaries.
Cardiac cycle	- the series of events that occurs through one heart beat. - during this cycle, there is both a phase of relaxation (diastole), where the heart is filling with blood, and a phase of contraction (systole), where the heart contracts and ejects the blood.

Systolic/diastolic blood pressure	
Vascular system	
Skeletal muscle pump	
Thoracic pump	
Red/white blood cells	
✱ Hemoglobin	- a specialized protein found in erythrocytes, each gram of hemoglobin in the blood can bind to 1.34 mL of O₂. - average concentration is ~16 mg/100 mL of blood
Platelets	
✱ Cardiac output (Q)	- refers to the volume of blood that is pumped out of the heart in 1 minute. - measured L/min - calculated as the product of stroke volume & heart rate.
✱ Stroke volume (SV)	- the amount of blood that is ejected from the left ventricle in a single beat - measured in mL.
Frank-Starling Law	
Ejection fraction (EF)	
✱ Heart rate (HR)	- the number of times the heart contracts in 1 minute.
Blood pressure	
Hypertension	
Bradycardia	
Cardiovascular disease	

External/internal/cellular respiration	
Conductive/respiratory zones	
Alveoli (alveolar sacs)	— grope-like structures found within the lungs. ⤷ provide a large surface area for the diffusion of gases into and out of the blood.
Diaphragm	
Ventilation (V_E)	
Tidal volume (V_T)	
Respiratory frequency (f)	
Respiratory control centres	
Static/dynamic lung volumes	
Gas exchange	
Diffusion	— the movement of a gas, liquid or solid from a region of high concentration to a region of low concentration through random movement. ⤷ diffusion can only occur if a difference in concentration exists (called a concentration gradient)
Partial pressures	
Diffusion pathway	
Henry's Law	
Oxygen transport	
Blood pH	— a measure of how acidic or how basic the blood is. ⤷ generally blood pH is maintained very close to a pH of 7.4

✳	a-vO₂ diff	— the difference between the amount of O_2 in the artery and vein reflects the amount of O_2 delivered to the muscle.
	Asthma	
	Chronic obstructive pulmonary disease (COPD)	
✳	Oxygen consumption (VO₂)	— the amount of oxygen taken up and consumed by the body for metabolic process
✳	Maximal rate of oxygen consumption (VO₂max)	— the maximum volume (v) of oxygen (O_2) in (mm) that the human body can use in 1 minute, per kg of body weight, while breathing air at sea level.
✳	Respiratory exchange ratio	— the ratio between the amount of carbon dioxide produced and the amount of oxygen consumed is used to calculate the respiratory exchange ratio.
	Ventilatory threshold	
✳	Lactic acid	— the main product of glycolysis is pyruvate (pyruvic acid) — under aerobic conditions, pyruvate leads to the complete breakdown of glucose, in the beginning of the 3rd — in the absence of adequate oxygen, the process is system. halted at the glycolysis stage.
✳	Lactate threshold	→ pyruvic acid is converted to lactic acid and exhaustion or pain in the muscles begins to set in. — a point where blood lactate concentrations begin to rise during excercise
✳	Onset of blood lactate accumulation (OBLA)	— the point at which blood lactate levels begin to accumulate very rapidly. (shortly after the blood lactate threshold is reached).
✳	Oxygen deficit	— the amount of oxygen taken in during stressful excercise minus the amount that would otherwise have been required for steady-state aerobic excercise.
✳	Excess post-exercise oxygen consumption (EPOC)	— the additional oxygen taken in during the recovery period in order to restore the balance.
	Hyperbaric oxygen therapy	
	Passive/active recovery techniques	

Internal Anatomy of the Heart

The heart is a complex organ formed from specialized muscle tissue called myocardium.

Mission: To gain familiarity with the heart's key internal components, label the illustration below. Some labels may need to be used more than once. Next, colour parts of the heart and the arrows to indicate the circulation of oxygenated (red pencil crayon) and deoxygenated (blue pencil crayon) blood through the heart.

Name:
Rose

Date:
Dec. 9. 2015

Look in the Book! Page: 111

Labels

- ☑ Aorta
- ☑ Aortic semilunar valve
- ☑ Bicuspid (mitral) valve
- ☑ Chordae tendinae
- ☑ Inferior vena cava
- ☑ Interventricular septum
- ☑ Left atrium

- ☑ Left pulmonary artery
- ☑ Left pulmonary veins
- ☑ Left ventricle
- ☑ Papillary muscles
- ☑ Pulmonary semilunar valve
- ☑ Right atrium
- ☑ Right pulmonary artery

- ☑ Right pulmonary veins
- ☑ Right ventricle
- ☑ Superior vena cava
- ☑ Thoracic aorta (descending)
- ☑ Tricuspid valve

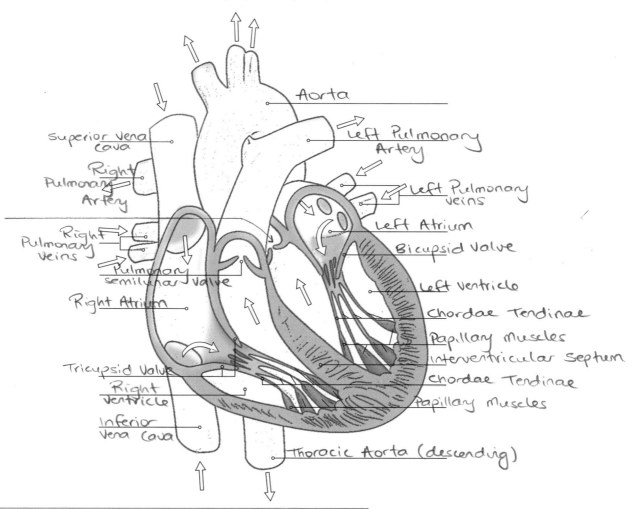

Internal anatomy of the heart and the blood pathway through the heart.

The Electrical Conduction System of the Heart

Name:

Date:

Look in the Book! Page: 112

The electrical conduction system of the heart is an intricate and continuous system that allows the heart to function properly.

Mission: To gain a better understanding of the process of electrical conduction and to identify the components involved, label the illustration below and colour the nerves (yellow pencil crayon).

Labels

- ☐ Atrioventricular (AV) node
- ☐ Bundle of HIS (AV bundle)
- ☐ Internodal pathways
- ☐ Purkinje fibres
- ☐ Right and left bundle branches
- ☐ Sinoatrial (SA) node

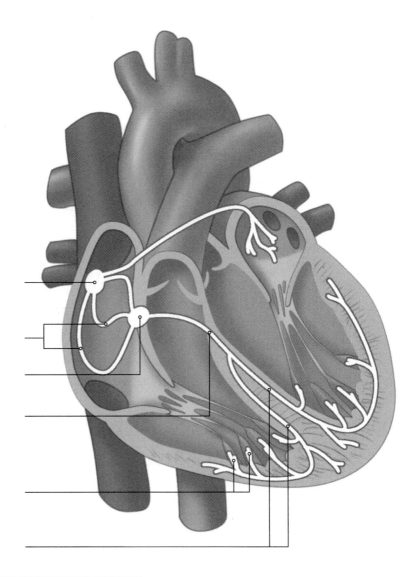

The electrical conduction system of the heart.

The Anterior Structure of the Heart

The anterior view of the heart reveals the coronary vessels, as well as other major structures of the heart.

Mission: Label the illustration below using the list of labels provided.

Name:

Date:

Look in the Book! Page: 113

Labels

- ❏ Anterior interventricular branch of left coronary artery
- ❏ Aorta
- ❏ Branches of left pulmonary artery
- ❏ Branches of right pulmonary artery
- ❏ Great cardiac vein
- ❏ Inferior vena cava
- ❏ Left atrium
- ❏ Left pulmonary artery
- ❏ Left pulmonary veins
- ❏ Left ventricle
- ❏ Pulmonary trunk
- ❏ Right atrium
- ❏ Right coronary artery
- ❏ Right pulmonary veins
- ❏ Right ventricle
- ❏ Small cardiac vein
- ❏ Superior vena cava
- ❏ Thoracic aorta (descending)

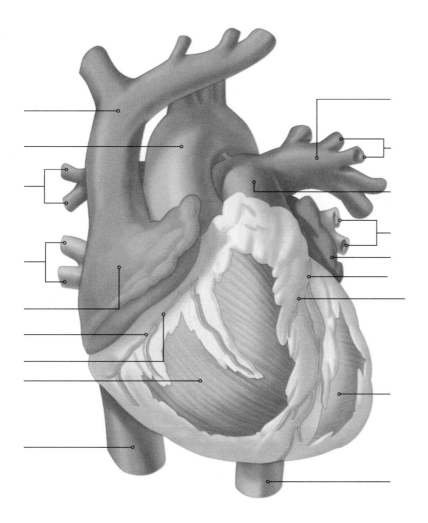

Anterior view of the coronary vessels, including other major heart structures.

The Respiratory System

The respiratory system is composed of many interconnected parts or structures that allow the passage of air. The actual structure of the respiratory system can be divided into two main zones.

Name:

Date:

Look in the Book! Pages: 120–121

Mission: Label the illustration below using the list of labels provided, and indicate the two main structures.

Labels

- ☐ Alveolar sacs
- ☐ Conductive zone
- ☐ Epiglottis
- ☐ Larynx
- ☐ Mouth
- ☐ Nasal cavity
- ☐ Pharynx

- ☐ Pulmonary arteriole (carrying deoxygenated blood)
- ☐ Pulmonary venule (carrying oxygenated blood)
- ☐ Respiratory bronchiole
- ☐ Respiratory zone
- ☐ Right and left primary bronchi

- ☐ Secondary bronchi
- ☐ Smooth muscle
- ☐ Terminal bronchiole
- ☐ Tertiary bronchioles
- ☐ Trachea

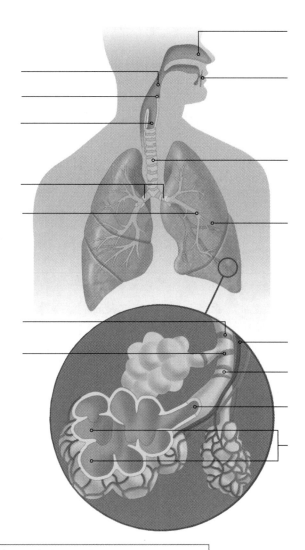

The main structures of the respiratory system.

External and Internal Respiration

Name:

Date:

Look in the Book! Pages: 125–127

External respiration involves the exchange of O_2 and CO_2 in the lungs. Internal respiration refers to the exchange of gases at the tissue level where O_2 is delivered and CO_2 is removed.

Mission: To gain a better understanding of the direction and purpose of the external and internal respiration pathways, label the illustration below. Some labels may need to be used more than once. Next, colour the oxygenated (red pencil crayon) and deoxygenated (blue pencil crayon) blood to demonstrate blood flow.

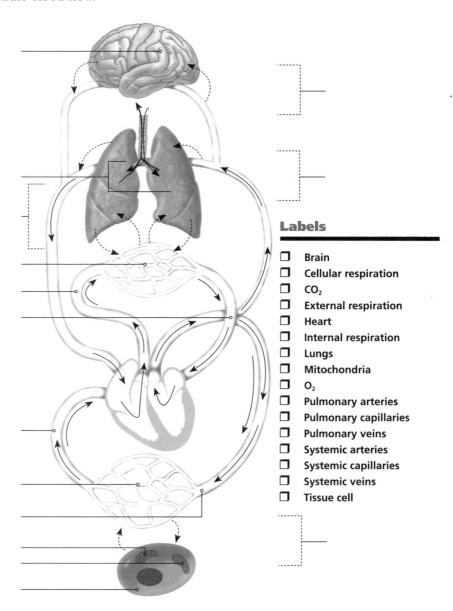

Labels

☐ Brain
☐ Cellular respiration
☐ CO_2
☐ External respiration
☐ Heart
☐ Internal respiration
☐ Lungs
☐ Mitochondria
☐ O_2
☐ Pulmonary arteries
☐ Pulmonary capillaries
☐ Pulmonary veins
☐ Systemic arteries
☐ Systemic capillaries
☐ Systemic veins
☐ Tissue cell

The main structures of the respiratory system.

Crossword on the Cardiovascular and Respiratory Systems

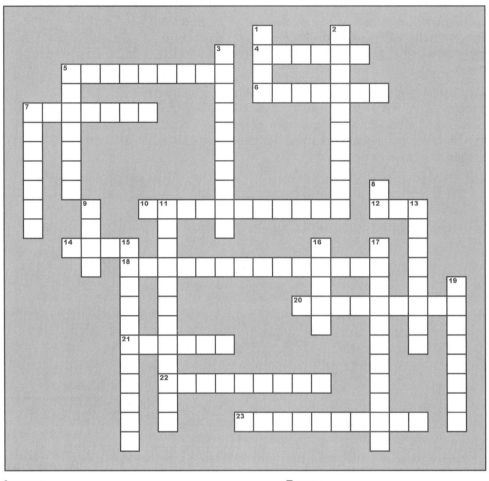

Across

4. Without this element, there would be no bodily tissue
5. Veins that carry oxygen-rich blood
6. Phase of contraction in the cardiac cycle
7. Shortness of breath
10. The combination of inspiration and expiration
12. This bundle is also known as the atrioventricular bundle
14. Acronym referring to recovery oxygen uptake
18. Process referring to the effects of chemical compounds on blood flow
20. This pathway is the site of movement for gases going from the lungs into the blood, from the blood to the tissue, and back
21. Acid that builds in the muscles during anaerobic exercise
22. The atrioventricular valve on the right side of the heart
23. The specialized muscle tissue of which the heart is composed

Down

1. An area of the brain stem important in the regulation of ventilation
2. A specialized protein found in erythrocytes
3. Controversial type of oxygen therapy
5. This type of recovery is attained through total rest
7. He has the highest VO_2max score on record
8. A measure of how acidic or basic blood is
9. Acronym for family of common respiratory diseases
11. The most abundant blood cells
13. As myocardium or cardiac muscle cells are said to act
15. Blood vessels of one-cell thickness
16. The upper chambers of the heart
17. Along with the apneustic, the pons contains this specialized respiratory centre
19. Tissue-level exchanges of gas comprise this form of respiration

CHAPTER 8

Unit 1 Career Choices

Investigate a career in one of the fields covered in Unit 1. Ideally, you should interview someone working within the field for this assignment.

1 Career and description

_____

_____

_____

_____

2 List at least two post-secondary institutions in Ontario and/or Canada that offer programs for this career.

_____

_____

_____

3 Choose one of the above institutions and determine the required courses in the first year of study for this program.

_____

_____

_____

4 What is the total length of the education needed to begin this career? Is an internship or apprenticeship required?

_____

_____

_____

5 What is the demand for individuals qualified for this occupation? If possible, provide some employment data to support your answer.

_____

_____

_____

6 What is the average starting salary for this career? What is the top salary? On what do salary increases depend in this career?

_____

_____

_____

7 List occupational settings where a person with these qualifications could work.

_____   _____

_____   _____

Unit 1 Crossword Challenge

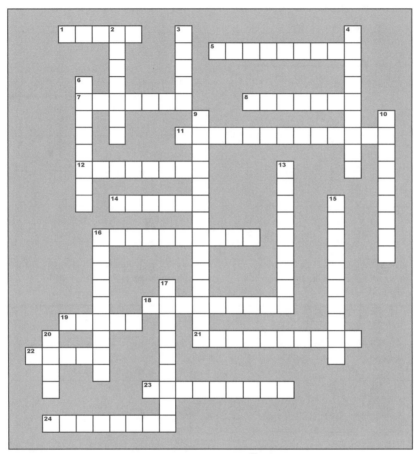

Across

1. Skeleton comprised mainly of the vertebral column, much of the skull, and the rib cage
5. The opposite of abduction
7. Type of joint bound tightly together with connective tissue, which allows no movement
8. Nervous system through which our awareness of the external environment operates
11. Term describing the movement of circling your arms in the air
12. Muscles that extend the limbs and increase the angle between two limbs
14. Muscles characterized by a high percentage of Type IIA and Type IIB fibres
16. Thread-like structures that run along the length of the muscle fibre
18. Tough bands of white, fibrous tissue that attach one or more bones together
19. Tendon organs that terminate where tendons join to muscle fibre
21. Also known as growth plates
22. Unit comprising the motor neuron, its axon, and the muscle fibre it stimulates
23. Large specialized muscle that separates the chest cavity from the abdominal cavity
24. Glucose is converted to this when it is stored within skeletal muscle and the liver

Down

2. System for resynthesizing ATP that takes place in the mitochondria
3. Cycle comprising a series of eight chemical reactions during which two ATP molecules are produced
4. Biological system that consists of glands
6. Nerves that carry information from sensory receptors to the central nervous system
9. Type of cartilage found mainly between the vertebrae of the spine
10. The point where the muscle attaches to the bone that is moved most
13. Shaft of the bone
15. A polysynaptic reflex that involves the withdrawal of a body part from a painful stimulus
16. Cavity found inside the shaft of the long bone
17. Movement of a gas, liquid, or solid from a region of high concentration to one of low concentration through random movement
20. Cycle in which lactic acid is converted to pyruvate for future conversion to glucose and glycogen

UNIT 2

HUMAN PERFORMANCE AND BIOMECHANICS

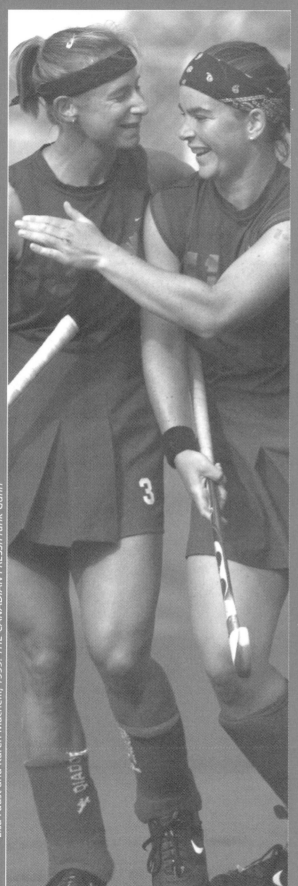

Lisa Faust and Karen Macneill, 1999. *THE CANADIAN PRESS/Frank Gunn*

10

Nutrition for Performance

Learning Objectives

The exercises in this section of the workbook will help to reinforce your knowledge of the following topics covered in the *Exercise Science* textbook:

- The importance of nutritional awareness for athletes and those who are physically active
- Macronutrients (proteins, carbohydrates, and fats) and miconutrients (vitamins, minerals, and water)
- Key vitamins and minerals
- Canada's Food Guide to Healthy Eating
- Dietary Reference Intakes
- Cholesterol and lipoproteins (including high-density and low-density lipoproteins)
- The "energy equation," and the process of counting calories
- How to develop a diet that matches performance requirements
- Your metabolic rate and how to calculate it
- How to estimate daily caloric needs
- The concept and calculation of Body Mass Index (BMI)
- Food labelling
- The controversy surrounding the "Zone Diet"
- The problem of obesity in Canada
- Weight management for athletes
- The role of nutrition in athletic performance, including competitive meals
- Dehydration and fluid replacement during athletic performance
- The concept of carbo-loading
- Heat cramps, heat stroke, and heat exhaustion

Section Quiz

Name: _____ Date: _____

Multiple-Choice Questions

Mission: Circle the letter beside the answer that you believe to be correct.

1. Which one of the following statements best describes carbohydrates?
   (a) they break down into amino acids
   (b) they contain 9 calories per gram
   (c) they contain 4 calories per gram
   (d) they have two subgroups called complete and incomplete

2. Which one of the following best describes proteins?
   (a) they contain 4 calories per gram
   (b) they can be grouped into complete and incomplete
   (c) there are 20 or so different types
   (d) all of the above

3. Which one of the following statements can be said about fats?
   (a) they contain 4 calories per gram
   (b) they can be grouped into complete and incomplete
   (c) they contain 9 calories per gram
   (d) none of the above

4. Which one of the following vitamins are fat-soluble vitamins?
   (a) C, D, and E
   (b) A, B, C, and K
   (c) B and C
   (d) A, D, E, and K

5. Which of the following best describes iron?
   (a) it aids in fat metabolism and can be found in most fruits and vegetables
   (b) most humans, especially women, get more than enough iron in their everyday diet
   (c) it helps build muscle, and can be found in all nutritional supplements
   (d) it helps carry oxygen and can be found in liver, tuna, and green leafy vegetables

6. Basal metabolic rate can be simply defined as
   (a) the rate at which your cardiovascular system uses energy
   (b) the rate at which all your muscle, taken together, use energy on a daily basis
   (c) the sum of all the essential energy needs for one's body to function
   (d) a rate of energy consumption that only applies to those who work out

Short-Answer Questions

Mission: Briefly answer the following questions in the space provided:

1. Why are certain amino acids referred to as essential?

2. What are the three macronutrients?

3. What are the three micronutrients?

4. What percentage of our daily caloric intake should come from carbohydrates, fats, and proteins?

5. What is the difference between the seven key minerals and "trace" minerals?

6. What happens to arteries in the condition known as arteriosclerosis?

7. List some ways in which the body loses water.

Essay Questions

Mission: On a separate piece of paper, develop a 100-word response to the following questions.

1. Name several food items that are an excellent source of iron and explain why iron is so important for female athletes.

2. What is the importance of hydration in training and competition? What beverage best fulfils the body's needs and why?

3. Explore the reasons for the rise in the levels of obesity in Canada. How can these best be addressed?

Terminology Review

Defining Key Terms

Name:
Date:

Mission: Briefly explain the meaning of the following key terms:

Key Term	Definition
Macronutrients/micronutrients	
Complete/incomplete proteins	
Complex/simple carbohydrates	
Glycemic index	
Saturated/polyunsaturated fats	
Vitamins	
Minerals	
Water	
Canada's Food Guide	
Dietary Reference Intakes (DRIs)	
Cholesterol	
Atherosclerosis	
Energy equation	
Calorie	

Daily caloric need	
Metabolic rate (MR)	
Basal metabolic rate (BMR)	
Resting metabolic rate (RMR)	
Harris-Benedict Equation	
Body Mass Index (BMI)	
Nutritional labelling	
Low-fat food diets	
Transfats	
Obesity/underweight	
Weight management	
Reflex dilation of skin	
Sweating reflex	
Dehydration	
Carbo-loading	
Heat cramps	
Heat exhaustion	
Heatstroke	

Body Mass Index

The Body Mass Index (BMI) is a tool used by researchers and medical practitioners, allowing them to assess the extent to which individuals are balancing the energy equation.

Name:
Date:
Look in the Book! Page: 151

Mission: Locate the point on the chart where your height and weight intersect to estimate your BMI and determine your BMI zone. Have five of your classmates, friends, or family do the same (write their initials on the chart).

BMI Zones

- **Zone A** (< 20) — may be associated with health problems for some people;
- **Zone B** (20–25) — good weight for most people;
- **Zone C** (25–27) — may lead to health problems in some people;
- **Zone D** (>27) — increased risk of developing health problems.

What are the limitations that the BMI present?

_____

_____

_____

_____

_____

_____

_____

_____

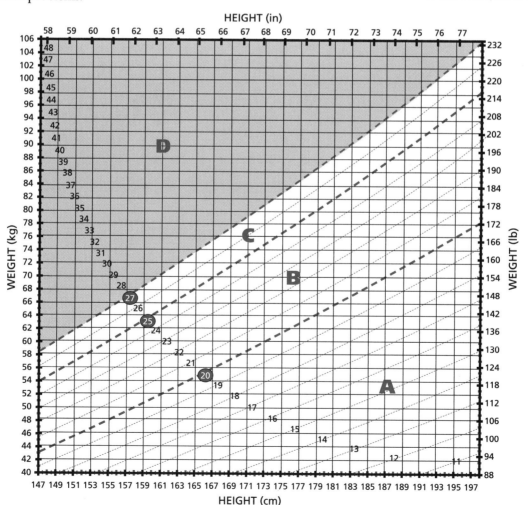

Estimating Resting Metabolic Rate and Daily Caloric Need

Name:
Date:
Look in the Book! Pages: 150–151

The resting metabolic rate (RMR) is an estimate of the amount of energy an individual's body requires while at rest. By determining one's RMR it is possible to determine the daily caloric need required to sustain one's current body weight.

Step 1:
Using the Harris-Benedict equation [RMR = constant + (___× ht. in cm) + (___× wt. in kg) – (___× age)], insert the required data in the appropriate table below (males/females) so as to compute your RMR.

Step 2:
Estimate your daily caloric need by completing the appropriate calculations: multiply RMR by 1.4 if you are sedentary; multiply RMR by 1.6 if you are moderately active; multiply RMR by 1.8 if you indulge in hard exercise/vigorous sports.

Resting Metabolic Rate for Males

Constant					66.5
Height	5	×	cm.	+	
Weight	13.7	×	kg.	+	
Subtotal				Subtotal	
Age	6.8	×	yrs.	–	
				RESTING METABOLIC RATE =	

Resting Metabolic Rate for Females

Constant					665
Height	1.9	×	cm.	+	
Weight	9.5	×	kg.	+	
				Subtotal	
Age	4.7	×	yrs.	–	
				RESTING METABOLIC RATE =	

RMR		Factor	Daily Caloric Need
	×		kcal/day

Making a Nutritional "Smoothie"

Eating wisely and learning how to achieve the right nutritional balance is key to maintaining a healthy body weight, and furthering your goal of optimum performance.

Name: _____

Date: _____

Look in the Book!
Pages: 146–147, 149, 152

Step 1: In a small group (2–5 students), choose foods listed in the table below to make a blended smoothie. (You may use different food items upon the approval of your teacher.) Complete the table by filling in the required information for each of the foods listed.

Step 2: On the following page, complete the food label by providing the nutritional information of your creation.

Step 3: Create a name as well as a brief promotional description that focuses on the nutritional value that your smoothie provides.

Tip: Use the following website to acquire your nutritional food values: http://www.dietitians.ca/ public/content/eat_well_live_well/english/index.asp

Ingredient	Approx. Grams Used	Carbo-hydrate per Gram	Fat per Gram	Protein per gram	Total Energy	Choles-terol	Sodium	Vitamin A	Vitamin C	Calcium	Iron	Fibre
Ice cream/ frozen yoghurt												
Banana												
Apple												
Chocolate syrup												
Pineapple juice												
Yoghurt												
Kiwi												
Strawberry												
Cantaloupe												
Peach												
Watermelon												
Totals												

_____

_____

_____

_____

_____

Nutrition Facts

Per _____mL (_____g)

Amount	% Daily Value

Calories _____

Fat _____g _____%

   Saturated _____g

   + Trans _____g _____%

Cholesterol _____mg

Sodium _____mg _____%

Carbohydrate _____g _____%

   Fibre _____g _____%

   Sugars _____g

Protein _____g

Vitamin A _____%   Vitamin C _____%

Calcium _____%   Iron _____%

Nutrition and Physical Activity

Name:
Date:

Look in the Book!
Pages: 146–147, 149, 156–159

Eating wisely is only one step of the process to achieving optimal performance. It is necessary to match your daily energy intake with your daily energy expenditure.

Step 1: In the space provided below, insert your resting metabolic rate score and calculate your daily caloric need using a factor based on your level of activity (see Exercise 10.4).

Step 2: In the chart provided below, record your food intake for a three-day period. Then write in your estimated average daily energy intake from food after the three days and compare this with your daily caloric need calculation. These figures will not be the same. If the difference is great, speculate as to why there is such a great difference—perhaps you are more active than you realized (or perhaps not as active).

*Your three-day food values can be acquired from: http://www.dietitians.ca/public/content/eat_well_live_well/english/eatracker

Resting Metabolic Rate	
Daily Caloric Intake Estimate	
Estimated daily energy intake from food after 3 days (taken from bottom of page 117)	

Food	Approx. Grams Used	Carbo-hydrate per Gram	Fat per Gram	Protein per Gram	Total Energy	Vitamin A	Vitamin B	Calcium	Iron
Day 1 Food Intake									

Food	Approx. Grams Used	Carbo-hydrate per Gram	Fat per Gram	Protein per Gram	Total Energy	Vitamin A	Vitamin C	Calcium	Iron
DAY 1 TOTALS									

Day 2 Food Intake

Food	Approx. Grams Used	Carbo-hydrate per Gram	Fat per Gram	Protein per Gram	Total Energy	Vitamin A	Vitamin C	Calcium	Iron
DAY 2 TOTALS									

Food	Approx. Grams Used	Carbo-hydrate per Gram	Fat per Gram	Protein per Gram	Total Energy	Vitamin A	Vitamin B	Calcium	Iron
Day 3 Food Intake									
DAY 3 TOTALS									
OVERALL TOTALS									

Nutrient Sources

It is important to understand how the human body can obtain key nutrients and vitamins from the food we eat.

Mission: To further your understanding of key nutrients and vitamins, fill in the missing information in the summary tables below.

Name:
Date:
Look in the Book! Pages: 141–143

Macronutrient	Calories per Gram	Major Subdivisions
Carbohydrates		
Protein		
Fat		

Vitamin	Main Food Sources
A	
B1	
B2	
B3	
B6	
B12	
C	
D	
E	
K	
Iron	
Calcium	
Phosphorous	

Ben Johnson, 1988. THE CANADIAN PRESS/STF/Fred Chartrand

11

Performance-Enhancing Substances and Techniques

Learning Objectives

The exercises in this section of the workbook will help to reinforce your knowledge of the following topics covered in the *Exercise Science* textbook:

- The three basic forms of performance-enhancing substances, or ergogenic aids (nutritional, pharmacological, and physiological aids)

- The basic subgroups of nutritional aids (vitamins and minerals; proteins and amino acid supplements; carnitine; creatine; and caffeine)

- The basic subgroups of pharmacological aids (pain-masking drugs, anabolic steroids, prohormones, human growth hormone, and erythropoietin)

- The role of the World Anti-Doping Agency in fighting drug use in sport

- The role of the Canadian Centre for Ethics in Sport in opposing illegal dug use and other unethical sport practices

- The International Olympic Committee's list of banned pharmacological substances

- The drug policies of various professional sports

- The use of physiological aids such as blood doping and drug masking

- The Dubin Inquiry and its impact on Canadian sport

- Drug testing practices in sport

- The ethical implications of drug use in sport

Section Quiz

Name: _____ Date: _____

Multiple-Choice Questions

Mission: Circle the letter beside the answer that you believe to be correct.

1. The artificial development of muscle tissue is promoted by the use of
   (a) anabolic steroids
   (b) erythropoietin
   (c) blood doping
   (d) caffeine

2. Athletes who compete in endurance sports may try to enhance their performance by taking
   (a) anabolic steroids
   (b) erythropoietin
   (c) beta-blockers
   (d) human growth hormone

3. Which of the following ergogenic techniques does not involve ingesting a substance?
   (a) drug masking
   (b) creatine
   (c) blood doping
   (d) human growth hormone

4. Which of the following performance-enhancing substances is difficult to detect?
   (a) human growth hormone
   (b) synthetic testosterone
   (c) erythropoietin
   (d) all of the above

5. Which of the following substances have athletes used to promote fat loss?
   (a) carnitine
   (b) protein supplements
   (c) creatine
   (d) caffeine

6. Which of the following ergogenic aids is used to enhance aerobic athletic performance?
   (a) blood doping
   (b) creatine
   (c) erythropoietin
   (d) a and c

7. The Canadian Centre for Ethics in Sport is concerned with
   (a) an ethical clean up of the sporting world
   (b) promoting fair play through educational outlets
   (c) opposing the use of drugs in sport
   (d) all of the above

Short-Answer Questions

Mission: Briefly answer the following questions in the space provided:

1. What must an Olympic competitor do if he or she wishes to use medicines that contain banned substances?

   _____

2. What method is used to test for banned substances?

   _____

3. What do beta blockers do?

   _____

4. Which common stimulant has been banned by the International Olympic Committee? Why?

   _____

5. What are the general negative side effects of ingesting extra human growth hormone?

   _____

6. Name four pain-masking agents used by athletes.

   _____

7. Which governing body banned Ben Johnson for life from competing in track and field?

   _____

8. What did the Dubin Inquiry seek to ascertain?

   _____

Essay Questions

Mission: On a separate piece of paper, develop a 100-word response to the following questions.

1. Describe one ergogenic aid from each classification (nutritional, pharmacological, physiological). In which sports would athletes benefit from the use of these aids?

2. Describe the drug policies of three of the five major-league sports.

3. Summarize Canada's drug scandal at the 1988 Seoul Olympics and explain the worldwide significance of this event.

Terminology Review

Defining Key Terms

Mission: Briefly explain the meaning of the following key terms:

Name:

Date:

Key Term	Definition
Nutritional supplements	
Protein and amino acid supplements	
Carnitine	
Creatine	
Caffeine	
Deceptive advertising	
Doping	
Pain-masking agents	
World Anti-Doping Agency	

Anabolic steroids	
Prohormones	
Human growth hormone (HGH)	
Canadian Centre for Ethics in Sport (CCES)	
Erythropoietin (EPO)	
Restricted pharmacological substances	
Drug policies	
Blood doping	
Drug masking	
Dubin Inquiry	
Drug testing	

The Effects of Performance-Enhancing Drugs and Techniques

Name:
Date:
Look in the Book! Pages: 165, 167, 169, 171

When the rewards of winning take precedent over the principle of fair play, athletes may resort to banned drugs and techniques to improve their performance.

Mission: Use the space provided in the table below to briefly identify and describe the use and effects, as well as the health risks associated with the substances listed in the left-hand column.

Type	Use and Effects	Health Risks
Anabolic agents		
Diuretics		
Narcotics		
Stimulants		
Hormones		
Blood doping		
Beta-blockers		

The Canadian Centre for Ethics in Sport—Research Exercise

Name:

Date:

Look in the Book! Pages: 168, 173

The Canadian Centre for Ethics in Sport (CCES) is engaged in a variety of national and international initiatives with leading sport organizations, public authorities, and the private sector in promoting ethical conduct.

Mission: Use the space provided in the table below to briefly identify and describe the goals of the following initiatives found on the CCES website (www.cces.ca).

CCES Initiative	Goals
True Sport Strategy	
The Sport We Want Symposium	
Sport Dispute Resolution Centre of Canada	
True Sport Foundation	
Bodysense Program	
Public Service Announcements	
Research and Discussion Papers	
World Anti-Doping Agency	
World Anti-Doping Code	
International Anti-Doping Arrangement	
Governmental	

Lindsay Alcock, 2002. THE CANADIAN PRESS/COA/Andre Forget

12

Technological Influences on Human Performance

Learning Objectives

The exercises in this section of the workbook will help to reinforce your knowledge of the following topics covered in the *Exercise Science* textbook:

- The impact that various scientific practices have had on sport performance
- The field of ergonomics and its role in sport
- How technology has improved the design and construction of personal protective equipment in a number of sports
- How technology has improved the design and construction of sports equipment such as clothing, playing surfaces, and so on
- The impact of advances in computer technology on sport

Section Quiz

Name: _____ Date: _____

Multiple-Choice Questions

Mission: Circle the letter beside the answer that you believe to be correct.

1. Helmets can reduce the energy absorbed by the skull in a cycling mishap (when riding at a common cycling speed of 15 km per hour) by
   (a) 15 percent
   (b) 25 percent
   (c) 90 percent
   (d) 50 percent

2. Athletes can use equipment that manufacturers claim will compress muscles, thereby limiting tissue vibration, in
   (a) track and field
   (b) swimming
   (c) race car driving
   (d) a and b

3. The Polara golf ball was banned by the U.S. Golf Association because
   (a) of its cellular construction
   (b) it reduced the skills necessary to play golf
   (c) of its asymmetrical shape
   (d) it increased the likelihood of hooks and slices

4. Ten Olympic records were broken in the speed skating competition at the Nagano Winter Olympics in 1998 because of
   (a) innovative bodysuits
   (b) an improved ice surface
   (c) clap skates
   (d) computerized timing equipment

5. The most critical material invention in sportswear was that of
   (a) Lycra
   (b) elastic
   (c) cotton
   (d) plastic

6. In recent years, the re-design of football equipment has been crucial because
   (a) rule changes have allowed players to wear less protection
   (b) rule changes have allowed greater physical contact
   (c) players have demanded less expensive equipment
   (d) heat-related injuries have become increasingly common

7. As bicycles have become more efficient, which traditional element have designers eliminated?
   (a) gear shifters
   (b) crossbars
   (c) hand brakes
   (d) rubberized tires

Short-Answer Questions

Mission: Briefly answer the following questions in the space provided:

1. Describe the role of an ergonomist in sport.

   _____

2. Describe the evolution of fabrics in sportswear.

   _____

3. What are the three main evolutionary changes in track events?

   _____

4. Describe how the clap skate has enhanced performance in speed skating.

   _____

5. Outline the controversy over the introduction of the new soccer ball, Fevernova, at the 2002 World Cup soccer.

   _____

6. What are the drawbacks to artificial turf?

   _____

7. Describe an example of an equipment design innovation that challenged the integrity of the sport when it was introduced.

   _____

8. Which sports have already used virtual reality simulators to help their athletes train?

   _____

Essay Questions

Mission: On a separate piece of paper, develop a 100-word response to the following questions.

1. Discuss the dilemma for sports organizations in their relationship with technology.

2. Explain how the evolution of equipment has enhanced human performance with respect to three sports.

3. Examine how coaching has been affected by the revolutionary changes in the application of computer technology to sport.

Terminology Review

Defining Key Terms

Name:
Date:

Mission: Briefly explain the meaning of the following key terms:

Key Term	Definition
Ergonomics	
Repetitive stress injury	
Personal protective equipment	
Equipment revolution	
Wicking properties	
Clap skate	
Full-body swimsuits	
Lifting shirt	
Artificial turf	
Motion analysis	
Virtual reality technologies	

The Equipment Revolution

The creation of new sports equipment is dramatically changing athletic performance, including the cost of participating, the skills necessary to succeed, and the injuries associated with a particular sport.

Name:

Date:

Look in the Book!
Pages: 176–179, 181

Mission: Use the space provided in the table below to briefly identify and describe the equipment changes and criticism/drawbacks associated with the sports listed in the left-hand column. Then, choose three pieces of equipment from other sports and fill in the required information. A sample entry is provided below.

	Equipment Changes	Criticism/Drawbacks
Hockey stick	Early North American wood sticks; more advanced wood/fibreglass design; graphite sticks	Hockey "purists" say graphite offers less control; too much curve in blade leads to poor shooting technique
Tennis racquet		
Soccer ball		
Swimsuits		
Athletic shoes		
Track surfaces		
Skates		
Bicycle		

Sport Organizations and Technology

Name:
Date:
Look in the Book! Pages: 179, 181

Many sport analysts argue that technologically improved equipment erodes the particular skills and traditions of sports and results in the dramatic change of an athlete's performance and/or ability.

Mission: Use the space provided in the table below to briefly identify the sport organization affected by the equipment innovation (listed in the left-hand column), and describe the reason for controversy. Then, choose another example of a controversial sport equipment and fill in the required information. Answer the question that follows.

Equipment	Sport	Reason for Controversy
Polara golf ball		
Full-body swimsuits		
Clap skates		
Inzer lifting shirt		

To what extent do you believe that improved athletic performance is due to the improved engineering and materials now used in sports equipment instead of an athlete's personal accomplishment in achieving higher skill levels? Give examples to support your answer.

_____

_____

_____

_____

Crossword on Technological Influences on Human Performance

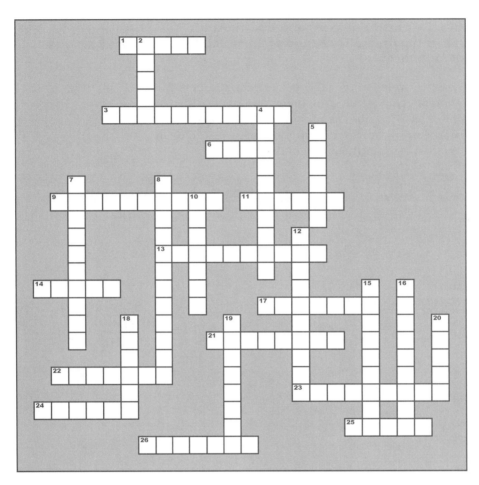

Across

1. This part of the clap skate is spring-loaded
3. "Reality" that uses models to create totally new views of real events
6. Dynamic that pulls a cyclist backward
9. Stress injury affecting tendons, nerves, muscles, and other soft body tissue
11. Sport that introduced controversial Fevernova ball
13. Turf reputed to cause injuries to ligaments, joints, and tendons
14. What gasoline does at temperatures reaching 1,149°C
17. Material formerly used to make baseball helmets
21. Synthetic material used in modern tennis racquets
22. Property of athletic clothing describing their ability to draw moisture away from the skin
23. Item used to clock track events before the introduction of digital timing
24. Fibre used to construct the structural parts of a race car
25. Entire athletic garments are now made from this elasticized material
26. Body part emulated by the seams of the Fastskin swimsuit

Down

2. Designer of controversial shirt for weightlifters
4. This science is sometimes called "human-factors engineering"
5. Mandatory protective gear in the NHL
7. Advances in materials can now protect football players from this potentially fatal condition
8. The reduction of friction by lessening wind contact
10. Users can interact realistically with this technologically created reality
12. Ergonomists use this term to describe individual differences
15. Type of base that prevents common foot and leg injuries for softball players
16. Personal equipment that measures hip undulations or strides and thereby distance travelled
18. Athletes now benefit from precision analysis of this
19. What athletic socks are now designed to eliminate
20. The human touch of this key sports figure is being challenged by technology

Donovan Bailey, 2001. THE CANADIAN PRESS/Chuck Stoody

13

Training Principles and Methods

Learning Objectives

The exercises in this section of the workbook will help to reinforce your knowledge of the following topics covered in the *Exercise Science* textbook:

- Definition of athletic training and its parameters
- The F.I.T.T. principle (Frequency, Intensity, Time, and Type) of developing a training program
- The role of cardiorespiratory fitness measurement in designing training schedules
- The role of the three energy systems in training
- The six principles of training (Overload, Progression, Specificity, Individual Difference, Reversibility, and Diminishing Returns), and their integration into an individual training regimen
- The six methods of training (periodization, concurrent, interval, Fartlek, resistance, and plyometrics)
- The general adaptation syndrome (GAS), and its role in athletic training
- Environmental factors and their impact on training
- Other important factors that can have an effect on training, such as rest, recovery, avoiding injury, maintaining interest, and avoiding burnout and/or overtraining

Section Quiz

Name: _____ Date: _____

Multiple-Choice Questions

Mission: Circle the letter beside the answer that you believe to be correct.

1. The acronym F.I.T.T.
   (a) was coined by Canadian Dr. David M. Chisholm
   (b) captures the four basic building blocks of an exercise plan
   (c) stands for frequency, intensity, type, and time of training
   (d) all of the above

2. The formula whereby one's age is subtracted from 220 is
   (a) the most accurate way of predicting maximal heart rate
   (b) recommended only for elite athletes
   (c) an accurate assessment of heart rate
   (d) an estimation of maximal heart rate

3. The baseline values for training frequency within the F.I.T.T. principle are
   (a) 1-2 times per week
   (b) 3-5 times per week
   (c) 3-7 times per week
   (d) 1-5 times per week

4. Which type of activity utilizes the anaerobic system?
   (a) sprints
   (b) high speed, explosive movements
   (c) long-distance running
   (d) both a and b

5. What is the recommended number of sets for an expert athlete seeking to attain hypertrophy as outlined by the ACSM?
   (a) greater or equal to five
   (b) greater or equal to three
   (c) greater or equal to one
   (d) greater or equal to four

6. Which principle states that loads must be increased in order for adaptation to occur?
   (a) Individual Differences
   (b) Overload
   (c) Specificity
   (d) S.A.I.D

7. Which type of training involves multiple system training (sometimes called "cross training")?
   (a) concurrent
   (b) Fartlek
   (c) interval
   (d) plyometric

Short-Answer Questions

Mission: Briefly answer the following questions in the space provided:

1. What are some of the potential benefits and drawbacks of Fartlek training?

   _____

2. What is PNF stretching? How does it work?

   _____

3. What is involved in interval training?

   _____

4. How could the Overload Principle be implemented into an existing training program?

   _____

5. Outline the parameters of the F.I.T.T. Principle.

   _____

6. Define the term "repetition maximum."

   _____

7. Name three long-term steady exercises for which the aerobic system supplies the energy.

   _____

8. Name three variables that should be taken into account when considering a weight-training program.

   _____

Essay Questions

Mission: On a separate piece of paper, develop a 100-word response to the following questions.

1. Using the HRR and MHR method, calculate a THR of 75 percent for a sixteen-year-old individual who has a resting heart rate of 80 beats per minute. State why one method is more accurate than the other.

2. Outline how the concept of periodization works.

3. The General Adaptation Syndrome (GAS) was devised in the mid-1950s by stress researcher Hans Selye. Explain the three stages that our body goes through in response to stress according to this theory.

Terminology Review

Defining Key Terms

Mission: Briefly explain the meaning of the following key terms:

Name:

Date:

Key Term	Definition
Resting heart rate (RHR)	
Target heart rate (THR)	
Maximal heart rate (MHR)	
Heart rate reserve (HRR)	
Borg Scale of Perceived Exertion	
F.I.T.T. Principle	
One repetition maximum (1RM)	
Repetition maximum (RM)	
Principle of Overload	
Principle of Progression	
Specificity Principle (the S.A.I.D. Principle)	
Principle of Individual Differences	

Principle of Reversibility	
Principle of Diminishing Returns	
Periodization	
The General Adaptation Syndrome (GAS)	
Concurrent training	
Interval training	
Fartlek training	
Resistance training	
Plyometrics training	
Cold stress and heat stress	
Thermoregulation	
Heat exchange	
Acclimatization	
Proprioceptive neuromuscular facilitation	
Burnout and overtraining	

Training Principles and Methods Research

Name:
Date:

Look in the Book!
Pages: 189, 191–197, 199

Training needs vary greatly depending on both the objectives and the physical attributes of the individual involved.

Mission: Select three different articles that deal with a specific aspect of training to improve performance in a sport or activity. Each article should focus on the same topic (e.g., weight training, stretching, interval training for recreational walkers, etc.) and aimed at varying levels of ability: one article for beginner, one article for intermediate, and one article for advanced participants. List your comparisons in the table below, using the column labelled "Criteria" as your guideline. A sample entry is provided below.

Criteria	Sample	Article 1	Article 2	Article 3
Name of magazine	Recreational Walker's World Magazine			
Article title	Interval training: "Just one workout a week can make a big difference!"			
Author/ qualifications	Dr. Peter Walker, Ph.D., exercise physiologist, U. of Alberta			
Overall claim	Incorporating one interval workout a week can help the recreational walker improve fitness and can add enjoyment to his or her exercise schedule.			
Body focus (i.e., energy system, muscle group, etc.)	Primary: cardiovascular system Secondary: leg muscle strength/ endurance			

Criteria	Sample	Article 1	Article 2	Article 3
Steps to success/ program outline	Walkers begin by adding faster "bursts" of 3–5 minutes into ordinarily steady-state walking; rest intervals begin at 2–4 minutes and are then decreased. Pulse rate monitoring also recommended.			
Duration of program	12-week cycle is recommended, although author also offers 3- and 6-week cycle schedules.			
Advantages of the strategies outlined	Incorporating intervals may break up monotony of constant steady walking for many. Faster walking interspersed with rest intervals will improve cardiovascular capacity according to theory of interval training.			
Problems with the strategies outlined	Program may be too "intense" for many recreational walkers. Extra fatigue incurred during these workouts may decrease enjoyment for many.			
General comments	Very well organized; author seems to understand aims of average recreational walker. Emphasis on enjoyment a big plus. Many walkers may not be aware of alternative training modes like this.			
Your overall evaluation of the article's effectiveness (Scale 1–10)	8.5			

The Effect of Environmental Factors on Training and Performance

Name:
Date:
Look in the Book! Pages: 199–201

Environmental factors such as extreme temperatures, high humidity, or high altitude can have a significant impact on physical training and physical performance.

Mission: Research how the various environmental factors listed in the left-hand column of the table can have a significant impact on physical training and physical performance, using historical or current sporting events as the basis of your research findings. A sample entry has been included to assist you.

Environmental Factor	Effects on the Body and Training
High altitude	At the track and field competition in the1968 Olympic Games in Mexico City, every long-distance event was won in a time significantly slower than the world record. Athletes born and raised at high altitudes dominated; those from sea-level areas attempted to train at altitude to prepare but almost none of their efforts were successful. Athletes in sprints, however, recorded many excellent times due to the "thinner" air.
Cold climates	
Hot climates (with high humidity)	
Air quality	

Crossword on Training Principles and Methods

Across

2. Muscle condition resulting from inactivity
3. Type of training that involves box jumping
4. Cool-down sessions can reduce the build-up of this acid
5. Type of stretching that involves bouncing
6. Swedish word for "speed play" training
7. Interval training pioneer
9. Training principle that states that performance outcomes must match training exercises
11. Term used to describe the breaking down of training into time-specific segments
13. Process in which sweat is vaporized from the skin into the environment
14. The maximal amount of weight an individual can lift for one repetition
18. Most athletes follow a routine of this type of exercise to increase muscle flexibility
20. The first person to break the 4-minute mile
22. What the "I" in F.I.T.T. represents
23. Person who devised the scale of perceived exertion

Down

1. Term for state in which training and/or competition performance stops improving
2. Process whereby the body adjusts to high altitude
8. Group of neurons located at the base of the brain that maintain the body's temperature
10. Type of training that combines resistance and endurance training
11. Performing your workouts faster each week is an example of this training principle
12. A method of training that involves using weight
15. Sleep and rest are essential to this element of any training regimen
16. Long-distance running, cycling, and swimming train this energy system
17. Another name for the heart rate reserve method
19. A "vehicle" used to make the body more efficient
21. This type of exchange is achieved by radiation, conduction, and evaporation

14

Personal Fitness and Training

Steve Nash, 2002. THE CANADIAN PRESS/Kevin Frayer

Learning Objectives

The exercises in this section of the workbook will help to reinforce your knowledge of the following topics covered in the *Exercise Science* textbook:

- Ways of determining a person's goals and level of commitment before embarking on a training program

- How to develop measurable objectives for a training program

- Methods of assessing a person's lifestyle prior to beginning training

- Tools for assessing personal fitness, including the CPAFLA protocol

- Ways of testing for specific areas of fitness, including cardiovascular fitness, body composition, muscular strength and endurance, and flexibility

- Basic guidelines for developing an exercise program for the improvement of both aerobic and anaerobic capacity

- The design of specialized exercise plans aimed at improving musuclar strength and endurance as well as cardiovascular conditioning, managing body weight, and enhancing flexibility

- How to develop specialized fitness plans for individuals with varying needs and at varying levels of fitness

- Pertinent safety issues in designing fitness programs

Section Quiz

Name: _____ Date: _____

Multiple-Choice Questions

Mission: Circle the letter beside the answer that you believe to be correct.

1. Which of the following is an example of a fitness objective?
   (a) developing a more active lifestyle
   (b) recovering from an injury
   (c) improving athletic performance
   (d) all of the above

2. Which of the following fitness appraisals is a test for muscular endurance?
   (a) Body Mass Index
   (b) grip strength
   (c) push-ups
   (d) all of the above

3. Circuit training is effective if you are seeking to
   (a) develop cardiorespiratory fitness and lay the foundation for sport-specific aerobic activity
   (b) develop cardiovascular fitness and reduce the incidence of sport-specific injuries
   (c) improve your heart rate reserve percentage
   (d) increase the time in which you can endure anaerobic activity

4. Anaerobic exercise should include
   (a) low levels of resistance training
   (b) speed and agility
   (c) strength and power development
   (d) both b and c

5. Flexibility is important in exercise because it
   (a) aids in increasing muscle hypertrophy
   (b) plays a major role in the maintenance of muscle balance
   (c) helps you to strengthen your muscles and reduce the risk of injury
   (d) increases the range of motion in your muscles

6. If aerobic training is a primary objective, the days between workouts should be no more than
   (a) one
   (b) two
   (c) three
   (d) four

7. The benefits of stretching include
   (a) increasing the ROM of joints
   (b) helping to nourish the joint's connective tissue
   (c) enhancing muscle length
   (d) all of the above

8. Which of the following is the best preventative method of avoiding overtraining?
   (a) adequate short-term recovery
   (b) proper variation
   (c) careful monitoring
   (d) all of the above

Short-Answer Questions

Mission: Briefly answer the following questions in the space provided:

1. Outline the three stages involved in developing a sound fitness training program.

2. What are three possible objectives of an individual's exercise program?

3. What are the elements of a healthy lifestyle?

4. Describe various testing methods to assess cardiovascular endurance.

5. Outline CPAFLA's approach to healthy body composition testing.

6. In designing an exercise program, what are the two main criteria for selecting appropriate exercises?

7. What are the three steps to consider when using interval training in an exercise program?

8. Why is a cooling-down period very important in an anaerobic program?

Essay Questions

Mission: On a separate piece of paper, develop a 100-word response to the following.

1. Design a personal anaerobic fitness program to suit an athlete in the sport of your choice.

2. Summarize the components of fitness that are emphasized in the Canadian Activity, Fitness and Lifestyle Approach and describe how they are tested.

3. The best solution to losing excess fat is to have an exercise program that combines aerobic exercise and light resistance training. Design a program for an individual who has cleared the PAR-Q questionnaire that would facilitate a reasonable loss of fat over a period of 8 weeks.

Terminology Review

Defining Key Terms

Mission: Briefly explain the meaning of the following key terms:

Name: _____

Date: _____

Key Term	Definition
Fitness objectives	
Motivational readiness	
FANTASTIC Lifestyle Checklist	
Performance-related fitness	
Health-related fitness	
The Canadian Physical Activity, Fitness and Lifestyle Appraisal (CPAFLA)	
Cardiovascular endurance	
Body composition	
Muscular strength	
Muscular endurance	
Flexibility	
Léger "Beep Test"	

Crossword on Personal Fitness and Training

Across

2. High levels of this acid are produced during anaerobic training
4. The flexibility of this body part can be measured by the Trunk Forward Flexion Test
9. Aspect of exercises that affects fatigue, safety, and results
10. The ability of a joint to move freely through its full range of motion
11. Type of training that achieves the greatest amount of work with the least fatigue
12. A solid aerobic base should be established prior to this type of training
14. Desires to meet needs in specific ways
17. Endurance of this type is generally regarded as the best indicator of overall health
19. Test for aerobic fitness developed by Dr. Luc Léger
20. The mCAFT is one example of this type of test
22. The ability of a muscle to perform repeated or sustained contractions over a period of time
23. Maximal uptake of this element is most precisely determined through direct gas analysis in a laboratory

Down

1. A type of anthropometric measurement
3. Tests such as the T-test measure this physical quality
5. Acronym for the current version of the 1979 Canadian Standardized Test of Fitness
6. Readiness for physical fitness training determined by the Stages of Change Questionnaire
7. Trying to improve this is key for those striving to succeed in sport or work
8. Muscular quality defined as the maximum tension or force a muscle can exert in a single contraction
13. These must be clear before designing a fitness program
15. The most important but taxing part of an aerobic program
16. Diseases due to these kinds of choices are the major causes of disability and death
18. The resistance provided by free weights and stack weights
19. Key values assessed for selected components of fitness against which progress can be measured
20. Tissue that stores fat
21. A screening device administered prior to a fitness assessment

Personal Fitness Assessment and Exercise Program Design

Name:

Date:

Look in the Book! Pages: 205–223

Gauging your own fitness level and adjusting your lifestyle to attain certain fitness goals is an important aspect of practising a healthy active lifestyle.

Mission: In this section of the workbook you will perform a series of fitness appraisals to determine areas where you need to improve your fitness level.

1. Physical Activity Readiness

First, fill out the PAR-Q & YOU Physical Activity Readiness Questionnaire on page 144 to identify any health-related problems.

Next, complete the Health and Physical Activity Participation Questionnaire on page 145. With this information, you may then proceed to carry out a series of health-related fitness appraisals of your choosing.

2. Body Composition Appraisals

CPAFLA offers five ways to assess body composition. These are: (1) Body Mass Index (BMI), (2) Waist Circumference (WC), (3) BMI Modified by Sum of Five Skinfolds (SO5S), (4) BMI Refined by WC, and (5) BMI, WC, and SO5S. You can choose the appraisal or appraisals that you want to perform in order to arrive at your Health Benefit Zone (HBZ) rating. These appraisals begin on page 146.

3. Aerobic (Cardiorespiratory) Appraisals

For persons aged 15–21, CPAFLA recommends only the mCAFT appraisal for aerobic fitness. This is a "sub-maximal" appraisal, which means you will not be going "all-out." It begins on page 148.

4. Musculoskeletal Appraisals

CPAFLA recommends six musculoskeletal appraisals: (1) Hand Grip Strength, (2) Vertical Jump; (3) Push-Ups, (4) Partial Curl-Ups, (5) Sit-and-Reach, and (6) Back Extension. These appraisals begin on page 150.

5. Composite Scoring

Finally, you can use your various musculoskeletal fitness scores to find two overall Composite Scores—one for overall musculoskeletal fitness and one for overall back fitness.

6. Interpreting your results

Once you have completed the appraisals, you can interpret your results by answering the following:

- In which appraisal did you achieve your best results?

- In which appraisal were your results the weakest?

- Why do you think this was so?

- Did your results equal your expectations of what you thought you were capable of?

- Your reactions as to how you place on the "Health Benefit Zones."

- With reference to specific components of fitness, how could you improve your overall results?

7. Design Your Own Fitness Program

You are now ready to design an exercise program to meet your personal needs.

Use Table 14.10 on page 222 of your *Exercise Science* textbook as a template. Apply the F.I.T.T. principle and other training principles (found in Section 13 of your textbook) to design an eight-week program to suit your needs.

Re-appraise after the eight weeks to determine improvements you have made in your fitness.

Physical Activity Readiness
Questionnaire - PAR-Q
(revised 2002)

PAR-Q & YOU

(A Questionnaire for People Aged 15 to 69)

Regular physical activity is fun and healthy, and increasingly more people are starting to become more active every day. Being more active is very safe for most people. However, some people should check with their doctor before they start becoming much more physically active.

If you are planning to become much more physically active than you are now, start by answering the seven questions in the box below. If you are between the ages of 15 and 69, the PAR-Q will tell you if you should check with your doctor before you start. If you are over 69 years of age, and you are not used to being very active, check with your doctor.

Common sense is your best guide when you answer these questions. Please read the questions carefully and answer each one honestly: check YES or NO.

YES	NO		
☐	☐	1.	Has your doctor ever said that you have a heart condition <u>and</u> that you should only do physical activity recommended by a doctor?
☐	☐	2.	Do you feel pain in your chest when you do physical activity?
☐	☐	3.	In the past month, have you had chest pain when you were not doing physical activity?
☐	☐	4.	Do you lose your balance because of dizziness or do you ever lose consciousness?
☐	☐	5.	Do you have a bone or joint problem (for example, back, knee or hip) that could be made worse by a change in your physical activity?
☐	☐	6.	Is your doctor currently prescribing drugs (for example, water pills) for your blood pressure or heart condition?
☐	☐	7.	Do you know of <u>any other reason</u> why you should not do physical activity?

If

you

answered

YES to one or more questions

Talk with your doctor by phone or in person BEFORE you start becoming much more physically active or BEFORE you have a fitness appraisal. Tell your doctor about the PAR-Q and which questions you answered YES.

- You may be able to do any activity you want — as long as you start slowly and build up gradually. Or, you may need to restrict your activities to those which are safe for you. Talk with your doctor about the kinds of activities you wish to participate in and follow his/her advice.
- Find out which community programs are safe and helpful for you.

NO to all questions

If you answered NO honestly to <u>all</u> PAR-Q questions, you can be reasonably sure that you can:
- start becoming much more physically active – begin slowly and build up gradually. This is the safest and easiest way to go.
- take part in a fitness appraisal – this is an excellent way to determine your basic fitness so that you can plan the best way for you to live actively. It is also highly recommended that you have your blood pressure evaluated. If your reading is over 144/94, talk with your doctor before you start becoming much more physically active.

DELAY BECOMING MUCH MORE ACTIVE:
- if you are not feeling well because of a temporary illness such as a cold or a fever – wait until you feel better; or
- if you are or may be pregnant – talk to your doctor before you start becoming more active.

PLEASE NOTE: If your health changes so that you then answer YES to any of the above questions, tell your fitness or health professional. Ask whether you should change your physical activity plan.

<u>Informed Use of the PAR-Q:</u> The Canadian Society for Exercise Physiology, Health Canada, and their agents assume no liability for persons who undertake physical activity, and if in doubt after completing this questionnaire, consult your doctor prior to physical activity.

No changes permitted. You are encouraged to photocopy the PAR-Q but only if you use the entire form.

NOTE: If the PAR-Q is being given to a person before he or she participates in a physical activity program or a fitness appraisal, this section may be used for legal or administrative purposes.

"I have read, understood and completed this questionnaire. Any questions I had were answered to my full satisfaction."

NAME _____

SIGNATURE _____   DATE_____

SIGNATURE OF PARENT _____   WITNESS _____
or GUARDIAN (for participants under the age of majority)

Note: This physical activity clearance is valid for a maximum of 12 months from the date it is completed and becomes invalid if your condition changes so that you would answer YES to any of the seven questions.

CSEP
SCPE   © Canadian Society for Exercise Physiology   Supported by: Health Canada Santé Canada

continued on other side...

Source: Canadian Physical Activity Readiness Questionnaire (PAR-Q) © 2002. Used with permission from the Canadian Society for Exercise Physiology www.csep.ca.

‖‖⮞ Healthy Physical Activity Participation Questionnaire

Answer the following questions. Circle your score for each answer and total up your points for the three questions. Use this point score to determine your HBZ rating from the table at the bottom of the page.

Participation Questionnaire: (Circle your answer)	POINT SCORE	
	Male	Female
1. Frequency: Over a typical seven-day period (one week), how many times do you engage in physical activity that is sufficiently prolonged and intense to cause sweating and a rapid heart beat?		
At least three times	3	5
Normally once or twice	2	3
Rarely or Never	0	0
2. Intensity: When you engage in physical activity, do you:		
Make an intense effort	3	3
Make a light effort	1	2
Make a moderate effort	0	0
3. Perceived Fitness: In a general fashion, would you say that your current physical fitness is:		
Good/Very Good	5	3
Average	3	1
Very Poor/Poor	0	0
ADD UP THE CIRCLED ITEMS:		
ENTER YOUR HBZ RATING:		

Health Benefits Zones: Physical Activity Participation			
Health Benefit Zone	**Total Score**		
Excellent	9–11	↑	Your physical activity participation falls within a range that is generally associated with optimal health benefits.
Very Good	6–8	↑	Your physical activity participation falls within a range that is generally associated with considerable health benefits.
Good	4–5	↑	Your physical activity participation falls within a range that is generally associated with many health benefits.
Fair	1–3	⬆	Your physical activity participation falls within a range that is generally associated with some health benefits but also with some health risks. Progressing from here into the "Good" zone is a very significant step to increasing the health benefits from your participantion.
Needs Improvement	0	↑	Your physical activity participation falls within a range that is generally associated with considerable health risks. Try to accumulate 30 minutes or more of moderate-intensity physical activity over the course of most days of the week.

Source: Canadian Physical Activity, Fitness & Lifestyle Approach: CSEP-Health & Fitness Program's Health-Related Appraisal & Counselling Strategy, Third Edition, © 2003. Reprinted with permission from the Canadian Society for Exercise Physiology.

Body Composition Appraisals

As mentioned earlier, CPAFLA offers five different methods to estimate body composition. These are listed below by least to most accurate.

Chose the method that best suits your needs. Be aware that these appraisals are only reliable when conducted by a certified fitness consultant with CPAFLA training. For more information on certifications, visit www.csep.ca.

BMI Alone (least accurate)

Calculate your BMI using the formula below:

BMI   =   weight (kg) ÷ by height (m²)

  =   _____ (kg) ÷ _____ (m²)

Score _____   HBZ Rating _____

Once you have calculated your BMI, find your body composition point score (using columns 1 and 2 in the table at the top of the adjacent page). Then, find your HBZ rating from the table at the bottom of the adjacent page.

Waist Circumference Alone

Stand straight with your arms at your sides, while your partner places the measuring tape around the narrowest point of your waist (usually just above your belly button). Record the measurement to the nearest 0.5 cm.

For this WC appraisal, you can assume a BMI of 27. Go to the row "25.0–29.9" and then locate your WC score in the "WC" column and your points in Column B. Refer to the Health Benefit Zone table for your HBZ rating.

WC = _____ cm   BMI = _27_____

Score _____   HBZ Rating _____

BMI Refined by SO5S

For this appraisal you must perform a series of skinfold measurements (see box at the top of the next column).

Using the table on the next page, locate the row matching your BMI score. Then proceed across to the double column representing the SO5S scores. Find the row that matches your own SO5S results. Look now to Column C for the points associated with that combination of BMI and SO5S. Refer to the Health Benefit Zone table for your HBZ rating.

BMI = _____   SO5S = _____

Score _____   HBZ Rating _____

Sum of Five Skinfolds (SO5S)

Refer to Figure 14.2 on page 213 of your *Exercise Science* textbook.

Complete one round of the skinfold measurements before performing a second; and if the difference is greater than 0.4, do a third measurement and take the average. Be sure to take all skinfolds on the right side of the body and relax the muscles. Record your results below.

Triceps   ____ ____ ____   Average_____

Biceps   ____ ____ ____   Average_____

Subscapular____ ____ ____   Average_____

Iliac crest   ____ ____ ____   Average_____

Medial cafe ____ ____ ____   Average_____

SO5S = _____ mm

BMI Refined by WC

You may also combine your BMI and WC results for a better estimate of your body composition.

First, locate your BMI point score (in column 1) and then locate your WC measurement for that BMI in the "WC" column. Find your point score (in Column B). Record your "BMI with WC" points score below, and then refer to the Health Benefit Zone table for your HBZ rating.

BMI = _____   WC = _____ cm

Score _____   HBZ Rating _____

BMI, WC, and SO5S

You can also get a three-way score, using BMI, Waist Circumference, and Sum of Five Skinfolds.

Locate your "BMI with WC" (Column B) and enter the point value in the first part of the formula below. Then, locate your "BMI with SO5S" (column C) and enter that point value in the second part of formula. Perform the calculation to get a total score (out of 4) and refer to the Health Benefit Zone table for your rating.

$$\text{Score (out of 4)} = \frac{(\text{column B} \times 1.5) + (\text{column C})}{2.5}$$

$$\text{Score (out of 4)} = \frac{(\underline{\hspace{1cm}} \times 1.5) + (\underline{\hspace{1cm}})}{2.5}$$

Score _____   HBZ Rating _____

Scoring for Body Composition

BMI (kg/m²)	Points Column A	WC (cm) Males	WC (cm) Females	Points Column B	SOSS (mm) Males	SOSS (mm) Females	Points Column C
<18.5	3	All Girths		3	<25	<46	3
					25–54	46–83	4
					55–77	84–113	3
					>77	>113	2
18.5–24.9	4	<94	<80	4	<54	<83	4
		94–101	80–87	3	54–77	83–113	3
		>101	>87	1	>77	>113	2
25.0–29.9	3	<94	<80	4	<54	<83	4
		94–101	80–87	3	54–77	83–113	3
		>101	>87	1	>77	>113	2
30.0–32.4	2	<94	<80	4	<54	<83	4
		94–101	80–87	2	54–77	83–113	3
		>101	>87	0	>77	>113	2
32.5–35.0	1	<94	<80	4	<54	<83	4
		94–101	80–87	2	54–77	83–113	2
		>101	>87	0	>77	>113	1
>35.0	0	<94	<80	4	<54	<83	4
		94–101	80–87	2	54–77	83–113	2
		>101	>87	0	>77	>113	0

Health Benefit Zones: Body Composition

Health Benefit Zone	Symbol	Score		
Excellent	E	4	⬆	Your body composition falls within a range that is generally associated with optimal health benefits.
Very Good	VG	3	⬆	Your body composition falls within a range that is generally associated with considerable health benefits.
Good	G	2	⬆	Your body composition falls within a range that is generally associated with many health benefits.
Fair	F	1	⬆	Your body composition falls within a range that is generally associated with some health risk. Continuing to progress from here into the "Good" zone will further increase the health benefits associated with your body composition.
Needs Improvement	NI	0	⬆	Your body composition falls within a range that is generally associated with considerable health risk. Try to achieve and maintain a healthy body composition by enjoying regular physical activity and healthy eating. Progressing from here into the "Fair" zone is a very significant step to increasing the health benefits associated with your body composition.

Source: Canadian Physical Activity, Fitness & Lifestyle Approach: CSEP-Health & Fitness Program's Health-Related Appraisal & Counselling Strategy, Third Edition, © 2003. Reprinted with permission from the Canadian Society for Exercise Physiology.

CPAFLA has several aerobic fitness appraisals, but only the Modified Canadian Aerobic Fitness Test (mCAFT) is recommendd for ages 15–21. This appraisal is described in your *Exercise Science* textbook (page 211).

After you have performed the mCAFT appraisal, you can calculate your Aerobic Fitness Score using the formula below. You can then find your point score and your Health Benefit Zone rating for Aerobic Fitness.

To complete the AFS formula, you will need to know your oxygen consumption (O$_2$ cost), which will depend on the stage you reached during the appraisal. This can be determined from the table at the top of the next page, depending on the stage you reached.

 The mCAFT Appraisal

CPAFLA recommends that a heart rate monitor is used during the mCAFT appraisal. If not, use a 10-second count (either your radial or carotid artery).

You will complete one or more sessions of three minutes until you reach your predetermined Ceiling Heart Rate (see table on this page). You must stop once you have reached your ceiling.

The pace is determined for you by the recording. The recording also tells you when to stop and take your pulse to see if you have reached your ceiling.

You have two choices in terms of steps—"two-steps" or "one-step." The "one-step" variation is more suitable for taller individuals or those that see themselves as being more fit.

Ceiling Heart Rates

Age	Heart Rate*	
	10 Sec. Count	Monitor Reading
15	29	174
16	28	173
17	28	173
18	28	172
19	28	171
20	28	170
21	28	169

85% of predicted maximum (220-age). Determined for each age and to balance accuracy and safety, rounding 10 sec. count was determined as follow: ≤.8 round down and >.8 round up.

Aerobic Fitness Score

Use the following equation to calculate your Aerobic Fitness Score, then refer to the tables on the adjacent page to find your HBZ rating.

AFS = 10 [17.2 + (1.29 × O$_2$ cost) –

(0.09 × wt. in kg) – (0.18 × age in years)]

= 10 [17.2 + (1.29 × _____) –

(0.09 × _____) – (0.18 × _____)]

= _____ HBZ Rating _____

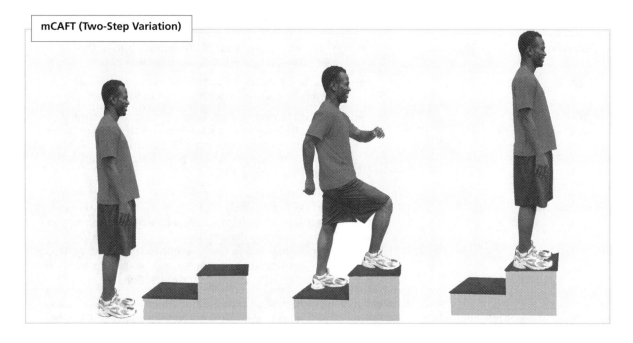

mCAFT (Two-Step Variation)

O₂ Cost in mL/kg/min for Different Stages of the mCAFT

Stage	Females	Males
1	15.9	15.9
2	18.0	18.0
3	22.0	22.0
4	24.5	24.5
5	26.3	29.5
6	29.5	33.6
7	33.6	36.2
8	36.2	40.1

Determination of Health Benefit Zones from Aerobic Fitness Score (Ages 15–19)

Zone	Males	Females
Excellent	574+	490+
Very Good	524–573	437–489
Good	488–523	395–436
Fair	436–487	368–394
Needs improvement	<436	<368

Health Benefits Zones: Aerobic Fitness

Health Benefit Zone	Symbol		
Excellent	E	⬆	Your aerobic fitness falls within a range that is generally associated with optimal health benefits.
Very Good	VG	⬆	Your aerobic fitness falls within a range that is generally associated with considerable health benefits.
Good	G	⬆	Your aerobic fitness falls within a range that is generally associated with many health benefits.
Fair	F	⬆	Your aerobic fitness falls within a range that is generally associated with some health benefits but also some health risks. Progressing from here into the "Good" zone and beyond requires accumulating 30 minutes or more of vigorous physical activity over the course of most days of the week. This is a very significant step to increasing the health benefits from aerobic fitness.
Needs Improvement	NI	⬆	Your aerobic fitness falls within a range that is generally associated with considerable health risks. Try to accumulate 30 minutes or more of moderate-intensity physical activity over the course of most days of the week.

Source: Canadian Physical Activity, Fitness & Lifestyle Approach: CSEP-Health & Fitness Program's Health-Related Appraisal & Counselling Strategy, Third Edition, © 2003. Reprinted with permission from the Canadian Society for Exercise Physiology.

Complete the following six musculoskeletal appraisals to determine your muscular strength and/or endurance and flexibility. When finished, you can also go on to comute a "Composite Score."

If you suffer from any back or joint ailment, you should not perform these appraisals.

1. Hand Grip Strength

Hold the dynamometer in a straight-arm position slightly away from the body and squeeze to exert maximum force. Exhale while squeezing.

Record your scores to the nearest kilogram. Circle the best score from each hand and add them together as your Two-Hand Max Total. Use the tables on the following page to find your HBZ rating for this appraisal.

RH _____ LH _____

RH _____ LH _____

Two-Hand Max Total _____ kg

HBZ Rating _____

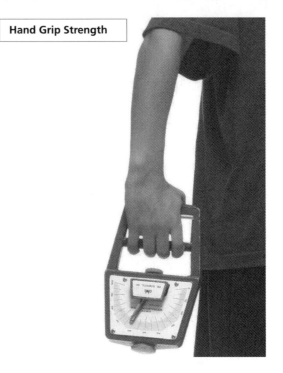

Hand Grip Strength

2. Vertical Jump

For this appraisal, stand sideways to a wall on which a measuring tape has been placed. With your feet flat on the floor, reach as high as possible. Have a partner record this beginning height.

Next, assume a ready position with your body at a safe distance from the wall. Move into a semi-squat position (a pre-jump is not permitted) and jump as high as possible, touching the tape at the peak height of your jump. Have your partner record this height.

Complete this three times and have your partner mark the highest jump on the results sheet. A rest of 10–15 seconds is recommended between each trial. To determine your height jumped, subtract the beginning height from the peak height. You may also obtain an HBZ rating by using your net height jumped.

Leg Power. After completing this appraisal, use the equation below to determine your leg power. Use the tables on the adjacent page to find your HBZ rating.

Peak Leg Power (watts)

= [60.7 × jump height (cm)] +

= [45.3 × body mass (kg)] – 2055

= _____ watts

HBZ Rating _____

Vertical Jump

Healthy Musculoskeletal Fitness Norms (Ages 15–19)

	Grip Strength (kg)	Push-Ups (#)	Sit-and-Reach (cm)	Partial Curl–Ups (#)	Vertical Jump (cm)	Leg Power (Watts)	Back Extension (sec)
Males							
Excellent	≥108	≥39	≥39	25	≥56	≥4644	158–180
Very Good	98–107	29–38	34–38	23–24	51–55	4185–4643	135–157
Good	90–97	23–28	29–33	21–22	46–50	3858–4184	119–134
Fair	79–89	18–22	24–28	16–20	42–45	3323–3857	91–118
Needs Improvement	≤78	≤17	≤23	≤15	≤41	≤3322	≤90
Females							
Excellent	≥68	≥33	≥43	25	≥40	≥3167	169–180
Very Good	60–67	25–32	38–42	22–24	36–39	2795–3166	141–168
Good	53–59	18–24	34–37	17–21	32–35	2399–2794	122–140
Fair	48–52	12–17	29–33	12–16	28–31	2156–2398	91–121
Needs Improvement	≤47	≤11	≤28	≤11	≤27	≤2155	≤90

Health Benefit Zones: Musculoskeletal Fitness

Health Benefit Zone	Symbol	Score		
Excellent	E	4	↑	Your musculoskeletal fitness falls within a range that is generally associated with optimal health benefits.
Very Good	VG	3	↑	Your musculoskeletal fitness falls within a range that is generally associated with considerable health benefits.
Good	G	2	↑	Your musculoskeletal fitness falls within a range that is generally associated with many health benefits.
Fair	F	1	↑	Your musculoskeletal fitness falls within a range that is generally associated with some health risk. Continuing to progress from here into the "Good" zone and beyond will further increase the health benefits associated with your musculoskelatal fitness.
Needs Improvement	NI	0	↑	Your musculoskeletal fitness falls within a range that is generally associated with considerable health risks. Progressing from here into the "Fair" zone requires utilizing your major muscle groups more vigorously against resistance two to three times per week. This is a very significant step to increasing the health benefits from musculosceletal fitness.

Source: Canadian Physical Activity, Fitness & Lifestyle Approach: CSEP-Health & Fitness Program's Health-Related Appraisal & Counselling Strategy, Third Edition, © 2003. Reprinted with permission from the Canadian Society for Exercise Physiology.

|||⟩ 3. Push-Ups

For this appraisal, correct performance is imperative, and the appraisal should be stopped when you are unable to maintain the correct push-up technique over two consecutive repetitions. Be sure to exhale on the effort phase of the push-up.

Use the Healthy Musculoskeletal Fitness Norms and Health Benefit Zones for Musculoskeletal Fitness tables on the previous page to determine your point score and HBZ ratings.

Number of push-ups completed _____

HBZ Rating _____

Push-up (Modified)

Note: CPAFLA recommends that females perform the modified push-ups and males perform the standard push-ups. However, females can perform the standard push-ups just as males can.

|||⟩ 4. Partial Curl-Ups

Refer to page 214 of your *Exercise Science* textbook for a description of this appraisal. Use the cadence of 50 beats per minute on a metronome to set the performance rate.

Use the tables on the previous page to determine your score and HBZ ratings.

Number of curl-ups completed _____

HBZ Rating _____

Partial Curl-up

||||➡ 5. Sit-and-Reach

Refer to the appraisal protocol on page 215 of your *Exercise Science* textbook and record your results in the space provided below.

Again, use the tables on page 151 to determine your HBZ ratings.

Trial 1 _____ cm

Trial 2 _____ cm

HBZ Rating _____

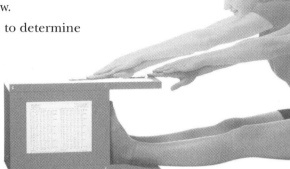

Sit-and-Reach

||||➡ 6. Back Extensions

The back extension appraisal is new to the CPAFLA protocol. If you suffer from any back ailment, you should not perform these appraisals. Do not attempt this appraisal on your own.

The appraisal is stopped once you are unable to maintain the correct technique.

1. Your partner must have a clock (with a second hand) or a stopwatch to record the time.

2. Lie on a bench as shown in the illustration, with your hands braced on the floor holding up your upper torso.

3. When ready, bring your arms to your chest. Maintain this horizontal position for as long as you can. Be sure to breathe normally throughout this appraisal.

4. Hold that position until you are unable to keep your body perfectly straight or you feel unduly stressed (for a maximum of 180 seconds). Record your time and refer to the tables on page 151 to find your HBZ rating.

Time _____

HBZ Rating _____

*Pre-Screen Test: CPAFLA recommends the following pre-screening test to be done before attempting this appraisal.

- *lie face down on a mat*
- *extend right leg up and back; place down*
- *extend left leg up and back; place down*
- *repeat in comination with an extension of the opposing arm.*

If you experience any discomfort or pain during those movements, do not perform the back extension appraisal.

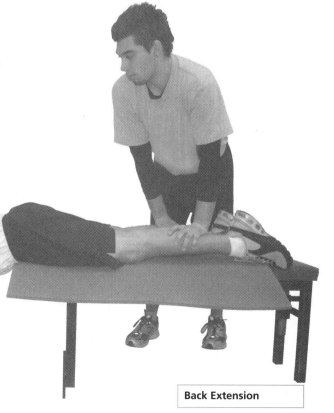

Back Extension

Musculoskeletal Fitness—Composite Score

You have successfully completed a number of CPAFLA musculoskeletal appraisals and obtained a raw score for each test. You may now combine these scores into a "Composite Score," which will give an overall picture of your musculoskeletal fitness.

Use the table at the top of the adjacent page to help you find your Composite Score.

Gather Your Results

1. Gather all the results from each of your musculoskeletal appraisals and write each result in the first column. Enter the HBZ rating for each appraisal in column 2 ("E' for Excellent or "NI" for "Needs Improvement," etc.). Skip the appraisals that you did not complete.

2. In the next column, you need to write in "weighted scores" for each appraisal that you performed. You can find the weighted score in the Weighted Scores chart. For example, if your rating was "Excellent" for "Grip Strength," your weighted score is "8" (in this case, the score is the same for males and females).

3 Add up all your weighted scores and write that total in line "(a)."

With these numbers in hand, you may now find your Composite Score for Musculoskeletal Fitness. Follow the steps below:

1. For each of the appraisals that you completed, circle the numbers in the "Maximum Attainable Weighted Scores" column (there is a column for males and another column for females). Add up the "maximums" for all the appraisals that you completed (i.e., the ones that you circled). Write in that total under the column on line "(b)."

2. To get your Composite Score, you need to refer to the Nomogram at the bottom of the next page. Locate your your Weighted Score across the top of the Nomogram and then find your "Maximum Attainable Weighted Score" down the left hand side. Your Composite Score is where those two lines intersect. For example, if your "Total Weighted Score Achieved" was "13" and your "Maximal Attainable Score" was "20," then your final Composite Score is "3." Write this result on line "(c)" (it is out of 4).

3. Simply refer to the Health Benefit Zones table below to get your Composite Rating for Musculoskeletal Fitness. Circle your overall HBZ rating on line "(d)."

Health Benefit Zones: Composite Scoring for Musculoskeletal Fitness

Health Benefit Zone	Symbol	Score		
Excellent	E	4	↑	Your musculoskeletal fitness falls within a range that is generally associated with optimal health benefits.
Very Good	VG	3	↑	Your musculoskeletal fitness falls within a range that is generally associated with considerable health benefits.
Good	G	2	↑	Your musculoskeletal fitness falls within a range that is generally associated with many health benefits.
Fair	F	1	↑	Your musculoskeletal fitness falls within a range that is generally associated with some health risk. Continuing to progress from here into the "Good" zone and beyond will further increase the health benefits associated with your musculoskelatal fitness.
Needs Improvement	NI	0	↑	Your musculoskeletal fitness falls within a range that is generally associated with considerable health risks. Progressing from here into the "Fair" zone requires utilizing your major muscle groups more vigorously against resistance two to three times per week. This is a very significant step to increasing the health benefits from musculosceletal fitness.

Source: Canadian Physical Activity, Fitness & Lifestyle Approach: CSEP-Health & Fitness Program's Health-Related Appraisal & Counselling Strategy, Third Edition, © 2003. Reprinted with permission from the Canadian Society for Exercise Physiology.

Composite Scoring—Healthy Musculoskeletal Fitness

Age _____	Male/Female (circle one)				
	Measurement	HBZ Rating	Weighted Score	Maximum Attainable Weighted Scores	
				Male	Female
Grip Strength (kg)				8	8
Push-Ups (#)				8	4
Sit-and-Reach(cm)				4	8
Partial Curl-Ups(#)				4	4
Leg Power (Watts)				4	4
Back Extension (s)				4	4

(a) Total Weighted Score Achieved _____

(b) Total Maximum Attainable Weighted Score _____ _____

(c) Composite Musculosceletal Fitness Score (out of 4) _____

(d) Composite Musculosceletal Fitness Rating (circle one)   E   VG   G   F   NI

Weighted Scores

	Male					Female				
	E	VG	G	F	NI	E	VG	G	F	NI
Grip Strength	8	6	4	2	0	8	6	4	2	0
Push-Ups	8	6	4	2	0	4	3	2	1	0
Sit-and-Reach	4	3	2	1	0	8	6	4	2	0
Partial Curl-Ups	4	3	2	1	0	4	3	2	1	0
Leg Power	4	3	2	1	0	4	3	2	1	0
Back Extension	4	3	2	1	0	4	3	2	1	0

Nomogram

Total Weighted Score Achieved

Maximal Weighted Attainable Score	32	31	30	29	28	27	26	25	24	23	22	21	20	19	18	17	16	15	14	13	12	11	10	9	8	7	6	5	4	3	2	1	0
32	4	4	4	4	3	3	3	3	3	3	3	3	3	2	2	2	2	2	2	2	1	1	1	1	1	1	1	1	1	0	0	0	0
28					4	4	4	4	3	3	3	3	3	3	3	2	2	2	2	2	2	2	1	1	1	1	1	1	1	0	0	0	0
24							4	4	4	4	3	3	3	3	3	3	2	2	2	2	2	2	1	1	1	1	1	1	1	0	0	0	0
20													4	4	4	3	3	3	3	3	2	2	2	2	2	1	1	1	1	1	0	0	0
16																	4	4	4	3	3	3	3	2	2	2	1	1	1	1	0	0	0
12																					4	4	3	3	3	2	2	2	1	1	1	0	0
8																									4	4	3	3	2	1	1	0	0
4																													4	3	2	1	0

Source: Canadian Physical Activity, Fitness & Lifestyle Approach: CSEP-Health & Fitness Program's Health-Related Appraisal & Counselling Strategy, Third Edition, © 2003. Reprinted with permission from the Canadian Society for Exercise Physiology.

Composite Score—Healthy Back Fitness

To find your Composite Score for Healthy Back Fitness, you will need to follow steps similar to those for musculoskeletal fitness (described on the previous page). You will also need your Physical Activity Participation results (from page 145) and your Waist Circumference results (from page 147).

Once you have these, you may find your Composite Score for Healthy Back Fitness by following these steps:

1. Fill in the Composite Scoring table below using the Weighted Score table at the bottom of this page and the Nomogram on page 155.
2. Once you have your Composite Back Fitness Score (line "c" in the table below), refer to the Health Benefits Zones table (on page 154) to determine your Health Benefit Zone for Back Fitness.
3. Circle your HBZ Rating on line (d).

Composite Scoring—Healthy Back Fitness

Age				Male/Female (circle one)	
Appraisal Items	Measurement	Rating	Weighted Score	Maximum Attainable Weighted Scores	
				Male	Female
P.A. Participation				8	8
Waist Circum. (cm)				4	8
Sit-and-Reach (cm)				4	4
Partial Curl-Ups (#)				4	4
Back Extension (s)				8	8

(a) Total Weighted Score Achieved _____

(b) Total Maximum Attainable Weighted Score _____ _____

(c) Composite Back Fitness Score (out of 4) _____

(d) Composite Back Fitness Rating (circle one) E VG G F NI

Weighted Scores for Composite Back Fitness

	Male					Female				
	E	VG	G	F	NI	E	VG	G	F	NI
P.A. Participation	8	6	4	2	0	8	6	4	2	0
Waist Circumference	4	3	2	1	0	8	6	4	2	0
Sit-and-Reach	4	3	2	1	0	4	3	2	1	0
Partial Curl-Ups	4	3	2	1	0	4	3	2	1	0
Back Extension	8	6	4	2	0	8	6	4	2	0

Source: Canadian Physical Activity, Fitness & Lifestyle Approach: CSEP-Health & Fitness Program's Health-Related Appraisal & Counselling Strategy, Third Edition, © 2003. Reprinted with permission from the Canadian Society for Exercise Physiology.

Jesse Palmer, 2002. *THE CANADIAN PRESS/AP/Alan Mothner*

15

Biomechanical Principles and Applications

Learning Objectives

The exercises in this section of the workbook will help to reinforce your knowledge of the following topics covered in the *Exercise Science* textbook:

- The definition of the term "biomechanics" and its adaptation to exercise
- The contributions of Sir Isaac Newton to the field of physics and biomechanics
- The basic scientific models and theories used in biomechanics to describe and study human movement
- Linear and rotational motion
- The concept of the vector
- Lever systems and how they relate to the body
- The seven principles of biomechanics
- Applications of biomechanics to the world of sports, including the areas of performance improvement, injury prevention and/or rehabilitation, and fitness and/or personal training

Section Quiz

Name: _____ Date: _____

Multiple-Choice Questions

Mission: Circle the letter beside the answer that you believe to be correct.

1. Force is a vector and is commonly represented using an arrow. Which of the following quantities is not a vector?

    (a) 100 Newtons
    (b) 80 metres per second, North
    (c) 10 miles, East
    (d) 5 kilometres, South

2. Which of the following concepts of rotational motion can be compared to the linear concept of mass?

    (a) moment of force (torque)
    (b) angular velocity
    (c) moment of inertia
    (d) angular displacement

3. The moment of inertia depends on

    (a) the distribution of the mass in relation to the axis of rotation
    (b) the object's angular velocity
    (c) the moment of force
    (d) angular acceleration

4. Force is a push or a pull of

    (a) a certain magnitude in any direction
    (b) a certain magnitude in a particular direction
    (c) any magnitude, independent of direction
    (d) all the above

5. When the resistance is between the force and the fulcrum, the type of lever is

    (a) Class I
    (b) Class II
    (c) Class III
    (d) None of the above

6. The product of force applied over a time interval refers to

    (a) acceleration
    (b) momentum
    (c) impulse
    (d) none of the above

7. By increasing the moment of inertia during a spin, an ice skater's angular velocity

    (a) rapidly increases
    (b) decreases
    (c) remains the same
    (d) slowly increases

Short-Answer Questions

Mission: Briefly answer the following questions in the space provided:

1. Name and describe Newton's Three Laws of Motion.

    _____

2. List and describe the three classes of levers.

    _____

3. What are the four broad categories into which the seven principles of biomechanics can be grouped?

    _____

4. What does the principle of the application of force state?

    _____

5. What are the three key terms relating to angular motion?

    _____

6. What is the biomechanical formula for (1) force and (2) momentum?

    _____

7. What does the Conservation of Energy Principle state?

    _____

Essay Questions

Mission: On a separate piece of paper, develop a 100-word response to the following questions.

1. Name and describe the seven principles of biomechanics.

2. Name and describe six applications of biomechanics.

3. With reference to the information box on the "Fosbury Flop" and the "jump serve," explain how biomechanics has played a role in advancing human performance in the high jump and volleyball.

Terminology Review

Defining Key Terms

Name:
Date:

Mission: Briefly explain the meaning of the following key terms:

Key Term	Definition
Biomechanics	
Scientific models	
Equilibrium	
Conservation of energy	
Newton's Three Laws of Motion	
Centre of mass	
Linear (or translational) motion	
Rotational motion	

Acceleration	
Force as a vector	
Angular acceleration	
Moment of force (torque)	
Moment of inertia	
Radius of gyration	
Classes of levers	
Applied biomechanics	
Seven principles of biomechanics	1. _____ 2. _____ 3. _____ 4. _____ 5. _____ 6. _____ 7. _____

Seven Principles of Biomechanics

Individuals can gain insight into movement dynamics and begin to apply biomechanical analysis by utilizing the seven principles of biomechanics.

Name: _____

Date: _____

Look in the Book! Pages: 231–234

Mission: Perform each lab activity with a partner (or in a small group) and answer the accompanying "Biomechanically speaking ..." reflection question. Write in which of the seven principles of biomechanics applies to each lab activity, and be sure to use each principle only once. A sample entry is provided below.

Equipment needed: Physical education uniform, basketballs, measuring tape, pylons, footballs, floor hockey sticks and balls.

Lab Activity	Biomechanically speaking ...	Principle #
Stand with your feet together while your partner gently pushes against your shoulder.	... what can you do to be more stable and resist falling over? *Lower my centre of mass—either by bending my knees or spreading my feet apart more.*	**Principle # 1:** *STABILITY: The lower the centre of mass, the larger the base of support*
Stand behind the foul line and, using only your shoulder, elbow, and wrist joints, try to get a basketball in the basket.	... what do you need to do reach the basket more easily?	**Principle #**
Run as fast as you can for about 20 metres with your arms pressed against your sides.	... what do you need you do to run faster and more efficiently?	**Principle #**
Using a floor hockey stick and ball, attempt a slapshot using only a 30-cm wind-up.	... what do you need to do to make the slapshot more effective?	**Principle #**
Throw a perfect spiral with a football.	... what forces are preventing the ball from spiraling forever?	**Principle #**
Perform a modified or standard push-up slowly.	... what do you need to do to perform a "hand-clap" push-up?	**Principle #**
In your stocking feet, spin on one foot, keeping your arms away from your body.	... what can you do with your arms to spin faster while twirling?	**Principle #**

Measuring Human Motion

Determining and plotting the X and Y coordinates of joints reveals motion characteristics that can be used in the analysis of human movement.

Name:

Date:

On the adjacent page there are ten sequential photographs of a player kicking a soccer ball. To quantify human movement for analysis, the first step is to convert these visual images into numeric values. This process is called "digitizing," which simply refers to a method of obtaining an X and Y coordinate for each joint of interest.

Once obtained, these values can be used to create a stick figure plot of movement. This representation can then be used in subsequent exercises to gain valuable information about the movement.

Mission: Obtain the X and Y coordinate for the hip, knee, and ankle joints for the right leg. Use your ruler to measure the X and Y coordinates of these three joints in millimetres for each photograph. Use the bottom left corner of each figure as your graph origin and plot these values on the axes provided below. Three sample entries are included.

Note the path of each marker. The foot goes through a much larger movement than the knee and hip. In fact, the hip moves only a small amount and mostly in the forward direction. In general, most physical movement involves large motion at the end of segments, while the joints closer to the body remain relatively stable.

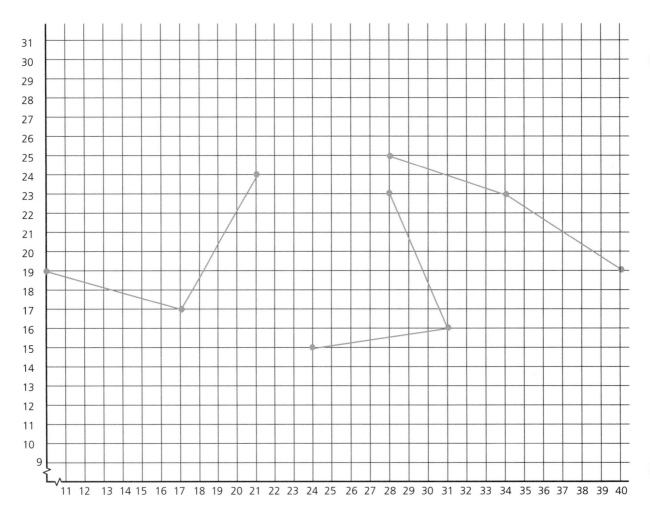

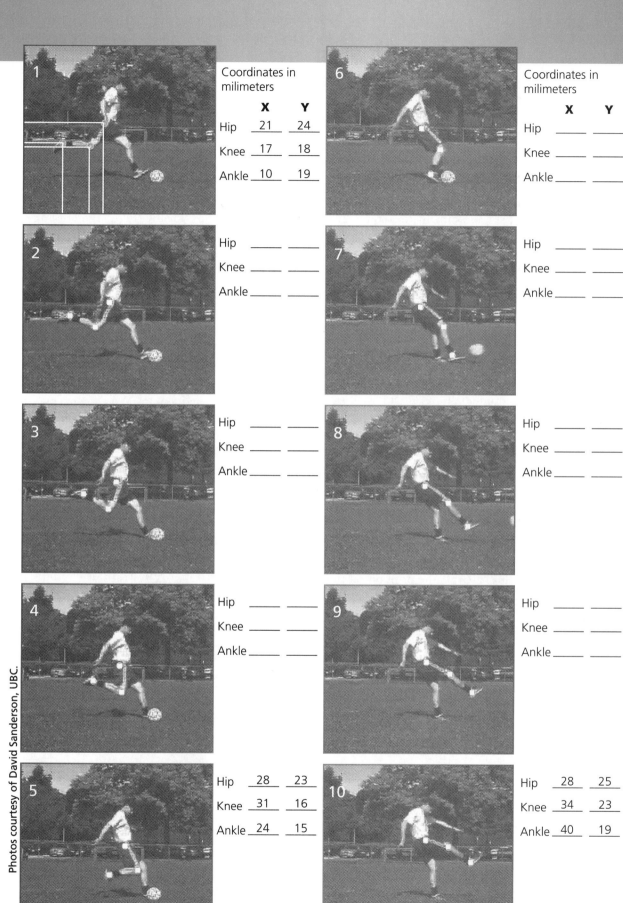

Photos courtesy of David Sanderson, UBC.

1

Coordinates in milimeters

	X	Y
Hip	21	24
Knee	17	18
Ankle	10	19

2

	X	Y
Hip		
Knee		
Ankle		

3

	X	Y
Hip		
Knee		
Ankle		

4

	X	Y
Hip		
Knee		
Ankle		

5

	X	Y
Hip	28	23
Knee	31	16
Ankle	24	15

6

Coordinates in milimeters

	X	Y
Hip		
Knee		
Ankle		

7

	X	Y
Hip		
Knee		
Ankle		

8

	X	Y
Hip		
Knee		
Ankle		

9

	X	Y
Hip		
Knee		
Ankle		

10

	X	Y
Hip	28	25
Knee	34	23
Ankle	40	19

Determining the Position of the Centre of Mass

Name:

Date:

The segmentation method can be used to compute the position of the centre of mass. This exercise will acquaint you with how this method works.

Can a resultant force such as gravity be considered to act through a single point in the body? The answer is "yes" and this point is called the centre of mass. If the object is of uniform density and shape, then this point will be in the geometric centre of the object. However the segmentation method must be used to compute the position of the centre of mass of the human body.

Mission: Compute the position of the centre of mass of the diver. To do this you must determine the position of the centre of mass of each segment with respect to the X and Y axes. Follow the steps to assist you in determining the segments.

- **Step 1:** On the photograph on the next page draw a straight line over each of the following segments: foot, shank (lower leg), thigh, trunk, head, and left and right upper arm, forearm, and hand (as shown in the small drawing to the right). These lines then represent a stick figure of the diver and we can use these lines plus some other measures to determine the position of the whole body centre of mass.

- **Step 2:** Using the data in the second column of the table below, identify the position on the straight line for the position of that segment's

centre of mass. For example, the position of the centre of mass for the thigh segment is measured as 37% of the distance to the hip end. Mark this location on the drawing.

- **Step 3:** On the large picture, using the lower left corner as the origin, measure and record the X and Y coordinates (in millimetres) for each segmental centre of mass location. Enter the X coordinate in column B and the Y coordinate in column D in the table.

- **Step 4:** For each segment, multiply the value in columns A and B and write this value in column C. For each segment multiply the value in columns A and D and write the result in column E.

- **Step 5:** Add all the values in column C and enter this sum in the bottom row. Do the same for column E. These two values represent the X and Y coordinates of the centre of mass for the diver. Plot this point (X and Y value) on the drawing.

> **Note:** The centre of mass need not fall within the boundaries of the body. Rather, the position is dependent upon the orientation of the arms and legs.

Segment	Centre of Mass Position
Head	46% from vertex (top)
Trunk	38% from neck
Upper Arm	51% from shoulder
Forearm	39% to elbow
Hand	82% to wrist
Thigh	37% to hip
Calf (shank)	37% to knee
Foot	45% to heel

THE CANADIAN PRESS/COA/S. Grant.

Segment	A	B	C	D	E
Head	.07				
Trunk	.51				
Right Upper Arm	.03				
Right Forearm	.02				
Right Hand	.01				
Left Upper Arm	.03				
Left Forearm	.02				
Left Hand	.01				
Thigh	.20				
Calf (shank)	.08				
Foot	.02				

Joint Angles

Name:

Date:

The X and Y coordinates of joints can be used to compute a joint angle, an important component of human movement analysis.

Angular Kinematics

A useful means of displaying human movement is to determine the angle between segments. For example, the knee angle is the angle between the thigh segment (from the hip joint to the knee joint) and the shank segment (from the knee joint to the ankle joint). When you watch your friends walk or run, you can see that the knee joint angle sometimes becomes smaller (flexes) and sometimes, larger (extends). The phases of flexion and extension play an integral role in permitting humans to walk or run smoothly.

Using the stick figure data constructed in Exercise 15.4, you can determine the knee joint angle for our soccer kick. For each of the ten stick figures that you plotted, use a protractor to measure the angle between the thigh segment and the shank segment. Enter these values in the table. To determine the angle measurement, place one of the arms of the protractor along the shank segment and record the angle between that segment and the thigh segment (as shown in the drawing below).

Now that you have the table complete, you can plot the joint angle versus picture number. Knowing that each picture was made about 0.07 seconds (1/15th of a second) apart, you can actually plot the angle versus time. Graph your data on the chart provided on the next page and compare your plot to the one provided.

Angular Displacement

In the plot you have created, you can see that the knee angle goes through some phases where the angle decreases and then increases. The phase where the angle decreases is called **flexion**. The angle is getting smaller so that the moment of inertia of the whole leg is reduced (see Section 15 of the textbook). This reduction in moment of inertia makes it easier for the athlete to develop high rotational velocity.

Once the knee has been flexed to a small angle, it is then extended to a maximum of close to 180°. This phase of extension results in a very high velocity of the foot which ensures that the force at contact with the ball is very large. Ensuring that these motions occur at the right time is a task facing all athletes.

Measuring the angular displacement of limbs and joints provides a key step in the analysis of human movement.

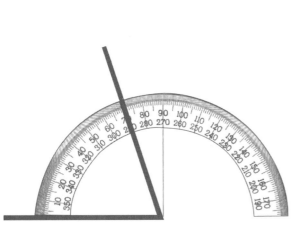

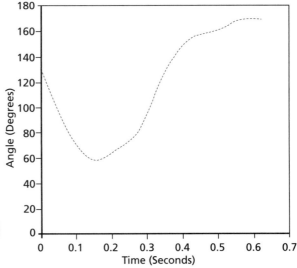

Picture Number	Time (Seconds)	Knee Joint Angle
1	0.00	
2	0.07	
3	0.14	
4	0.21	
5	0.28	
6	0.35	
7	0.42	
8	0.49	
9	0.56	
10	0.63	

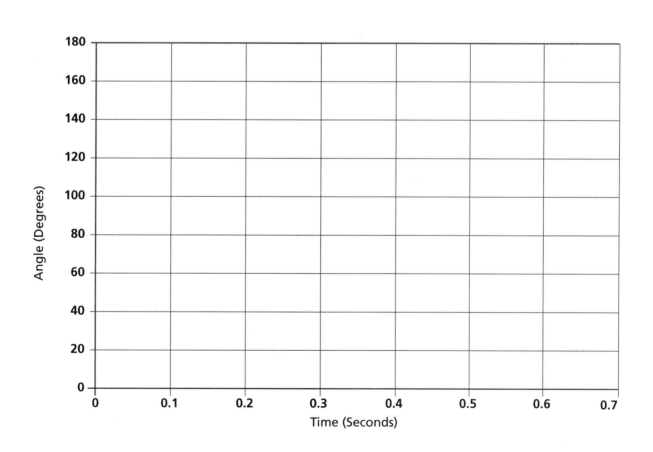

Joint Angular Velocity

Name:

Date:

In the previous exercise, you computed and plotted the joint angle as a function of time. In this exercise, you will take the next step and determine the angular velocity of the joint. This process, called differentiation, can be done by drawing a set of straight lines tangent to the curved joint angle-time plot.

The slope of a curved line can be estimated by drawing a straight line tangent to the curved line at the point of interest. This would be termed the *instantaneous slope*. Another method is to estimate the average slope between points, thereby calculating an average velocity. Using either of these methods allows computation of the angular velocity of a joint from the angular displacement data.

In the small drawing below, the curved line represents an example of the angular position of the knee joint during a movement. To compute the angular velocity of this movement, first place two points along the curve. Then draw a straight line between these points. To compute the slope of this straight line, record the rise (change in joint angle, or Δ Angle) and the run (change in time, Δt). You know from your textbook that angular velocity is the rate of change of angle. Thus, by calculating the slope of this line, you have calculated the angular velocity.

As this is an average value of the slope, you must plot this half way between the two points. When you do this for a series of points, you can create a graph of angular velocity and time. Such data are very important to the biomechanist in the search for a deeper understanding of human movement.

The goal of this exercise is to determine the slope of the angle-time graph from Exercise 15.6. There are a number of steps to perform.

First, copy the angle data from the previous exercise into the second column of the table. Now, on the plot, in Exercise 15.6, draw a straight line between each successive point. For each of these lines, determine the rise (change in joint angle, or Δ Angle) and enter the value in the fourth column of the table. Because each point in your plot was exactly the same distance apart in time, the run for every point is the same (0.07 seconds). The final step is to divide the rise (Δ Angle) by the run (Δt) and enter these numbers in the final column of the table.

Once the table has been completed, you can create a new graph by plotting the point number and its associated velocity value on the graph provided on the next page. It should look like the plot at the bottom of the previous column.

Now that you have plotted the data, you should note how high joint angular velocities can be. In fact, in normal activities such as walking, the knee joint will reach peak angular velocity of about 300 degrees/second, and values as high as 2,000 degrees/second have been recorded in some martial arts movements.

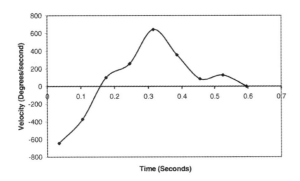

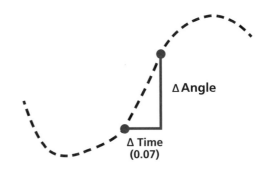

Time (Seconds) from Exercise 15.6	Angle (Degrees) from Exercise 15.6	Time (Seconds—average value)	Δ Angle	Slope Δ Angle / Δ Time
0.00		0.000		
0.07		0.035		
0.14		0.105		
0.21		0.175		
0.28		0.245		
0.35		0.315		
0.42		0.385		
0.49		0.455		
0.56		0.525		
0.63		0.595		

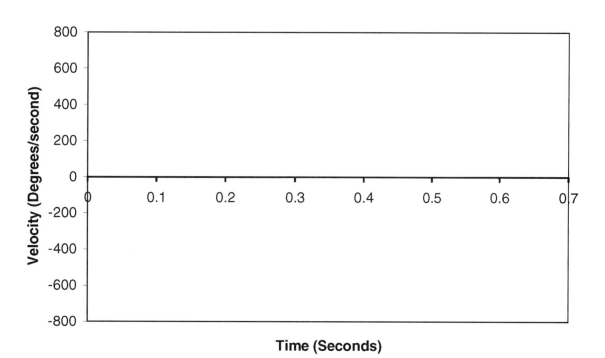

Linear Kinetics of Walking

Name:

Date:

Sir Isaac Newton identified three laws that govern motion, and these laws also apply to human motion, including everyday movements such as walking.

When you walk, your feet land on the ground. When you are in contact with the ground, Newton's third law states that there will be a reaction force from the ground applied to you. In a biomechanics lab, we can record the force between your feet and the ground and use these recordings to help us understand the biomechanics of walking.

Consider watching a friend walk. He might look like the person in the picture on the next page. The three lines indicate the force between his left leg and the ground. The diagonal line is the resultant force, while the two other lines represent the vertical and horizontal components of that force.

If we record the forces, the graph would look like the one shown below. The top line represents the vertical component of the ground reaction force, while the bottom line represents the fore-aft component of the ground reaction force. The vertical component, of course, points upward all the time. If it did not, then you would fall to the floor. The fore-aft component is interesting because it points first negatively and then positively. According to Newton's second law, F = ma, this force would result in a negative acceleration in the first half and then a positive direction in the second half. This would mean that, for each step you take, you first slow down (negative acceleration) and then speed up (positive acceleration). Analysis of this type of data helps us understand how people walk.

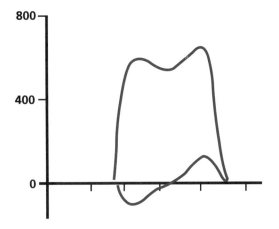

Newton's Laws: F = ma

In this exercise, you have two force-time curves, one for a person with a below-knee amputation walking on a prosthetic leg and one for an individual with two intact legs (the "control"). The plot shows the force-time data for the horizontal force—the fore-aft force as shown as the bottom line in the diagram on this page. The force is initially negative. The force then has a single moment when it is zero. The final phase of the force is positive.

Calculating Acceleration

You can calculate the acceleration of the individual if you know the mass and the force.

Newton's second law states that

$$F = ma \text{ (which can be rearranged as } a = F/m)$$

The control person had a mass of 62.69 kg while the person with the prosthetic had a mass of 69.72 kg. Using the force-time values observed at each stage of a stepping action, it is possible to determine the peak negative and peak positive acceleration of the person.

Sample Data

The full data set for this experiment consists of 100 observations over the course of one stepping action by each of the two individuals. From these two sets of observations, it is possible to compute acceleration at each stage and create a graph resembling the bottom line on the left. It is also possible to determine peak positive and negative accelerations for the two individuals.

Twenty observations from the full dataset are provided on the next page. **(1) compute the accelerations using a calculator; (2) indicate peak negative and positive accelerations; and (3) plot the data on the graph on the next page**—it should resemble the lower line in the graph on the left.

Finally, it is interesting to note that the actual peak accelerations were smaller for the person with the amputation (as one might well expect). Why? Perhaps because he was not walking as quickly as the control person.

Linear Kinetics of Walking

% Stance Phase	Control person (with no prosthetic)			Person with prosthetic		
	Force	Mass	Acceleration (a = F/m)	Force	Mass	Acceleration (a = F/m)
0	6.571	62.69 kg		24.345	69.72 kg	
5	-30.34	62.69 kg		-28.217	69.72 kg	
10	-129.686	62.69 kg		-78.106	69.72 kg	
15	-161.108	62.69 kg		-120.814	69.72 kg	
20	-158.618	62.69 kg		-131.195	69.72 kg	
25	-119.965	62.69 kg		-99.507	69.72 kg	
30	-81.925	62.69 kg		-62.544	69.72 kg	
35	-51.458	62.69 kg		-35.848	69.72 kg	
40	-29.4	62.69 kg		-23.833	69.72 kg	
45	-13.097	62.69 kg		-17.516	69.72 kg	
50	-5.614	62.69 kg		-6.656	69.72 kg	
55	5.811	62.69 kg		6.194	69.72 kg	
60	20.603	62.69 kg		13.234	69.72 kg	
65	39.59	62.69 kg		18.183	69.72 kg	
70	76.468	62.69 kg		35.035	69.72 kg	
75	117.534	62.69 kg		62.141	69.72 kg	
80	148.851	62.69 kg		92.545	69.72 kg	
85	164.084	62.69 kg		123.814	69.72 kg	
90	136.533	62.69 kg		133.684	69.72 kg	
95	59.828	62.69 kg		106.535	69.72 kg	
100	7.166	62.69 kg		10.663	69.72 kg	

	Control	Prosthetic
Peak negative acceleration		
Peak positive acceleration		

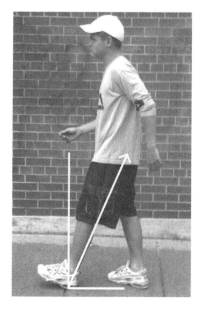

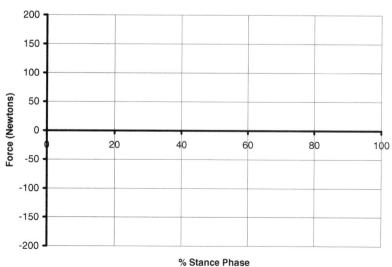

Impulse-Momentum— Hitting a Baseball

Name:

Date:

In order for an object to experience a change in momentum, an impulse must be applied.

Impulse-momentum relationship

Newton's Second Law states that F = ma. That is, when a force is applied to an object of mass "m" it will accelerate, and the acceleration will be proportional to the mass. That acceleration is the rate of change of velocity with respect to time, $a = \Delta v/\Delta t$. (The Greek symbol Δ is used to denote a change.) Therefore Newton's Second Law can be restated as the impulse-momentum relationship.

With simple substitution, we see that F = m $(\Delta v/\Delta t)$, and when we multiply both sides by "Δt" we arrive at the impulse-momentum relationship namely,

$$F\Delta t = m\Delta v$$

In words, this means that, when a force is applied over a time interval (Δt), the momentum of the object (mv) will change. If the force is in the opposite direction from the velocity, then the momentum will be reduced. If it is in the same direction, then the momentum will be increased.

The average force of this collision can be determined from this relationship, where

$$F_{average} = mv_f - mv_i / \Delta t$$

In the analysis of sporting movements, this is a key relationship to understand.

Larry Walker. THE CANADIAN PRESS/AP/David Zalubowski

FΔt = mΔv

Consider hitting a baseball with a bat. The bat is swung by the player, and when it contacts the ball, a force from the bat is applied to the ball that causes the ball to accelerate—that is, change its velocity. Because the ball was moving initially towards the batter, this acceleration will be in the opposite direction and be large enough first to stop the ball and then to continue accelerating it so that it flies to the field. In other words, there will be a change in the ball's momentum.

Now, consider a typical recreational baseball game. The pitcher throws the ball (with a mass of .2 kg) at you, and it is moving at 70 mph (110 kph). You swing the bat and strike the ball perfectly, hitting it to the outfield at a velocity of 75 mph (120 kph). The ball was in contact with the bat for only 0.8 milliseconds. *Using the impulse-momentum relationship, estimate the average force of contact and complete the table to the left.* (When you complete the table, you must convert the speed of the ball from mph to m/s.)

In fact, it amounts to a lot of force. Using Newton's Second Law (F = ma), you can determine that the acceleration of the ball is about 80,951 m/s^2 – or 8,251 times the acceleration of gravity!

Mass of baseball (m)	0.2	kg		
Velocity of pitch (-v_i)*		mph (÷2.239)	=	m/s
Velocity of bat (mv_f)		mph (÷2.239)	=	m/s
Duration of bat-ball contact ($\triangle$t)	0.8	msec (÷1000)	=	s
Momentum after pitch (mv_i)		kg/m/s		
Momentum after hit (mv_f)		kg/m/s		
Average Force (mv_f - mv_i)/$\triangle$t		Newtons		

Remember that because velocity is a vector it has direction and magnitude. Therefore, consider the velocity after the pitch as being a negative velocity and after being struck by the bat it will have a positive velocity.

CHAPTER 16

Unit 2 Career Choices

Investigate a career in one of the fields covered in Unit 2. Ideally, you should interview someone working within the field for this assignment.

1 Career and description

_____

_____

_____

_____

2 List at least two post-secondary institutions in Ontario and/or Canada that offer programs for this career.

_____

_____

_____

3 Choose one of the above institutions and determine the required courses in the first year of study for this program.

_____

_____

_____

4 What is the total length of the education needed to begin this career? Is an internship or apprenticeship required?

_____

_____

_____

5 What is the demand for individuals qualified for this occupation? If possible, provide some employment data to support your answer.

_____

_____

_____

6 What is the average starting salary for this career? What is the top salary? On what do salary increases depend in this career?

_____

_____

_____

7 List occupational settings where a person with these qualifications could work.

_____   _____

_____   _____

CHAPTER 17

Unit 2 Crossword Challenge

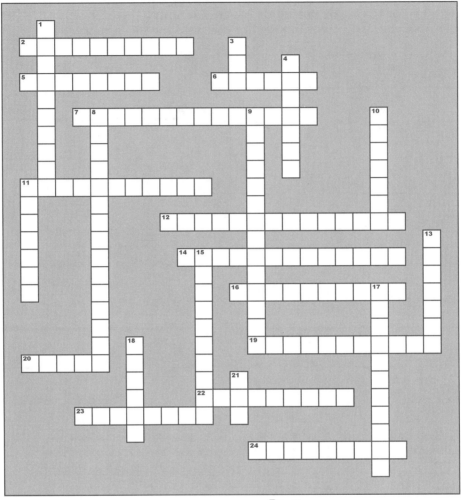

Across

2. Type of training that combines resistance and endurance training; also called cross-training
5. Another name for heart rate reserve method
6. Movement in a particular direction
7. Our direct sources of energy, consisting of carbohydrates, proteins, and fats
11. Term referring to the ability of a joint to move freely through its full range of motion
12. Type of endurance that is the best indicator of overall health
14. Term used to describe the breaking down of training into time-specific segments
16. Condition resulting from a complete failure of the body's heat-regulatory system
19. Dietary supplements that may contain hidden amount of steroids and other banned substances
20. He led inquiry into the use of illegal performance-enhancing drugs in Canada
22. Widely advertised as a "fat burner"
23. Performing this on motion helps athletes improve performance
24. Rate that measures the energy that needs to be consumed to sustain essential bodily functions

Down

1. Movement about an axis
3. Acronym for the ratio of a person's weight in kilograms to the square of his or her height in metres
4. Swedish word for "speed play" training
8. Process whereby the body adjusts to high altitude
9. Natural protein hormone produced in the kidneys
10. The moment defined as resistance to angular motion
11. Levers are classified based on its location in relation to the force
13. Users can interact realistically with this technological reality
15. Science sometimes called "human-factors engineering"
17. What a Calorie is also known as
18. Acronym for Canadian test that provides a simple, safe, and standardized approach to assessing major components of fitness
21. The maximal amount of weight an individual can lift for one repetition

UNIT 3

MOTOR LEARNING AND SKILLS DEVELOPMENT

Wayne Gretzky, 2001. THE CANADIAN PRESS/Aaron Harris

18

Human Growth and Development

Learning Objectives

The exercises in this section of the workbook will help to reinforce your knowledge of the following topics covered in the *Exercise Science* textbook:

- The four key components of human development: physical, cognitive, motor/skills, and social

- The relationship between age and physical development, and the various ways of measuring age (chronological, skeletal, and developmental)

- The study of human morphology and the three morphological types (mesomorph, ectomorph, and endomorph)

- The four basic stages of human growth and development: infancy/toddler, childhood, puberty/adolescence, and adulthood

- The four basic phases of human movement: reflexive, rudimentary, fundamental, and sport-related

- The various rates of growth for different body parts, including the cephalocaudal and proximodistal sequences

- Various factors that influence physical growth, including glandular/hormonal activity, heredity, nutrition/diet, physical activity, and sociocultural factors

- Jean Piaget's "Four Stages of Cognitive Development"

- The stages of human social development, including tools for assessing this development in children

Section Quiz

Name: _____ Date: _____

Multiple-Choice Questions

Mission: Circle the letter beside the answer that you believe to be correct.

1. Human physical development encompasses

    (a) an individual's ability to interpret information
    (b) the ability to perform a wide range of tasks
    (c) relationships with peer, friends, and others
    (d) none of the above

2. Skeletal age

    (a) is indicated by the degree of ossification of bones
    (b) can be predicted according to chronological age
    (c) can be affected by diet, disease, and injury
    (d) all of the above

3. Which stage of human growth witnesses the most rapid physical development?

    (a) childhood
    (b) developmental
    (c) rudimentary
    (d) reflexive

4. People are considered to "grow into their bodies" during

    (a) the sport-related movement phase
    (b) puberty
    (c) the fundamental movement phase
    (d) adolescence

5. Which system secretes hormones to the body's various organs and tissues?

    (a) reproductive system
    (b) nervous system
    (c) endocrine system
    (d) lymphatic system

6. The most accepted model of the stages of cognitive development was developed by

    (a) Piaget
    (b) Erikson
    (c) Bandura
    (d) McLellan

7. What is the greatest difficulty in trying to draw links between genetic heredity and growth?

    (a) science has proven that there is absolutely no link between genetic heredity and growth.
    (b) these links do not give sufficient weight to environmental factors
    (c) it is easy to offend people by trying to make such connections
    (d) in most cases, it is impossible to track growth patterns in large populations.

Short-Answer Questions

Mission: Briefly answer the following questions in the space provided:

1. List the four key components of human development

    _____

2. What are the differences between chronological, skeletal, and developmental age?

    _____

3. Identify and provide a short description of the three classic body types.

    _____

4. List the four key stages of human development.

    _____

5. Describe how a lack of physical activity can affect human growth.

    _____

6. Who developed the four-stage model of cognitive development? What are the four stages contained in it?

    _____

Essay Questions

Mission: On a separate piece of paper, develop a 100-word response to the following questions.

1. Using the four basic areas of human development (physical, cognitive, motor/skills, and social), pick any person you know (e.g., a friend, relative, classmate, etc.) and write a brief report about their current level of development within each area.

2. What are the three morphological types? What is the benefit of using this system of body classification? Does it have any drawbacks?

3. Discuss the role that sport participation and team membership can play in social interaction and relationship building.

Terminology Review

Defining Key Terms

Name:

Date:

Mission: Briefly explain the meaning of the following key terms:

Key Term	Definition
Components of human development	
Chronological age	
Skeletal age	
Developmental age	
Morphology	
Stages of human development	
Phases of human movement	
Factors affecting physical growth	
Cognitive development	
Piaget's four stages of cognitive development	
Socialization	

Crossword on Human Growth and Development

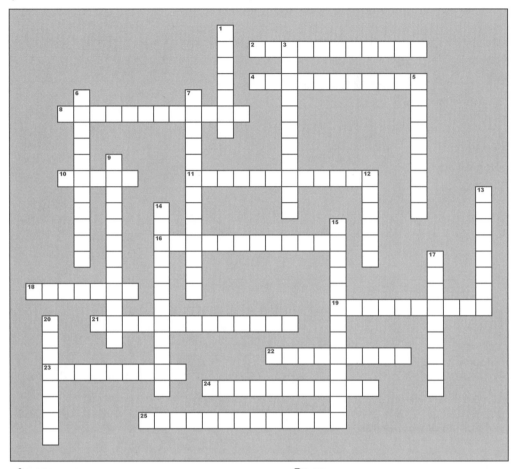

Across

2. Games held in the same year as the "regular" Olympic Games
4. A sumo wrestler belongs to this body type classification
8. For Piaget, this is the ability to adapt to one's environment
10. Type of development that combines cognitive and physical development
11. This can have an adverse effect on muscle growth and bone formation during childhood and adolescence
16. Stage defined by Piaget characterized by motor activity without the use of symbols
18. Stage of human growth that sees profound changes in human appearance (e.g., growth of body hair)
19. Categorization developed to help classify physical appearance and structure
21. Process by which humans form attachments with others
22. A diet lacking in these will impede growth
23. This period is relatively long in humans in comparison to other mammals
24. Movement phase in which humans begin to develop basic movement skills
25. Sequence in which growth progresses fastest in the head, followed by the trunk, and then the extremities

Down

1. Relative to other stages, the fastest growth occurs in this one
3. Basic activities such as crawling and walking develop during this movement phase
5. Development that includes awareness of one's self
6. Along with genetics, the major factor impacting human growth and development
7. Age as expressed in one's ability to perform certain tasks
9. Participation in team sports can further the development of this trait among young athletes
12. This process is usually complete by adulthood
13. Genetic lineage
14. As this process occurs, skeletal age increases
15. Sequence that describes how body movements originating close to the centre of the body seem to develop earlier than those farther away
17. Movement phase in which humans first show controlled motor development
20. Operational stage defined by Piaget in which logical thinking develops

Motor Development Observation Lab

Name:

Date:

Look in the Book! Pages: 247–250

An important concept inherent in motor/skills development is that, within any given group of people, there can be a wide variation in development and skill levels.

Mission: Arrange with your teacher for you to observe Grade 9 or 10 students during a physical education class in which the students will be learning and/or practising a sport or specific skill.

Select a partner. Then, at random and in agreement with your partner, select ten students in the class. Assign each of them a number or otherwise identify them. After you and your partner have selected your observation group of students and have agreed on your identification system, go to opposite ends of the gym.

Independent of your partner, observe your group of ten students "in action" for 30 minutes.

(Remember to perform your observations unobtrusively and without consulting your partner. You will be able to compare notes at the end of the exercise.)

During your observation period, complete the table below as thoroughly as possible. Notes and observations should be detailed (you may use a separate sheet of paper if needed).

When you return to class, discuss your observations with your partner. Did you agree on your assessment of each student? Why or why not? What factors might explain some of the differences in assessment that occurred?

Motor Development Assessment Table

Grade level under observation: _____

Date: _____

Instructor for class: _____

Individual (Use Number)	1	2	3	4	5	6	7	8	9	10
Sport or skill(s) being practised										
Estimated height of student (Tall/medium/short)										
Estimated weight of student (Heavy/average/underweight)										

Individual (Use Number)	1	2	3	4	5	6	7	8	9	10
Morphological type (Rough categorization) (Ectomorph—ECTO; Mesomorph—MESO; Endomorph—ENDO)										
Strength (Rate overall physical strength from 1 to 5—weak to strong)										
Balance (Rate overall balance from 1 to 5—very unstable to very stable)										
Coordination/agility (Rate overall coordination/agility from 1 to 5—very poorly coordinated/severely lacking in agility to very well coordinated/extremely agile)										
Overall skill level (General rating of how well or poorly student performed the sport or skill from 1 to 5—very poor to excellent)										
Notes for comparing your assessment with your partner at the end of the exercise										

Adapting Sport Skills to Match Development Levels

Name:
Date:
Look in the Book! Pages: 249–251, 253–254

It is generally accepted that humans develop in four different ways—physically, cognitively, in terms of the motor skills they acquire, and socially. Coaches need to understand these various dimensions and adapt their training methods accordingly.

Mission: Imagine yourself as the coach of the group of athletes whose ages and sport are indicated on the chart below. Fill in as much information as possible about how you would endeavour to teach the sport skills indicated based on the appropriate age levels.

In each case, indicate how you would address the four developmental areas—physical, cognitive, motor/skills, and social—and modify your instruction to the indicated age level. Keep in mind that you can modify equipment, basic rules of the sport, and many other factors in your attempts to match these activities to the appropriate age and/or developmental level. A sample entry is provided below.

Note: Assume that all of the athletes have "come through the ranks" of the various age levels—that is, a tennis player at Level 2 (aged 7–9) has already participated at Level 1; a soccer player at Level 3 (aged 9–11) has already participated at Levels 1 and 2, and so on. One entry has been completed to provide you with an example.

Sport Skill	Age Level	Modification
1. Hitting a baseball	Level 1 (under 5 years)	▫ use a "tee," as player of this age may have difficulty hitting moving pitch ▫ use light bat to allow for lack of physical strength ▫ work with the athlete to develop his or her swing without a ball, encouraging him or her to "visualize" contact repeatedly ▫ gradually introduce slow-moving pitch with larger ball for more advanced players ▫ "social" aspects of this skill may be hard to develop as the skill is essentially individual
2. Kicking a soccer ball	Level 1 (under 5 years)	

3. Heading a soccer ball	Level 2 (5–7 years)	_____ _____ _____ _____
4. Passing a hockey puck	Level 2 (5–7 years)	_____ _____ _____ _____
5. Executing a cartwheel in gymnastics	Level 3 (7–9 years)	_____ _____ _____ _____
6. Tossing a "spiral" pass in football	Level 3 (7–9 years)	_____ _____ _____ _____
7. Executing a jump shot in basketball	Level 4 (9–11 years)	_____ _____ _____ _____
8. Executing a sand-trap shot in golf	Level 4 (9–11 years)	_____ _____ _____ _____

Scott Shaw, 2001. THE CANADIAN PRESS/Jackques Voissinot

19

Motor Learning and Skill Acquisition

Learning Objectives

The exercises in this section of the workbook will help to reinforce your knowledge of the following topics covered in the *Exercise Science* textbook:

- How humans acquire both simple and complex motor skills
- Basic principles of motor learning and skill acquisition
- Stages of motor learning, including Fitts and Posner's classic three-stage model
- Various factors affecting skill development
- Singer's five-step process to learning a skill
- The role of evaluation and feedback in learning a skill
- Skill categories, including locomotor, manipulative/handling, and stability-balancing
- Ways of analyzing and observing skills
- Adapting skill development to match a person's level of skill, including the processes of shaping and chaining

Section Quiz

Name: _____ Date: _____

Multiple-Choice Questions

Mission: Circle the letter beside the answer that you believe to be correct.

1. The process through which a person develops the ability to perform and refine a task or skill is commonly called

   (a) physical development
   (b) psychological development
   (c) rudimentary learning
   (d) motor learning

2. "Individuals differ widely in terms of how quickly and easily they learn new motor skills" defines the principle of

   (a) motor development
   (b) individual differences
   (c) stages of learning
   (d) skill development

3. What is the name given to the body's "mechanism" that coordinates the mental commands and physical responses needed to produce movement?

   (a) effector
   (b) decision
   (c) memory
   (e) perceptual

4. What do motor learning researchers consider to be the two basic divisions of motor activity?

   (a) planned and spontaneous
   (b) voluntary and involuntary
   (c) psychological and physical
   (d) instant and delayed

5. Feedback gained by knowledge of performance is also called

   (a) knowledge feedback
   (b) kinematic feedback
   (c) performance feedback
   (d) predictable feedback

6. The process of encouraging a learner to learn a skill gradually is called

   (a) chaining
   (b) linking
   (c) shaping
   (d) moulding

7. The two types of chaining are

   (a) basic and advanced
   (b) forward and backward
   (c) critical and important
   (d) beginning and automatic

Short-Answer Questions

Mission: Briefly answer the following questions in the space provided:

1. Explain the principle of individual differences. What factors can contribute to the way that this principle comes into play with people learning a skill?

   _____

2. What are the five stages in Singer's five-step method of skills teaching?

   _____

3. Why is skill transferability important when learning new skills?

   _____

4. What is the difference between open and closed skills?

   _____

5. Discuss how the chaining process can assist an individual to learn a more complex skill.

   _____

   _____

Essay Questions

Mission: On a separate piece of paper, develop a 100-word response to the following questions.

1. Outline the "classic" stages-of-learning model developed by Fitts and Posner and summarize each stage. Do you think this model accurately reflects the way people learn a new skill? Why or why not?

2. Choose one factor widely held to be an impediment to skill development, and describe a situation in which this factor is preventing an athlete from refining his or her skills in a specific sport. Suggest ways in which this inhibiting factor could be overcome.

3. Using a specific sport skill, describe how you would take a beginner through Singer's five-step approach to learn that skill.

Terminology Review

Defining Key Terms

Mission: Briefly explain the meaning of the following key terms:

Name:

Date:

Key Term	Definition
Motor learning	
Automatic/controlled motor activity	
Principle of individual differences	
Stages-of-learning model	
Factors affecting skill acquisition	
Five-step method of skills teaching	
Feedback	
Skill transferability	
Basic skill categories	
Open/closed skills	
Stages of skill observation	
Shaping	
Chaining	

Crossword on Motor Learning & Skill Acquisition

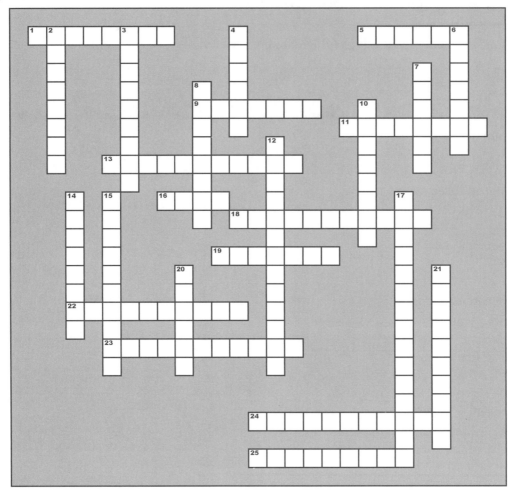

Across

1. The information a learner obtains regarding his or her performance
5. These supply the body with information regarding external stimuli
9. Singer's term for picturing the correct execution of a skill
11. This curve represents how well we learn a skill
13. Crowd noise is an example of this type of performance-inhibiting factor
16. Skill performed in an unpredictable environment
18. Movements needed to prepare for a skill
19. Physiologist who developed the two-dimensional system of skills classification
22. Skill development stage in which performance becomes "automatic"
23. Process by which instructors can assess the skills of learners
24. Skill development stage in which learners begin to refine skills
25. Term that describes how well we manipulate objects with our hands and feet

Down

2. Name for the mechanism that coordinates the mind and body
3. Motor activity that involves very little thought
4. Superstar who needed to refine important skill
6. Process by which learners are encouraged to develop a skill gradually
7. Co-developer with Fitts of the "classic" stages-of-learning model
8. Beginners make many; those at autonomous skill levels, very few
10. The first step in skills teaching in Singer's five-step model
12. "Keeping your mind on the game" is a popular way of expressing this key aspect of learning a skill
14. The instant at which a golfer's club hits the ball
15. Performing this when learning a skill allows you to understand what you are doing wrong
17. The ability to apply skills learned in one sports context in another sports context
20. Key mental function that allows us to recall past events
21. Motor activity that requires thought and time to perform

Hockey Skills Observation

When coaches and athletes break down the phases of a skill and analyze those phases separately, they can look for ways to improve the execution of the skill as a whole. The next four exercises will allow you to become familiar with this process.

Name:

Date:

Look in the Book! Pages: 261–263

Skill Observation Checklist: Using the photographs above, identify the key elements of each phase of the skill and indicate training exercises that might result in improvement at each phase.

Phase	Key Elements of Phase	Training Exercises
Preliminary movements		
Backswing movements		
Force-producing movements		
Critical instant		
Follow-through		

Soccer Skills Observation

Skill Observation Checklist: Using the photographs above, identify the key elements of each phase of the skill and indicate training exercises that might result in improvement at each phase.

Phase	Key Elements of Phase	Training Exercises
Preliminary movements		
Backswing movements		
Force-producing movements		
Critical instant		
Follow-through		

Golf Skills Observation

Skill Observation Checklist: Using the photographs above, identify the key elements of each phase of the skill and indicate training exercises that might result in improvement at each phase.

Phase	Key Elements of Phase	Training Exercises
Preliminary movements		
Backswing movements		
Force-producing movements		
Critical instant		
Follow-through		

Tennis Skills Observation

Skill Observation Checklist: Using the photographs above, identify the key elements of each phase of the skill and indicate training exercises that might result in improvement at each phase.

Phase	Key Elements of Phase	Training Exercises
Preliminary movements		
Backswing movements		
Force-producing movements		
Critical instant		
Follow-through		

20

The Psychology of Sport

Dominique Bilodeau, 2001. THE CANADIAN PRESS/Jonathan Hayward

Learning Objectives

The exercises in this section of the workbook will help to reinforce your knowledge of the following topics covered in the *Exercise Science* textbook:

- The basic principles and definition of sport psychology, including why psychological factors are important for athletes and coaches in both training and competition
- The relationship between physical and mental factors in sport
- How psychologists define performance states
- Key terms in sport psychology, including arousal, anxiety, relaxation, concentration, and motivation
- Psychological factors that can affect sport performance, including self-talk, imagery/ visualization, hypnosis, the regulation of arousal and relaxation, motivation, goal setting, and improving concentration
- The role of the audience and fatigue on an athlete's performance
- Orlick's "Wheel of Excellence"
- The impact of sport psychology on young athletes
- Various roles and careers open to sport psychologists

Section Quiz

Name: _____ Date: _____

Multiple-Choice Questions

Mission: Circle the letter beside the answer that you believe to be correct.

1. Which of the following is a role of the sports psychologist?
    (a) teaching an athlete how to block out crowd noise
    (b) working with coaches and athletes to improve motivation
    (c) helping competitors to avoid feelings of anxiety that inhibit performance
    (d) all of the above

2. In the mind of the athlete, a complete absence of doubt, a narrow focus, a sense of effortlessness, and the feeling that time has "stood still," describes
    (a) "the zone"
    (b) ideal performance state
    (c) choking
    (d) both A and B are correct

3. An athlete who, before a competition, is sweating or feeling "butterflies" is likely experiencing
    (a) arousal
    (b) relaxation
    (c) anxiety
    (d) concentration

4. Feeling "psyched up" or "wired" is known more formally in sports psychology as
    (a) arousal
    (b) relaxation
    (c) anxiety
    (d) concentration

5. An athlete develops a broad picture of what success "feels like" when using
    (a) hypnosis
    (b) concentration
    (c) imagery
    (d) motivation

6. Techniques for improving an athlete's concentration include
    (a) positive self-talk
    (b) duplicating performance distractions in practice
    (c) use of cue words
    (d) all of the above

7. Which of the following is *not* one of Orlick's seven key elements of excellence?
    (a) confidence
    (b) distraction
    (c) focused connection
    (d) mental readiness

Short-Answer Questions

Mission: Briefly answer the following questions in the space provided:

1. Define concentration and give three ways a person can increase their level of concentration during competitions.

2. Define motivation and discuss why some athletes are more motivated than others.

3. Why is goal setting important for athletes? Why might objective or quantifiable goals be "better" than subjective goals?

4. What is "choking"? Why does it happen?

5. What are some important psychological points to remember when dealing with children in sports?

Essay Questions

Mission: On a separate piece of paper, develop a 100-word response to the following questions.

1. Research any three famous athletes who have benefitted from using psychological practices, and explain how they used sport psychology to their advantage.

2. Imagine you are a sports psychologist who has been hired to work with a top-level athlete who has recently been "choking" in major events. Outline the steps you would take in working with the athlete to attempt to overcome this impediment to his or her performance.

Terminology Review

Defining Key Terms

Mission: Briefly explain the meaning of the following key terms:

Name:

Date:

Key Term	Definition
Sport psychology	
Ideal performance state	
Arousal	
Anxiety	
Relaxation	
Concentration	
Motivation	

Role of the audience	
Fatigue	
Psychological skills training	
Self-talk	
Imagery and visualization	
Hypnosis	
Goal setting	
S.M.A.R.T. principle	
Wheel of Excellence	

Sports Psychology Poster Exercise

Name:

Date:

Look in the Book! Pages: 267– 274

Sport psychology is the study of the thought processes, feelings, and behaviour of people within the context of sports. It is an area with many subfields, and it includes a wide range of techniques that are used to enhance performance.

Mission: Review Section 20 in your *Exercise Science* textbook to familiarize yourself with the key topics in the field of sport psychology. Then, once in your assigned group (maximum of five students per group), choose an aspect of sport psychology that your would like to research. Topics/strategies may include:

- arousal and relaxation regulation
- hypnosis
- self-talk
- concentration development
- motivation improvement
- imagery/visualization
- relaxation techniques
- fatigue
- any other suitable topic approved by the instructor

In the space provided below, and on a separate sheet of paper if necessary, compile notes about the aspect you have selected. Information should include a definition of the field, the fundamentals of how it works to enhance performance, people who use it (athletes, coaches, and psychologists), and real-life examples of how it has been used to assist athletes.

Each student will have one period to research their topic, either in the school library or Internet computer lab, and research can be completed at home or at an outside library.

After individual research is completed, reconvene with your group to compile your findings into a poster. Each of the topics should be represented on the poster.

Submit the poster to your instructor as a group (be sure to include the names of all compilers). All group members should also hand in their individual research notes for evaluation.

Research Areas	Initial Notes
Description of selected topic or strategy	
How the strategy is used	
Famous coaches/athletes/ psychologists who use it	
When did it start being used?	
How it works	

Sport Psychology—Annotated Bibliography

Name:
Date:

An annotated bibliography is a brief synopsis of books or articles pertinent to a given topic of interest.

Mission: Select a topic of your own choosing and in the space provided annotate three different articles or books relating to your chosen topic. Keep a hard copy of the article or book for reference. A sample entry is provided below.

Author, Article Title, Source	Summary in Point Form
1. Lenihan, Brian P. (1996). A review of motivational practices among elite long- and middle-distance runners. *Australian Journal of Sport Psychology*, 58 (1), 33–39.	This article examines, via a set of 40 interview questions, the motivational practices of 100 elite, long- and middle-distance runners at the Atlanta Summer Olympics in 1996. Author Lenihan surveyed an equal number of male and female runners and attempted to cover as wide a geographical/ethnic cross-section as possible, in order to establish preliminary data on whether or not motivational practices have a gender/ethnic basis.
2.	
3.	
4.	

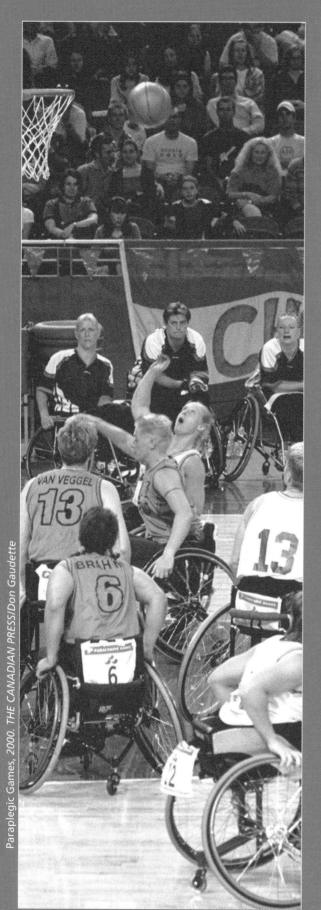

Paraplegic Games, 2000. THE CANADIAN PRESS/Don Gaudette

21

Coaching Principles and Practices

Learning Objectives

The exercises in this section of the workbook will help to reinforce your knowledge of the following topics covered in the *Exercise Science* textbook:

- The definition of the term "coach"
- Various styles adopted by coaches in pursuit of their roles, including authoritarian, business-like, "nice guy/gal," intense, and "easy-going"
- The differences between autocratic and democratic coaches
- The concept of "fair play" and its relation to coaching
- The roles and responsibilities of the coach in working with athletes
- The development of coaching skills
- How to build age-appropriate coaching strategies
- Guidelines for working with advanced athletes
- The differences between strategy, tactics, and planning in sport coaching
- The role of the National Coaching Certification Program in Canada
- Ethical and legal concerns for coaches
- How coaches and athletes can find the right working relationship
- Policies regarding the monitoring of coaches
- Opportunities for coaches in Canada

Section Quiz

Name: _____ Date: _____

Multiple-Choice Questions

Mission: Circle the letter beside the answer that you believe to be correct.

1. When working with an athlete, which is the most important consideration for a coach?
   (a) how working with the athlete will impact the coach's overall career
   (b) the athlete's commitment, in terms of time
   (c) whether or not the coach/athlete relationship will involve financial reimbursement for the coach
   (d) the athlete's age and ability level

2. When attempting to select a coach, an athlete should ask about the coach's
   (a) record with athletes of a similar background.
   (b) method of dealing with conflict
   (c) expectations for the athlete
   (d) all of the above

3. Which coaching style best describes a coach who tells his team that he is not interested in any feedback about how a game is progressing?
   (a) democratic coach
   (b) sympathetic coach
   (c) autocratic coach
   (d) business-like coach

4. A coach who encourages a cyclist to take a short-cut during a race violates which NCCP philosophy?
   (a) tactical decision-making ethics
   (b) the importance of coaching theory
   (c) knowledge of crucial coaching skills
   (d) fair play

5. One of the significant things about Danièle Sauvageau's coaching success is that
   (a) she has never played hockey herself
   (b) she has never coached Team Canada full time
   (c) she has never had an assistant coach
   (d) her teams never played together in non-Olympic years

6. A coach and athlete who sit down to make a competitive plan before an event are engaged in
   (a) tactical planning
   (b) strategic planning
   (c) unfair play
   (d) poor sportsmanship

7. Which best describes the role of the coach as outlined by the NCCP?
   (a) gives positive feedback
   (b) builds an athlete's self-esteem
   (c) encourages participation
   (d) all of the above

Short-Answer Questions

Mission: Briefly answer the following questions in the space provided:

1. Summarize the philosophy of fair play.

   _____

2. Choose three (of the eight) essentials of the role of the coach that you feel are the most important. Define each, and state why you think these three are the most important.

   _____

3. Which five skills or attributes are, in your opinion, the most important for a coach? Provide reasons for your answers.

   _____

4. Using your favourite sport, give an example of a good use of tactics by a coach and/or athlete, and one example of a poor tactical decision.

   _____

5. Define the term "ethical decision" as it relates to sport. List three ethical and three unethical decisions that could be made by a coach and his/her athlete.

   _____

   _____

   _____

Essay Questions

Mission: On a separate piece of paper, develop a 100-word response to the following questions.

1. Discuss why there is a problem with the "win at all costs" philosophy when coaching younger athletes.

2. On page 286 of the text, a number of questions that an athlete might ask a prospective coach are presented. In your opinion, how would an "ideal" coach respond to three questions of your choice?

Terminology Review

Defining Key Terms

Name: _____

Date: _____

Mission: Briefly explain the meaning of the following key terms:

Key Term	Definition
Coaching styles	
Autocratic coach	
Democratic coach	
National Coaching Certification Program (NCCP)	
Fair play	
Role of a coach	
Age-appropriate coaching strategies	
Strategy/tactics	
Standards of ethics and behaviour for coaches	
Coach-athlete relationship	

Crossword on Coaching Principles and Practices

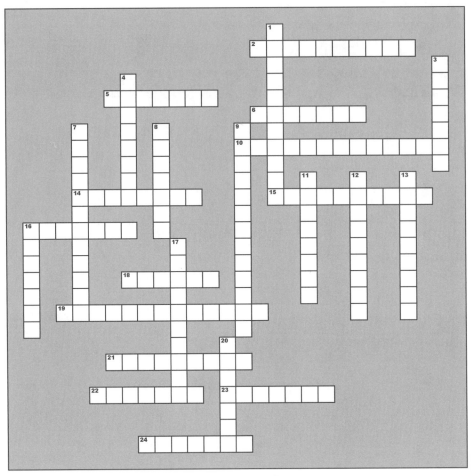

Across

2. The type of coach who involves athletes in most decisions
5. The bond between a successful coach and his or her athletes is based on this
6. Part of being a good coach and athlete is developing a sense of this towards the opponent
10. The type of coach who emphasizes discipline in practice and competition
14. Coaches with this type of attitude generally help young athletes to succeed
15. Working to maintain high levels of this is one of a coach's most important tasks
16. A more severe level of staleness
18. Coaches are often referred to as this by their athletes
19. The NCCP provides levels of this for coaches.
21. Name for the hands-on component of NCCP instruction for coaches
22. The practice of devising plans during actual competition
23. Deciding whether to use performance-enhancing drugs is an example of this type of decision
24. The type of coach who emphasizes winning above all

Down

1. Coaches can work to improve this by finding something to praise in every athlete's efforts
3. Coaches struggle with the decision to stress this over personal development
4. American coach who believed winning is "everything"
7. Allowing an athlete to determine aspects of his or her career fosters this
8. Under the fair-play philosophy, coaches must maintain this at all times
9. Most derive enjoyment and skill development from this
11. The practice of devising plans in advance of a competition
12. Former Olympic hockey coach; currently a police officer
13. An unpaid coach
16. Coaches who stress this see sport as only one aspect of life
17. The "do-as-I-say" approach to coaching
20. When coaching young athletes, building a relationship with these people is crucial

Coaching Styles

Name:
Date:
Look in the Book! Pages: 277–279, 281–282

There are as many different types of coaches as there are types of athletes. Coaches at all levels of sport adopt a wide range of coaching styles and approaches to working with athletes.

Mission: Select one of ten coaches from the list below (or one approved by your instructor) and answer the questions that follow. Additional research will be required.

- Pat Quinn
- Joe McAdoo
- Melody Davidson
- Teitur Thordarson

- Tom Johnson
- Ernie Whitt
- Laryssa Biesenthal
- Marcel Lacroix

- Michel Larouche
- Tanya Dubnicoff
- Any other coach approved by your teacher

Questions

1. For what sport is this coach best known?

2. Which one of the coaching styles outlined in the text does he or she demonstrate?

3. Is this coach best described as autocratic or democratic?

4. How does this coach motivate his or her athletes? Provide examples from actual competitions to support your answer.

5. Based on the discussion in the text about fair play and the ethical behaviour of coaches, would you say that this coach deals with matters in a fair and ethical manner? Again, give examples to justify your answers.

6. Indicate one instance in which this coach utilized a superior knowledge of strategies or tactics to the benefit of his or her athlete(s) in a competitive situation. Provide a brief description of when this happened.

7. If you were an athlete, would you like to work with the coach you selected? Why, or why not?

8. If you were a coach, would you attempt to emulate the coach you have chosen? Why, or why not?

Coaching Comparison

The style a coach adopts is often determined by the age/level of development of the athlete. Coaches use different techniques to elicit the best performance from athletes. This is your opportunity to familiarize yourself with various coaching techniques.

Name:

Date:

Look in the Book! Pages: 277–279

Mission: Choose two coaches and observe their coaching style during a practice session. As you observe the practice sessions, complete the following chart by placing a check mark in the box beside the appropriate coaching style each time you see that style exhibited by the coach. Remember to obtain approval from your teacher, and from each coach that you would like to observe before you begin the exercise.

Coach's Name _____

Sport _____

Age level of athlete(s) _____

Coaching Style	Definition	Coach 1	Coach 2
Authoritarian			
Business-like			
"Nice guy/gal"			
Intense			
"Easy-going"			

CHAPTER 22

Unit 3 Career Choices

Investigate a career in one of the fields covered in Unit 3. Ideally, you should interview someone working within the field for this assignment.

1 Career and description

_____

_____

_____

_____

2 List at least two post-secondary institutions in Ontario and/or Canada that offer programs for this career.

_____

_____

_____

3 Choose one of the above institutions and determine the required courses in the first year of study for this program.

_____

_____

_____

4 What is the total length of the education needed to begin this career? Is an internship or apprenticeship required?

_____

_____

_____

5 What is the demand for individuals qualified for this occupation? If possible, provide some employment data to support your answer.

_____

_____

_____

6 What is the average starting salary for this career? What is the top salary? On what do salary increases depend in this career?

_____

_____

_____

7 List occupational settings where a person with these qualifications could work.

_____   _____

_____   _____

CHAPTER 23

Unit 3 Crossword Challenge

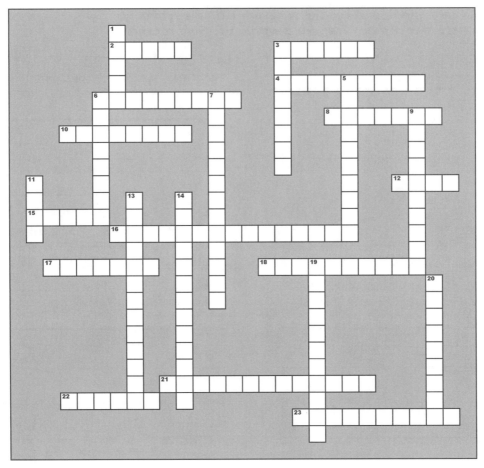

Across

2. Type of learning in which a person develops the ability to perform a task
3. Classification of skill performed in stationary environmental conditions
4. Motor activity that involves very little thought
6. Ethical and behavioural rules set by most sport leagues and associations for coaches
8. Psychological state in which an athlete feels ready to do his or her very best in competition
10. Information a learner obtains regarding how he or she is progressing in learning to perform a skill
12. Acronym for instructional courses offered by the Coaching Association of Canada
15. Performance state commonly known as "the zone"
16. The ability to use a skill learned in one sport context in another sport context
17. Process in which learners develop a skill gradually
18. Coach who encourages his or her athletes to be fully involved in decisions
21. Process in which humans form attachments to others
22. What Robert Singer's five-step method was created to teach
23. Motor activity that needs thought and time to perform

Down

1. Acronym for basic framework for establishing goals
3. Process in which complex skills are broken into separate and distinct parts
5. Categorization created by researchers to help classify people's appearance and physical structure
6. Age indicated by physical maturity of the skeleton
7. Age expressed by one's ability to perform certain tasks
9. Coach who adopts a "do-as-I-say" approach
11. Type of play that is one of the fundamental tenets of the National Coaching Certification Program
13. Age measured in years, months, and days
14. Psychological process in which athletes imagine themselves succeeding
19. How a coach or a teacher evaluates an athlete's skills
20. Development characterized by changes in a person's ability to interpret and process information

UNIT 4

THE EVOLUTION OF PHYSICAL ACTIVITY AND SPORT

Former Edmonton Grads Margaret MacBurney Vasheresse and Helen Northup Alexander. *THE CANADIAN PRESS/John Ulan*

24

History of Physical Education and Sport

Learning Objectives

The exercises in this section of the workbook will help to reinforce your knowledge of the following topics covered in the *Exercise Science* textbook:

- Basic trends in sport history
- The role of the Greeks and Romans in sport development
- Sport in the Americas
- The European legacy of sport, including the importance of the Victorian era
- Racially segregated and restricted sport
- Canadians who have excelled in Olympic competition
- Early Canadian sport pioneers
- The rise of North American pro sport leagues
- Major twentieth-century achievements by Canadians in sport
- The importance of the Commonwealth Games
- The development of physical education in Canadian schools and society
- How sport and physical activity have contributed to Canadian society
- The concepts of exploitation and sport equity

Section Quiz

Name: _____ Date: _____

Multiple-Choice Questions

Mission: Circle the letter beside the answer that you believe to be correct.

1. What is the Olympic Peace?
   (a) offerings all athletes had to bring in order to be allowed to compete
   (b) ceremonial clothing worn by early Olympians
   (c) truce called in order to allow athletes to travel to Olympia
   (d) the prize offered to victorious athletes in early Olympic competition

2. Physical education classes for children were instituted in 1420 in Europe by
   (a) Leonardo da Vinci
   (b) Pierre de Coubertin
   (c) Queen Victoria
   (d) an Italian physician

3. The Victorian gentleman athlete embraced the concepts of
   (a) fair play
   (b) amateurism
   (c) sport as a reflection of life
   (d) all of the above

4. Canadian winners at the Olympics include
   (a) Gaetan Boucher
   (b) Tom Longboat
   (c) Edward "Ned" Hanlan
   (d) George Beers

5. Professional teams arose when
   (a) amateurism was no longer valued
   (b) teams started paying their best players to ensure patrons returned
   (c) Olympic sports became open to the common man
   (d) the Victorian age was at its height

6. Which Canadian athlete was nicknamed the "Saskatoon Lily"?
   (a) Elizabeth Manley
   (b) Nancy Greene
   (c) Barbara Ann Scott
   (d) Ethel Catherwood

7. The Canadian hockey players who participated in games against the USSR represented
   (a) the free-market capitalist society
   (b) the hopes and dreams of many Canadian youth
   (c) warriors in a clash of sporting ideologies
   (d) all of the above

Short-Answer Questions

Mission: Briefly answer the following questions in the space provided:

1. Did Greek and Roman concepts of sport have any effect on each other? If so, what was it?

   _____

2. Define the concept of the "Renaissance man."

   _____

3. Why did the Victorians believe that participation in sports was harmful for women?

   _____

4. For what reasons did the NBA's Vancouver Grizzlies fail?

   _____

5. In what ways do the Canada Games serve young Canadian athletes?

   _____

6. Why is the principle of "equal access" an important concept in the world of sports?

   _____

   _____

   _____

Essay Questions

Mission: On a separate piece of paper, develop a 100-word response to the following questions.

1. Examine the Victorian beliefs with regard to sport.

2. What did the Olympic Charter emphasize? How did this affect the goals of the Olympic Movement?

3. Discuss the positive and negative aspects of athletes serving as role models for youth.

Terminology Review

Defining Key Terms

Name:

Date:

Mission: Briefly explain the meaning of the following key terms:

Key Term	Definition
Olympic Games	
Renaissance man	
Calisthenics	
Olympic Charter	
Olympic Movement	
International Olympic Committee	
National Hockey League	

Edmonton Commercial Graduates Basketball Club	
Canadian Football League	
Commonwealth Games	
Canada Games	
Crazy Canucks	
ParticipAction	
Marathon of Hope	
Terry Fox Run	
Man in Motion World Tour	
Role models	
Exploitation	
Sport equity	

Modern Olympic Timeline

Name:
Date:
Look in the Book! Pages: 298–300

Since their founding in 1896, the modern Olympic Games have been profoundly affected by political events. As well, they have provided chances for Canadian athletes to shine on the international sporting stage.

Mission: Fill in the chart below. Provide a significant political event (if any) occurring at the time of the Games, and the name(s) of the Canadian athlete(s) who won medals at the Games. Be sure to also include the name of the event, and medal achieved.

Note: The Olympics were not held in 1916, 1940, and 1944.

Summer Olympics		Political Events	Canadian Medalists
1896	Athens, Greece		
1900	Paris, France		
1904	St. Louis, USA		
1906	Athens, Greece		
1908	London, England		
1912	Stockholm, Sweden		
1920	Antwerp, Belgium		
1924	Paris, France		
1928	Amsterdam, The Netherlands		
1932	Los Angeles, USA		
1936	Berlin, Germany		
1948	London, England		
1952	Helsinki, Finland		
1956	Melbourne, Australia		
1960	Rome, Italy		
1964	Tokyo, Japan		
1968	Mexico City, Mexico		
1972	Munich, Germany		
1976	Montreal, Canada		
1980	Moscow, USSR		
1984	Los Angeles, USA		

		Political Events	Canadian Medalists
1988	Seoul, South Korea		
1992	Barcelona, Spain		
1996	Atlanta, USA		
2000	Sydney, Australia		
2004	Athens, Greece		
2008	Beijing, China		
2012	London, England		

Winter Olympics		Political Events	Canadian Medalists
1924	Chamonix, France		
1928	St. Moritz, Switzerland		
1932	Lake Placid, USA		
1936	Garmisch-Partenkirchen, Germany		
1948	St. Moritz, Switzerland		
1952	Oslo, Norway		
1956	Cortina d'Ampezzo, Italy		
1960	Squaw Valley, USA		
1964	Innsbruck, Austria		
1968	Genoble, France		
1972	Sapporo, Japan		
1976	Innsbruck, Austria		
1980	Lake Placid, USA		
1984	Sarajevo, Yugoslavia		
1988	Calgary, Canada		
1992	Albertville, France		
1994	Lillehammer, Norway		
1998	Nagano, Japan		
2002	Salt Lake City, USA		
2006	Torino, Italy		
2010	Vancouver-Whistler, Canada		

Canadian Sport Heroes and Their Achievements

Understanding the historical context of sport and physical activity can further your appreciation of current trends and events. The following exercise will acquaint you with the significant contributions made by Canadians in the history of sport.

Name:

Date:

Look in the Book! Pages: 299–301, 305–307, 309–313

Mission: Research the major achievements of the following Canadian sport figures, and fill in the table below.

Athlete	Major Achievements
James Naismith 1891	
Tom Longboat 1905–1915	
Barbara Ann Scott 1940s	
Russ Jackson 1950s–1960s	
Dick Pound 1960s–Present	
Arnie Boldt 1960s–1970s	

Nancy Greene 1960s–1970s	
Terry Fox 1980s	
Charmaine Crooks 1980s–1990s	
Wayne Gretzky 1980s–1990s	
Hayley Wickenheiser 1990s–present	
Clara Hughes 1990s–present	
Simon Whitfield 2000–present	
Cindy Klassen 2000–present	

Kara Lang, 2002. *THE CANADIAN PRESS/Adrian Wyld*

25

Women in Sport

Learning Objectives

The exercises in this section of the workbook will help to reinforce your knowledge of the following topics covered in the *Exercise Science* textbook:

- Basic trends and key events in the history of women in sport
- The growth of the Women's Amateur Athletic Federation
- Pioneering Canadian sportswomen
- The role of Title IX in women's sport
- The role of women in sport today
- Key athletes and events in contemporary Canadian women's sports
- Women in key positions in Canadian sports
- The media's impact on women in sport
- The concept of body image and its influence on women athletes
- The "female triad" and the dangers it poses
- The role of the Canadian Association for the Advancement of Women in Sport (CAAWS)

Section Quiz

Name: _____ Date: _____

Multiple-Choice Questions

Mission: Circle the letter beside the answer that you believe to be correct.

1. In the 1920s, women participating in sport were still fighting for the right to
   (a) wear sleeveless shirts
   (b) wear shorts
   (c) bare their legs
   (d) all of the above

2. A landmark sexual discrimination case in the Supreme Court was won by
   (a) Justine Blainey
   (b) Manon Rheaume
   (c) Hayley Wickenheiser
   (d) Alison Sydor

3. Gender discrimination of any kind is prohibited in schools in the United States by
   (a) Educational Amendments
   (b) American Sport Policy
   (c) U.S. Charter of Rights and Freedoms
   (d) Title IX

4. The Scott Tournament of Hearts
   (a) is the Canadian Women's Curling Championship
   (b) won a Gemini award in 2001 for the best live sporting event
   (c) has been won five times by Colleen Jones
   (d) all of the above

5. The majority of Canadian female sports teams
   (a) are coached by women
   (b) are officiated by women
   (c) are coached by men
   (d) are coached by former female athletes

6. The female triad can be broken by
   (a) early identification and intervention
   (b) expressing general concern for the individual's health
   (c) seeking the guidance of trained medical professionals
   (d) all of the above

7. The handbook and website **Speak Out! Act Now!** was released by
   (a) the Canadian Association for the Advancement of Women
   (b) the Coaching Association of Canada
   (c) the Harassment and Abuse in Sport Collective
   (d) the Canadian Centre for Ethics in Sport

Short-Answer Questions

Mission: Briefly answer the following questions in the space provided:

1. Which sport offers three inspiring tales of women who were allowed to compete successfully against men?

   _____

2. At which university was the first Physical Education Bachelor's Degree created? When?

   _____

3. Which federation merged with the Amateur Athletic Union of Canada?

   _____

4. Which female athlete cut off her hair and posed as a boy to join a hockey team?

   _____

5. What initiative was developed by the Canadian Heritage Ministry and released in 2002?

   _____

6. Which national women's team competed in the Women's Pacific Rim Championships?

   _____

7. What is needed to encourage women to enter leadership positions in sport?

   _____

Essay Questions

Mission: On a separate piece of paper, develop a 100-word response to the following questions.

1. Discuss the effects of Title IX for both American and Canadian female athletes.

2. Examine the issue of media coverage of women's sports. Discuss how it could be improved.

3. How has the Canadian Association for the Advancement of Women in Sport increased the rate of participation of girls and women in sport?

Terminology Review

Defining Key Terms

Name:
Date:

Mission: Briefly explain the meaning of the following key terms:

Key Term	Definition
Femininity	
Women's Amateur Athletic Federation	
Title IX	
Gender representation in leadership positions	
Media coverage of women's sports	
Body image	
Female triad	
Canadian Association for the Advancement of Women in Sport (CAAWS)	
On The Move	
ACTive	
Girls @ Play	

Crossword on Women in Sport

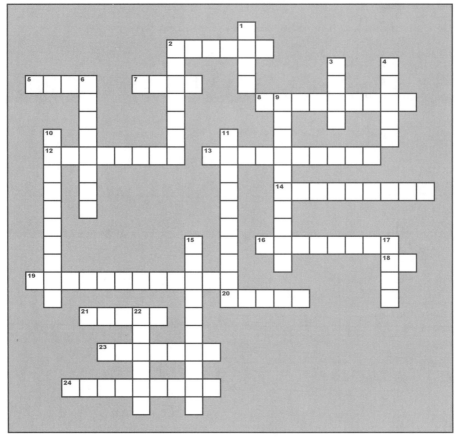

Across

2. This athlete turned from speed skating to cycling and then back to speed skating
5. Top athlete who became columnist
7. Sport federation that held the Under 19 World Cup championship for women
8. Head coach of Team Canada in hockey for the 2002 Winter Olympics
12. Creator of a diploma course in physical education at Margaret Eaton School
13. Term that no longer means weak, silent, unthinking waifs
14. Athlete named Canadian Women Athlete for the Half-Century
16. Official who took away Ben Johnson's ill-gotten gold medal
18. Title of American equal-opportunity legislation that affects both U.S. and Canadian athletes
19. Canadian female athlete signed by the Kirkkonummi Salamat team
20. Female health syndrome that includes osteoporosis
21. Women and girls are concerned with this societal aspect of the body
23. Athlete who fought for and won the legal right to participate on boys' teams
24. Dubbed the "Queen of Curling" following a gold medal win in the 1998 Nagano Olympic Games

Down

1. Number of women who competed in the first modern Olympic Games
2. First woman elected to the Executive of the Canadian Olympic Association
3. Acronym for the first national body commonly called the Canadian Parliament of Women's Sport
4. Acronym for organization that promotes sports and physical activity for Canadian women
6. Clothing invented to aid female sports participation
9. Term for condition in which menstrual periods are absent
10. Petitclerc won this 800-metre race included in the 2002 Commonwealth Games
11. First woman to referee an Olympic soccer game
15. Contributing factors to this type of eating include low self-esteem and perfectionism
17. CAAWS teamed up with this company to develop the Girls@Play program
22. Manon Rheaume made history playing this position

Female Role Models in Sports

Name:

Date:

Successful female athletes play a critical role in encouraging young female athletes to follow their dreams and develop their talent to the fullest.

Mission: For each of the following sports, identify a Canadian female role model and describe her achievements. If possible, include a local role model. If you are unable to identify a female role model for a sport listed below, give possible reasons why this sport lacks female participation.

Sport	Athlete/Achievements
Alpine skiing	
Baseball	
Basketball	
Cross-country skiing	
Curling	
Cycling	
Dance	

Diving	
Field hockey	
Figure skating	
Golf	
Hockey	
Rowing	
Sailing	
Speed Skating	
Sport of choice	
Sport of choice	

The Role of Female Athletes

Female sports pioneers have paved the way for the opportunities and successes enjoyed by many Canadian female athletes.

Mission: Choose ten Canadian female athletes from the list below and research their achievements/goals accomplished within their chosen sport, as well as their post-career contributions.

Name:

Date:

Look in the Book! Pages: 316–323

- ❑ Elizabeth (Liz) Ashton
- ❑ Angela Bailey
- ❑ Dorothea Beale
- ❑ Marilyn Bell
- ❑ Justine Blainey
- ❑ Debbie Brill
- ❑ Vicki Keith
- ❑ Becky Keller
- ❑ Silken Laumann
- ❑ Carol Anne Letheren
- ❑ Jocelyn Lovell
- ❑ Carolyn Waldo
- ❑ Ethel Catherwood
- ❑ Edmonton Grads
- ❑ The Firth Sisters
- ❑ Sylvie Frechette
- ❑ Elizabeth Manley

- ❑ Alice Milliat
- ❑ Ann Ottenbrite
- ❑ Sharon Wood
- ❑ Nancy Greene
- ❑ Abigail (Abby) Hoffman
- ❑ Sue Holloway
- ❑ Angella Issajenko
- ❑ Lori Kane
- ❑ Ann Peel
- ❑ Manon Rheaume
- ❑ Bobbie (Fanny) Rosenfeld
- ❑ Jamie Sale
- ❑ Barbara Ann Scott
- ❑ Kay Worthington
- ❑ Hayley Wickenheiser
- ❑ Chantal Petitclerc

- ❑ Cassie Campbell
- ❑ Beckie Scott
- ❑ Chandra Crawford
- ❑ Clara Hughes
- ❑ Cindy Klassen
- ❑ TA Loeffler
- ❑ Charmaine Crooks
- ❑ Sonia Denoncourt
- ❑ Ljiljana (Lilo) Ljubisic
- ❑ Margo Mountjoy
- ❑ Stephanie Dixon
- ❑ Pat Reid
- ❑ Marlene Stewart Streit
- ❑ Anne Merklinger
- ❑ Carla Qualtrough

Name of Athlete	Athletic Background	Achievements After Athletic Career
1.		
2.		
3.		

Name of Athlete	Athletic Background	Achievements After Athletic Career
4.		
5.		
6.		
7.		
8.		
9.		
10.		

26

Government Support for Sport and Physical Activity

Learning Objectives

The exercises in this section of the workbook will help to reinforce your knowledge of the following topics covered in the *Exercise Science* textbook:

- The historical relationship between the Canadian government and sport
- Why sport matters to governments at all levels
- The Mills Report and what it revealed about sport in Canada
- Canada's national Sport Policy and its key points
- How sport is organized in Canada at the various levels of government
- The role of Sport Canada
- The importance of the Canadian Olympic Committee
- The significance of National Sport Organizations (NSOs), Provincial Sport Organizations (PSOs), and Multi-Sport Service Organizations (MSOs)
- The Games of La Francophonie and their importance for the French-speaking world
- Canada's federal sport budget
- How Canada promotes women and youth in sport
- The role of Aboriginal people in Canadian sport
- Sport and the disabled in Canada
- The impact of finance and wagering on Canadian sport

Section Quiz

Name: _____ Date: _____

Multiple-Choice Questions

Mission: Circle the letter beside the answer that you believe to be correct.

1. A major report on Canadian sport, released in 1998, was entitled

   (a) Task Force Report on Sport
   (b) Promoting Physical Activity and Sport
   (c) Sport in Canada
   (d) Canadian Sport Policy

2. Sport Canada, the major granting agency for sports in Canada, is located within

   (a) the Athlete Assistance Program
   (b) each provincial and territorial government
   (c) Heritage Canada
   (d) the community of National Games Organizations

3. The Canadian Olympic Committee is one of the founding partners of

   (a) Sport Dispute Resolution Centres
   (b) National Sport Organizations
   (c) Provincial Sport Organizations
   (d) Canadian Sports Centres

4. The Games of La Francophonie are

   (a) open to Canadian and non-Canadian athletes
   (b) sponsored mainly by government bodies
   (c) a showcase for both sporting and cultural events
   (d) all of the above

5. Multi-Sport Service Organizations include

   (a) Athletics Canada
   (b) Canadian Centre for Ethics in Sport
   (c) International Amateur Athletics Federation
   (d) Tennis Canada

6. The most significant federal program involved with promoting a sports culture in younger age groups is

   (a) Outreach
   (b) Sport Participation Development Program
   (c) Run Jump Throw
   (d) Kids of Steel

7. Sporting equipment has been provided to recreation organizations, including many in rural Aboriginal communities, by the

   (a) UPS Olympic Sports Legacy Program
   (b) Human Resources Development Canada
   (c) Canadian Olympic Association
   (d) Aboriginal Sports Circle

Short-Answer Questions

Mission: Briefly answer the following questions in the space provided:

1. What is the primary goal of Sport Canada?

   _____

2. What is the main responsibility of the Canadian Olympic Committee?

   _____

3. What is the new approach developed by the federal government in funding NSOs?

   _____

4. Within which Ontario government department is responsibility for sport located?

   _____

5. In which international games are medals awarded for both athletic and artistic competition?

   _____

6. The Sport Participation Development Program provides financial support to National Sports Organization in which of their efforts?

   _____

7. What source of funds provides Sport Canada with 55 percent of its budget?

   _____

Essay Questions

Mission: On a separate piece of paper, develop a 100-word response to the following questions.

1. State the main recommendations of the *The Mills Report: Sport in Canada* and suggest how they can be implemented.

2. Outline the goals of the Canadian Sport Policy.

3. Describe the various organizations that comprise the "sport community" in Canada and their relationship to one another.

Terminology Review

Defining Key Terms

Name:

Date:

Mission: Briefly explain the meaning of the following key terms:

Key Term	Definition
Mills Report	
Sport Dispute Resolution Centre	
Canadian Sport Policy	
Sport Canada	
Canadian Olympic Committee	
Canadian Sport Centres	
National Sport Organizations (NSOs)	
Provincial Sport Organizations (PSOs)	

Multi-Sport Service Organizations (MSOs)	
Games of La Francophonie	
Athlete Assistance Program	
Royal Commission on the Status of Women in Canada	
Sport Participation Development Program	
Aboriginal Sports Circle	
Arctic Winter Games	
Canadian Paralympic Committee	
Special Olympics	
Sports Select and PRO-LINE	
Inter-Provincial Lottery Corporation	

The Sport Community in Canada

Name: _____

Date: _____

Look in the Book! Pages: 332–336

The sport community in Canada consists of a number of organizations that provide sport programming and activities at the municipal, provincial/territorial, national, and international levels.

Mission: To acquaint yourself with the organizations that provide sport programming on various levels, complete the following chart using a minimum of three examples for each level of sport indicated.

Local	Provincial	National	International
Local or community sport clubs	Provincial Games Organizations	National Games Organizations	Major Games Federations
_____	_____	_____	_____
_____	_____	_____	_____
_____	_____	_____	_____
_____	_____	_____	_____
School clubs and teams	Provincial Sport Organizations	National Sport Organizations	International Sport Federations
_____	_____	_____	_____
_____	_____	_____	_____
_____	_____	_____	_____
_____	_____	_____	_____
Post-secondary institutions clubs/teams	Provincial Multi-Sport Organizations	National Multi-Sport Organizations	General Assemblies of International Sports
_____	_____	_____	_____
_____	_____	_____	_____
_____	_____	_____	_____
_____	_____	_____	_____

Provincial Sport Organizations

Name:

Date:

Look in the Book! Pages: 335–336

Provincial Sport Organizations (PSOs) play an important role in providing sporting opportunities for Canadians.

Mission: To gain an understanding of how Provincial Sport Organizations operate, choose and research a provincial sport organization and then fill in the chart below.

Full name of PSO	
When the PSO was founded	
Number of local clubs represented	
Total current individual members	
Is the membership growing?	
Name of president	
Number of full-time staff	
Location of offices	
Website address	
Annual expenditure of the PSO	
Amount of funding received in most recent year	
Current programs offered	
Significant past achievements	

CHAPTER 27

Unit 4 Career Choices

Investigate a career in one of the fields covered in Unit 4. Ideally, you should interview someone working within the field for this assignment.

1   Career and description

_____

_____

_____

_____

2   List at least two post-secondary institutions in Ontario and/or Canada that offer programs for this career.

_____

_____

_____

3   Choose one of the above institutions and determine the required courses in the first year of study for this program.

_____

_____

_____

4   What is the total length of the education needed to begin this career? Is an internship or apprenticeship required?

_____

_____

_____

5   What is the demand for individuals qualified for this occupation? If possible, provide some employment data to support your answer.

_____

_____

_____

6   What is the average starting salary for this career? What is the top salary? On what do salary increases depend in this career?

_____

_____

_____

7   List occupational settings where a person with these qualifications could work.

_____   _____

_____   _____

CHAPTER 28

Unit 4 Crossword Challenge

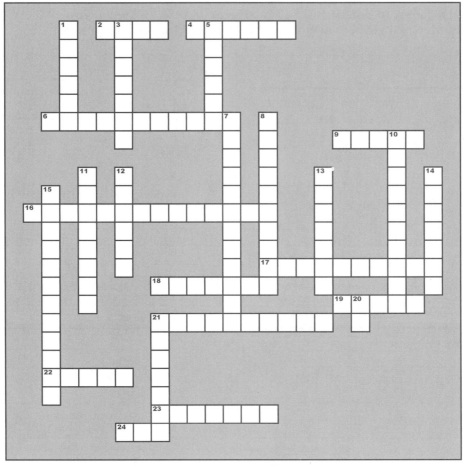

Across

2. Image concern confronting women and girls
4. Status achieved in sport when the same opportunities are equal to everyone
6. Era that produced people equally good at and interested in multiple things
9. Female syndrome that includes disordered eating habits, amenorrhea, and osteoporosis
16. A program created to encourage the Canadian public to become more physically active
17. Federal athlete program that helps athletes meet their living, training, and travel expenses
18. Olympics organized for persons with mental disabilities
19. Report prepared by the Sub-Committee on the Study of Sport in Canada
21. Concept no longer equated with weak, silent, unthinking women
22. Acronym for association founded in 1981 to promote sports and physical activity for women across Canada
23. Athlete who does not receive material rewards from sport
24. League that began its first season in 1917 with five hockey teams

Down

1. Program promoting physical activity for women and girls that provides opportunity for their participation
3. Games originated by the Greeks
5. Canada Games first held here in 1967
7. Relationship in which one party engages in the majority of the effort without receiving a fair share of the results
8. Level of sport organizations that form an intermediary between community and national sport organizations
10. Sports Circle that promotes indigenous games and traditional approaches to amateur sport
11. Level of sport organizations that support athletes in international competitions
12. Winter Games co-hosted in 2002 by Nuuk, Greenland, and Iqaluit, Nunavut
13. Canadian Committee that represents Canada within the IOC
14. Document detailing the goals of the Olympic Movement
15. Series of vigorous exercises and stretches originating in the Victorian era
20. Title of American equal-opportunity legislation affecting female athletes
21. Level of government that developed the Canadian Sport Policy in 2002

UNIT 5
SOCIAL ISSUES IN PHYSICAL ACTIVITY AND SPORT

Notes

29

The (Big) Business of Sport Entertainment

Learning Objectives

The exercises in this section of the workbook will help to reinforce your knowledge of the following topics covered in the *Exercise Science* textbook:

- The basic principles of sport's relationship to the world of business
- The differences between for-profit and not-for-profit sport
- The fundamental difference between amateur and professional sport
- The reasons behind rising player salaries in professional sport
- The importance of a winning team from an economic perspective
- The role played by the media in the sports-as-entertainment complex
- How television has impacted on sport
- The fundamentals of the sports-as-entertainment industry, including broadcasting rights, player endorsements, the role of sports marketing, and promotion
- Key figures in the sport industry: team owners, athletes, agents, and fans
- The role of advertising
- Sports "spin-offs" including replica products, food and beverage sales, alternative use of sports stadiums, charities, and the overall contribution of sport to local economies

Section Quiz

Name: _____ Date: _____

Multiple-Choice Questions

Mission: Circle the letter beside the answer that you believe to be correct.

1. Amateur athletes derive compensation for their efforts through

    (a) player contracts
    (b) endorsement deals
    (c) sale of merchandise and tickets
    (d) none of the above

2. Formerly for amateurs only, the Olympic Games now permits competition by professional

    (a) skaters and ice dancers
    (b) hockey and basketball players
    (c) baseball and softball players
    (d) boxers and wrestlers

3. The largest source of profits for big-business sports teams is

    (a) athlete endorsements
    (b) ticket sales
    (c) the use of games for the sale of various rights
    (d) concession sales

4. The WWE "Wrestlemania" events are broadcast as

    (a) regular over the air telecasts
    (b) conventional cable presentations
    (c) video features
    (d) exclusive pay-per-view engagements

5. Nike has received criticism for

    (a) the huge endorsement fees it has paid to celebrity athletes
    (b) the targeting of its marketing towards youth
    (c) the manufacturing of its product in Third World countries
    (d) its advertising at the Atlanta Olympic Games

6. Which of the following countries participated in the 1980 Olympics, held in Moscow, despite a political boycott?

    (a) Great Britain
    (b) United States
    (c) Canada
    (d) France

7. Pro sports teams contribute to their local economy by

    (a) increasing sales at restaurants and hotels close to stadiums
    (b) employing people in the local community
    (c) paying taxes to the government
    (d) all of the above

Short-Answer Questions

Mission: Briefly answer the following questions in the space provided:

1. On what is the distinction between for-profit and not-for-profit sport based?

2. What economic concept/theory is used by many to explain the high salaries in professional sports today? Explain.

3. The revenue generation of live sports events is similar to what other events?

4. What features are offered to viewers as part of the overall sport-as-entertainment package?

5. How do broadcasters recoup the massive sums they have paid for broadcasting rights to sporting events? What would happen if this avenue were not open to them?

6. Which trend in athlete endorsement and marketing was ushered in by Michael Jordan's huge endorsement contract?

Essay Questions

Mission: On a separate piece of paper, develop a 100-word response to the following questions.

1. How does a city stand to benefit from hosting the Olympic Games, thereby justifying the enormous cost of preparing a bid for the IOC?

2. Compare the "business" of sport in Eastern Europe at the height of the "Cold War," and of Cuba today, with that of North America and Europe.

3. Examine the arguments in favour of and against the role of a player's agent and explain at least three of them.

Terminology Review

Defining Key Terms

Mission: Briefly explain the meaning of the following key terms:

Name:

Date:

Key Term	Definition
For-profit/not-for-profit sport	
Amateur/professional athletes	
Media	
Sports-as-entertainment industry	
Broadcasting rights	
Endorsement	
Sport franchises	
Player's agent	
Fan loyalty	
Players' strikes	
Stadium concessions	
Charitable activities	

Crossword on the Business of Sport Entertainment

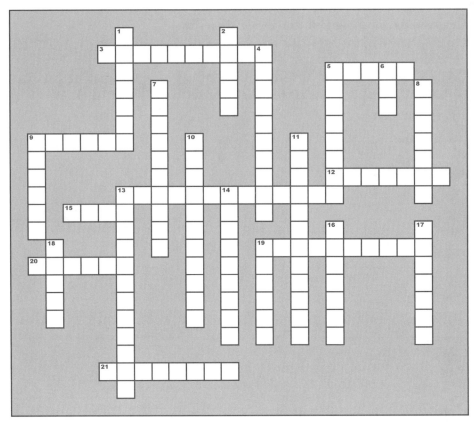

Across

3. Source of financial support for Cuban athletes
5. Negotiator of a player's salary with team owners
9. The other side of the economic theory that posits demand as a major force
12. Products such as team jerseys, supporter banners, scarves
13. Athletes who receive financial rewards for their efforts
15. What consumers must be when it comes to advertising
19. Activities for a cause in which athletes can serve as positive role models
20. Basketball player who refused to comment on Nike's labour practices
21. Along with TV and radio, the twentieth century has seen the birth and growth of sport coverage through this medium

Down

1. Pro teams try to build this among their fans
2. Collective name for television, radio, newspapers, and so on
4. Medium responsible for gradually reshaping the rules of sport
5. Athletes who receive no financial rewards for their efforts
6. Acronym for North American professional sports league with highest average salary
7. Sport organized primarily to make money
8. What the action produced by athletes in big-business sport is known as
9. "The beautiful game" (Pelé)
10. Nowadays, an integral part of professional sport and a major source of revenue
11. Rights to telecast games
13. Runner-up city in the bidding to host the 2010 Winter Olympics
14. High-profile WWE event
16. For many in sport, this is crucial
17. Pro sports teams make money through these streams
18. Golf star who endorsed GM Buick car
19. Former coach who is now the best-known non-player in the hockey world

Viewpoints on the Business of Sport

Name:
Date:
Look in the Book! Pages: 359, 361, 363, 365–366

Various athletes, agents, team owners, and media benefit from the large sums of money generated by professional sports events, and some trends in the "big" business of sport may have a varied impact on those involved.

Mission: Complete the chart below with one of the three responses: "PRO," "CON," or "NR" ("not relevant"), depending on whether you think that athletes/agents, team owners, sports fans, or broadcasters would be in favour of the sport trend indicated. Give reasons to support your opinions. A sample entry is provided below.

	Athletes/ Agents	Team Owners	Sports Fans	Broadcasters
In general, ticket prices need to be higher. ═══	PRO— expectation that increased revenue will lead to higher player salaries			
There needs to be more advertising on televised events. ═══	PRO— expectation of increased revenue			
Player's unions need to be strengthened. ═══	CON—becomes harder for average fan to attend events			
Top players' salaries are still too low. ═══	NR—Price of live admission is irrelevant to broadcaster			

Changes Inspired in Sport by Television

Name:

Date:

Look in the Book! Pages: 356–357

Of all the various forms of media, television has made the most significant and influential impact on the world of sport.

Mission: For each sport indicated in the chart below, list a fundamental change that occurred due to the influences of television coverage and/or the advertising that accompanies it. This can include: rules of the sport, the redesign of uniforms and/or equipment worn/used by the athletes, or even the duration and tempo of the sporting event. A sample entry is provided below.

Sport	Impact/Change Factor	When
1. NBA (Basketball)	"TV Time-outs" held approximately every 4 minutes to allow for more commercials during telecasts	1990s
2. NFL/CFL Football		
3. NHL Hockey		
4. Soccer		
5. Pro Boxing		
6. Pro Golf		
7. Auto Racing		
8. Pro Baseball		
9. Pro Tennis		
10. Track and field		

Jody Holden, 2000. THE CANADIAN PRESS/Scott Grant

30

School and Community Sport Programs

Learning Objectives

The exercises in this section of the workbook will help to reinforce your knowledge of the following topics covered in the *Exercise Science* textbook:

- Historical trends in the development of sport programs in Canadian schools and communities
- The rise of physical education as a subject in Canadian schools
- Early Canadian school and/or community sport pioneers
- Contemporary trends in Canadian school physical education
- Various organizations that support school physical education and sport in Canada
- The significance of sport scholarships for Canadian high-school athletes
- The basic structure of community sport programs in Canada
- Various notable Canadian sport leagues and clubs for youth
- Health and Physical Education Associations across Canada
- The growth of the YMCA and YWCA in Canada
- Significant community sport initiatives in Canada
- The role of recreational programs in helping "at-risk" youth
- How physical activity can improve overall health and personal development
- How sport helps in creating social networks
- Notable Canadians who have raised awareness of social issues through sport
- The health, social, and economic benefits of large-scale sport programs

Section Quiz

Name: _____ Date: _____

Multiple-Choice Questions

Mission: Circle the letter beside the answer that you believe to be correct.

1. In elite English private schools, physical education was

   (a) a vital part of every student's life
   (b) recognized as inherently valuable
   (c) a legitimate academic course
   (d) mainly a means for training military commanders

2. In 1910, physical education in Canadian public schools

   (a) was taught by retired military officers
   (b) featured drills, calisthenics, and gymnastics
   (c) prepared the masses for a lifetime of hard work
   (d) all of the above

3. An extensive plan for public education was developed in 1844 by

   (a) Egerton Ryerson
   (b) Thomas Arnold
   (c) Lord Strathcona
   (d) Matthew Arnold

4. According to Physical and Health Education Canada (formerly known as CAHPERD), what is the recommended weekly minimum of physical education instruction in schools?

   (a) 75 minutes
   (b) 150 minutes
   (c) 250 minutes
   (d) 100 minutes

5. The main focus of amateur hockey leagues is

   (a) learning team skills
   (b) teaching athletes to have fun
   (c) improving the competitive level of the sport
   (d) supporting amateur hockey in Canada

6. The PRYDE program features which sport to combat increasing youth inactivity?

   (a) boxing
   (b) basketball
   (c) judo
   (d) wrestling

7. At what activity do Canadian children spend most of their time?

   (a) watching television
   (b) sleeping
   (c) surfing the Net
   (d) reading

Short-Answer Questions

Mission: Briefly answer the following questions in the space provided:

1. How was the curriculum of Rugby College in England affected by its headmaster from 1828 to 1842?

2. What is the goal of the Canadian Intramural Recreation Association?

3. What factors must be considered by athletes who have been offered a sport scholarship?

4. What are the four key areas that organizers of community programs must consider. Why?

5. Name four major initiatives undertaken by the YMCA since its inception.

6. What is the most important feature of drop-in centres?

7. How many minutes of physical exercise do Canadians need per day to enjoy optimal health benefits?

Essay Questions

Mission: On a separate piece of paper, develop a 100-word response to the following questions.

1. Discuss the effect of budget cuts in the 1990s on physical education programs in schools.

2. Describe the role and work of the Canadian School Sport Federation.

3. Outline the issues that organizers of community programs must consider.

Terminology Review

Defining Key Terms

Mission: Briefly explain the meaning of the following key terms:

Name:

Date:

Key Term	Definition
Muscular Christianity	
Canadian Association for Health, Physical Education, Recreation and Dance (CAHPERD)—now known as Physical and Health Education Canada	
Canadian Intramural Recreation Association	
Canadian School Sport Federation	
Coaching Association of Canada (CAC)	
Sport Leadership Program	

Canadian Hockey Association (CHA)	
Community recreation centres	
Ophea (Ontario Physical and Health Education Association)	
Young Men's Christian Association (YMCA)	
Drop-in centre programs	
Midnight Basketball League	
Grass Roots Canada Basketball	
ESTEEM Team	
Quality of life	

Developing a Community Sport League

Name:

Date:

There are many organizational aspects to running school- and community-based sport programs. One must consider all the various costs involved, the facilities and equipment available for use, policies that govern play, and volunteer staff versus paid staff.

Mission: Begin by forming groups of 3 to 5 students. Imagine that your group has volunteered to act as the executive committee for a new soccer league for children thirteen years of age and under in your community. The league has been given $5,000 through a municipal grant to begin operations. You will also be able to collect registration fees from your players.

Your task is to begin to organize the league's first year of play. Some of the information below will be for organizational purposes; in some cases, you will be required to input dollar figures. Also,

you will need to decide which age divisions will incorporate mixed boys and girls play, and which will be single-sex only.

Finally, on the next page, complete an income and expense budget for the first year. Keep in mind that your expenses must not exceed what you take in. It is also a good idea to have some money left over for the following year's executive to work with. In some instances, research will be required (e.g., to discover the cost of field rental, insurance, and equipment in your community).

Kick-Off Youth Soccer League: Preparation Notes

President	
Vice-President	
Secretary	
Total target registration (Boys/Girls)	
What is the league's "philosophy" (e.g., "fun league" or "competitive league")? How will this philosophy be articulated to players and coaches?	
Number of age divisions and age breakdown (e.g., under-5; under-7; etc.) for girls-only, boys only, and mixed?	
How will the league be promoted and advertised to prospective players and their parents?	
Will officials be involved on a voluntary basis (e.g., parents and coaches) or will paid officials be required (e.g., referees)? If paid officials are needed, what is the cost per division?	
Cost of insurance for league?	
Cost of field(s) rental?	
Cost of uniforms purchase?	
Costs of equipment (e.g., balls, nets, etc.)?	
Registration fee per player: Are basic player photograph costs included in registration fee? Cost of trophies, awards to players? Cost of year-end party? Cost of coach/volunteer "appreciation night?"	
Cost (if any) of registering league with larger organization (e.g., Canadian Soccer Association)?	
What policies exist within the community recreation structure that will govern league play? (e.g., city-wide facilities policy on zero-tolerance for violence)?	
Other considerations	

Sample Income and Expenditure Statement

The income and expenditure statement below is from a real community tennis club. Use it to model your own expected "income and expenditure" statement for a hypothetical local club. Cross out the expenditure items that do not apply and substitute new expenditure items

and dollar figures as necessary for the club you are setting up.

If you wish to do this in a spreadsheet program, the sample below (which you can modify as required) is available at: www.thompsonbooks.com/hpe/incomesample.xls

COMMUNITY TENNIS CLUB

Statement of Income and Expenses and Members' Equity
For The Year Ended September 30, 2008

	(SAMPLE) 2008 $	
Income		
Membership fees	26,506.00	_____
Interest	798.00	_____
Other income	-	
	27,304.00	_____
Expenses		
Audit fee	-	
Bank charges	76.00	_____
Court steward fees	1,883.00	_____
Junior program	1,783.00	_____
Tennis balls	1,573.00	_____
Team expenses	170.00	_____
Trophies, prizes and gifts	-	_____
Repairs and maintenance	147.00	_____
Social events	3,323.00	_____
Insurance	1,148.00	_____
Ontario Tennis Association	-	_____
Postage and printing	826.00	_____
Telephone	-	_____
Shoe tags	442.00	_____
Meetings	-	_____
Website	88.00	_____
	11,459.00	_____
Excess of income over expenses	15,845.00	_____
Court renovations	56,817.00	_____
Excess of expenses over income	**(40,972.00)**	_____
Members' Equity		
Equity, beginning of year	77,353.00	_____
Equity, end of year	**36,381.00**	_____

American Sport Scholarships Available to Canadian Athletes

Name:

Date:

For Canadian high-school athletes, there are a number of important issues to consider when offered a sports scholarship to a university or college in the United States. The following exercise requires you to conduct research into the nature of these scholarships.

Mission: Choose four sports in which sports scholarships are available at U.S. colleges and universities. Use the Internet (two important sites to visit are the official sites of the National Collegiate Athletic Association at www.ncaa.org and www.ncaasports.com to do your research) and complete the chart below.

A sample entry using the sport of tennis has been provided in the table below.

Sport	Number of NCAA Division One Schools That Compete in this Sport	Number of Scholarships Available in NCAA Competition	A Canadian Athlete Currently Competing on Scholarship (incl. Hometown, and School Affiliation)	Current NCAA Division One Champion School in this Sport (Men and Women)
Women's Field Hockey	Total:77	Total: 1087	Maire Dineen (Toronto, ON) University of Maine	North Carolina
Sport 1:				

Sport	Number of NCAA Division One Schools That Compete in this Sport	Number of Scholarships Available in NCAA Competition	A Canadian Athlete Currently Competing on Scholarship (incl. Hometown, and School Affiliation)	Current NCAA Division One Champion School in this Sport
Sport 2:				
Sport 3:				
Sport 4:				

31

Social and Ethical Problems in Sport

Men's Speed Skating Team, 2002. THE CANADIAN PRESS/COC/Andre Forget

Learning Objectives

The exercises in this section of the workbook will help to reinforce your knowledge of the following topics covered in the *Exercise Science* textbook:

- The role that ethical and social considerations play in sport at all levels
- How Canada has developed its own strategy for the development of a policy in ethical conduct in sport
- The role of violence and aggression in sport
- Various modes of sports violence
- The numerous ways it is possible to cheat at sport, including recruitment violations, corruption of officials, and bribery
- The use of drugs in sport, including the history of drug use, drug-testing "mistakes," the World Anti-Doping Agency, and the use of "recreational" drugs
- The significance of tobacco and alcohol sponsorships for sporting events
- Gambling and its impact on sport

Section Quiz

Name: _____ Date: _____

Multiple-choice Questions

Mission: Circle the letter beside the answer that you believe to be correct.

1. The Ottawa-based Canadian Centre for Ethics in Sport is responsible for
    (a) co-creating the Canadian Strategy for Ethical Conduct in Sport
    (b) administering Canada's drug-free sport policy
    (c) policy making in the promotion of drug-free, fair, and ethical sport
    (d) all of the above

2. Factors that increase the likelihood of violence in sports include:
    (a) high scoring games
    (b) higher athletes salaries
    (c) decrease in ticket sales
    (d) fans having unrealistically high expectations of a team

3. During the 2002 World Cup, a Korean man did this to support his nation's soccer team.
    (a) lit himself on fire
    (b) went on a hunger strike
    (c) chained himself to the stadium
    (d) none of the above

4. In Canada, in order for athletes to retain amateur status, they cannot
    (a) deny any incentives offered
    (b) be over fifteen
    (c) accept any money or promised payment
    (d) refuse coaching assistance from the government

5. When attempting to persuade student-athletes to accept scholarships, coaches sometimes commit recruiting violations that can include
    (a) free hotel rooms
    (b) money
    (c) gifts
    (d) all of the above

6. Which of the following have been proven to enhance athletic performance?
    (a) cocaine
    (b) heroin
    (c) marijuana
    (d) none of the above

7. In Ontario, betting on sports for adult sports fans is
    (a) illegal
    (b) legal and unregulated
    (c) illegal but generally tolerated
    (d) legal but highly regulated

Short-answer Questions

Mission: Briefly answer the following questions in the space provided:

1. Why was the Canadian Strategy for Ethical Conduct in Sport created ?

    _____

2. What action did the NHL take against Marty McSorley for his attack against Donald Brashear?

    _____

3. What is the worst example of soccer fan violence in recent times?

    _____

4. List various methods athletes use to cheat?

    _____

5. What honour did the members of the Asahi baseball team, interned during the Second World War, recently receive?

    _____

6. According to the head of the CCES, Paul Melia, who is ultimately responsible for how an athlete does on a urine test?

    _____

    _____

Essay Questions

Mission: On a separate piece of paper, develop a 100-word response to the following questions.

1. Outline the goals of the Canadian Strategy for Ethical Conduct in Sport.

2. Discuss why bribery has entered the bidding process for the right to host the Olympic Games.

3. Summarize the history of steroid use in athletic competition.

Terminology Review

Defining Key Terms

Mission: Briefly explain the meaning of the following key terms:

Name:

Date:

Key Term	Definition
Canadian Strategy for Ethical Conduct in Sport	
Canadian Centre for Ethics in Sport	
Instrumental aggression	
Hostile aggression	
Cheating	
Recruiting violations	
Corruption of judges and officials	
World Anti-Doping Agency	
World Anti-Doping Code	
Athlete's Passport Program	
"Recreational" drug use	
Sports gambling	

Crossword on Social and Ethical Problems in Sport

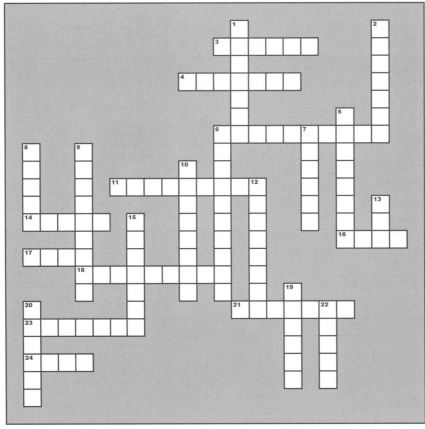

Across

3. Spectator violence among the fans of this sport is a large problem in England
4. Pete Rose of the Cincinnati Reds was banned from baseball for life because of this
6. Violations intended to entice players to choose a particular university
11. Because of their decision-making responsibilities, they are often the target of fan violence
14. Tennis player stabbed by fan of Steffi Graf
16. Along with Pelletier, this skater maintained dignity in a corrupt judging case
17. Toronto Maple Leaf renowned for fighting
18. Altering this necessity of sport is a form of cheating
21. Soccer player subsequently murdered for scoring on his own goal in World Cup soccer
23. "Recreational" substance often used by athletes to ease stress
24. Acronym for Canadian organization that develops policies on ethical issues in sport

Down

1. Type of aggression featuring the deliberate intent to harm another player
2. Many believe this needs to be reformed in many sports
5. In basesball, these players cheat by changing the flight properties of the ball
6. Canadian athlete stripped of his gold medal for marijuana use
7. A difficult thing for officials to determine when a player has been injured by another
8. Nine-time Olympic gold medallist accused of failing a drug test at 1988 U.S. Olympic Trials
9. Large sponsors of sporting events
10. Criminal charges were brought against this Bruins' player who smashed Donald Brashear over the head with his stick
12. The side effects of these drugs was unknown until the late 1950s
13. Acronym of professional sports league that opposes drug testing of players
15. Conduct that must be taught universally and from a young age
19. The first athletes charged with this were European swimmers in the 1860s
20. Rule-breakers have traditionally "succeeded" in this racing series
22. Team composed of Japanese-Canadians that came to dominate in the Pacific Northwest

Ethical Issues in Sport

Name:
Date:

There is a wide range of ethical considerations that emerge every day on the world sporting stage.

Mission: Using any media outlet that reports regularly on sport, research five recent examples of an ethical controversy in the world of sport, and complete the chart below. Sources for your research can include:

- any major Canadian newspaper (such as the *Globe and Mail, Toronto Star, National Post,* and so on) or even foreign newspapers (note that most newspapers have complete editions online);

- any sports magazine (such as *Sports Illustrated* or *The Hockey News*);

- any news broadcast on TV or radio that includes sports highlights;

- any live broadcast on TV or radio of a sporting event.

A sample entry is provided below.

Media Story	Summary of Events and Ethical Consideration in Question
1. "Teen charged in alleged hockey-stick assault" www.thestar.com/article/420798 (May, 02, 2008)	Seventeen-year-old hockey player charged with assault with a weapon after an alleged stick-swinging incident during an Ontario Minor Hockey Association game that ruptured the victim's spleen. Issue: Violence and aggression in sports
2.	
3.	
4.	
5.	
6.	

Drug Violations in International Sport

Name:

Date:

Some athletes are willing to use any means necessary to gain an advantage and have been caught using banned performance-enhancing substances. This violation has seriously affected, and in some cases ended, an athlete's career.

Mission: Using a variety of sources, fill in the following table with as much information as possible on five athletes who have been caught using performance-enhancing substances in the sports listed below. It is recommended that you do a quick review of Section 11 of the text (Performance-Enhancing Substances and Techniques) before completing the chart. A sample entry has been provided in the table below.

Sport	Athlete/Country	Event/Date Tested Positive	Result of Test (Action Taken)	Summary of Career After Testing Positive
1. Track and field (men)	Ben Johnson (Canada)	1988 Seoul Olympics, positive test came after win in men's 100 metre in world-record time	Stripped of gold medal; banned from sport for 3 years; also stripped of earlier world record	Attempted comeback; failed drug test again in 1993 and banned for life from track and field
2. Track and field (women)				
3. Weightlifting (men)				
4. Swimming (women)				
5. Any other sport of your choice (men or women)				

CHAPTER 32

Unit 5 Career Choices

Investigate a career in one of the fields covered in Unit 5. Ideally, you should interview someone working within the field for this assignment.

1 Career and description

_____

_____

_____

_____

2 List at least two post-secondary institutions in Ontario and/or Canada that offer programs for this career.

_____

_____

_____

3 Choose one of the above institutions and determine the required courses in the first year of study for this program.

_____

_____

_____

4 What is the total length of the education needed to begin this career? Is an internship or apprenticeship required?

_____

_____

_____

5 What is the demand for individuals qualified for this occupation? If possible, provide some employment data to support your answer.

_____

_____

_____

6 What is the average starting salary for this career? What is the top salary? On what do salary increases depend in this career?

_____

_____

_____

7 List occupational settings where a person with these qualifications could work.

_____   _____

_____   _____

CHAPTER 33

Unit 5 Crossword Challenge

Across

3. Olympic judges and officials may be guilty of this
6. Type of Christianity coined by Thomas Hughes
8. Their loyalty is the central asset of a sports franchise
9. Negotiator of a player's salary with team owners
11. The appearance of athletes in advertisements for products
12. Recreation centres that offer a common meeting ground
17. Rights to telecast games
19. Violations intended to entice players to choose a particular university
20. What the Coaching Association of Canada offers at various levels
22. Attempt to gain an unfair advantage in training or in competition
23. Athletes who receive no financial rewards for their efforts

Down

1. Canadian association that offers programs for training and certification of coaches
2. Food and beverage venues in stadiums
4. Athlete's program that allows athlete's to demonstrate their commitment to keeping sports clean of drug use
5. Type of aggression marked by the deliberate intent to harm another player
6. Collective term for television, radio, newspapers, and so on
7. Acronym for the Ottawa-based national charitable organization that promotes exercise in schools
10. The use of such drugs as marijuana, cocaine, or heroin
12. Activities in which athletes can serve as positive role models by raising funds
13. Canadian recreation association that seeks to reduce physical inactivity through sport in education
14. Athletes who receive financial rewards for their efforts
15. In Canada, this aspect of sport is legal but highly regulated
16. Type of aggression in which injury of another player is a side effect
18. Conduct promoted by the Canadian Centre for Ethics in Sport
21. Founded by Englishman George Williams in the 1840s

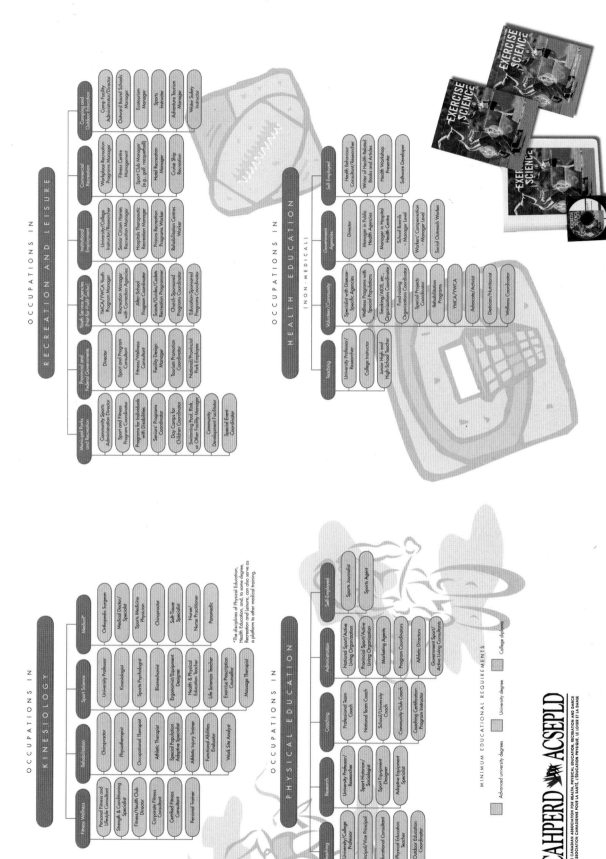

OCCUPATIONS IN RECREATION AND LEISURE

Camping and Outdoor Education:
- Camp Facility Administrator/Director
- Outward Bound Schools Manager
- Ecotourism Manager
- Sports Instructor
- Adventure Tourism Manager
- Water Safety Instructor

Commercial Recreation:
- Workplace Recreation Programs Manager
- Fitness Centre Management
- Sport Club Manager (e.g., golf, racquetball)
- Hotel Recreation Manager
- Cruise Ship Recreation

Institutional Employment:
- University/College Instructor/Researcher
- Senior Citizen Homes Recreation Manager
- Hospital Therapeutic Recreation Manager
- Prison Recreation Programs Worker
- Rehabilitation Centres Worker

Youth Service Agencies (Not-for-Profit Sector):
- YMCA/YWCA Youth Program Manager
- Recreation Manager with Correction Agencies
- Scouts/Guides/Cadets Recreation Programmer
- Church-Sponsored Programs Coordinator
- Education-Sponsored Programs Coordinator

Provincial and Federal Governments:
- Director
- Sport and Program Consultant
- Fitness/Wellness Consultant
- Facility Design Coordinator
- Tourism Promotion Coordinator
- National/Provincial Park Employee

Municipal Parks and Recreation:
- Community Sports Administration Director
- Sport and Fitness Program Coordinator
- Programs for Individuals with Disabilities
- Seniors' Programs Coordinator
- Day Camps for Children Coordinator
- Swimming Pool, Rink, or Other Facility Manager
- Community Development Facilitator
- Special Event Coordinator

OCCUPATIONS IN HEALTH EDUCATION (NON-MEDICAL)

Self-Employed:
- Health Behaviour Consultant/Researcher
- Writer of Health-Related Books and Articles
- Health Workshop Presenter
- Software Developer

Government Agencies:
- Director
- Manager in Public Health Agencies
- Manager in Hospital Health Centre
- School Boards – Manager Level
- Workers' Compensation – Manager Level
- Social Outreach Worker

Volunteer/Community:
- Specialist with Disease-Specific Agencies
- Wellness Programs with Special Populations
- Smoking/AIDS, etc. Organizations Coordinator
- Fund-raising Organizations Coordinator
- Special Projects Coordinator
- Rehabilitation Programs
- YMCA/YWCA
- Advocate/Activist
- Dietician/Nutritionist
- Wellness Coordinator

Teaching:
- University Professor/Researcher
- College Instructor
- Junior High and High School Teacher

OCCUPATIONS IN KINESIOLOGY

Medical*:
- Orthopedic Surgeon
- Medical Doctor/Specialist
- Sports Medicine Physician
- Chiropractor
- Soft-Tissue Specialist
- Nurse/Nurse Practitioner
- Paramedic

Sport Science:
- University Professor
- Kinesiologist
- Sports Psychologist
- Biomechanist
- Ergonomist/Equipment Designer
- Health & Physical Education Teacher
- Life Sciences Teacher
- Exercise Prescription Counsellor
- Massage Therapist

Rehabilitation:
- Chiropractor
- Physiotherapist
- Occupational Therapist
- Athletic Therapist
- Special Population Adaptive Specialist
- Athletic Injury Trainer
- Functional Abilities Evaluator
- Work Site Analyst

Fitness/Wellness:
- Personal Fitness and Lifestyle Consultant
- Strength & Conditioning Specialist
- Fitness/Health Club Director
- Corporate Fitness Consultant
- Certified Fitness Consultant
- Personal Trainer

*The disciplines of Physical Education, Health Education, and, to some degree, Recreation and Leisure, can also serve as a platform to other medical training.

OCCUPATIONS IN PHYSICAL EDUCATION

Self-Employed:
- Sports Journalist
- Sports Agent

Administration:
- National Sport/Active Living Organization
- Provincial Sport/Active Living Organization
- Marketing Agents
- Program Coordinators
- Athletic Directors
- Government Sport/Active Living Consultants

Coaching:
- Professional Team Coach
- National Team Coach
- School/University Coach
- Community Club Coach
- Coaching Certification Program Instructor

Research:
- University Professor/Researcher
- Sport Historian/Sociologist
- Sport Equipment Designer
- Adaptive Equipment Specialist

Teaching:
- University/College Professor
- Principal/Vice Principal
- Educational Consultant
- Physical Education Teacher
- Outdoor Education Coordinator

MINIMUM EDUCATIONAL REQUIREMENTS
- Advanced university degrees
- University degree
- College diploma

CAHPERD ACSEPLD
THE CANADIAN ASSOCIATION FOR HEALTH, PHYSICAL EDUCATION, RECREATION AND DANCE
L'ASSOCIATION CANADIENNE POUR LA SANTÉ, L'ÉDUCATION PHYSIQUE, LE LOISIR ET LA DANSE

TEP

www.thompsonbooks.com

◆ Exercise Science — Careers Chart

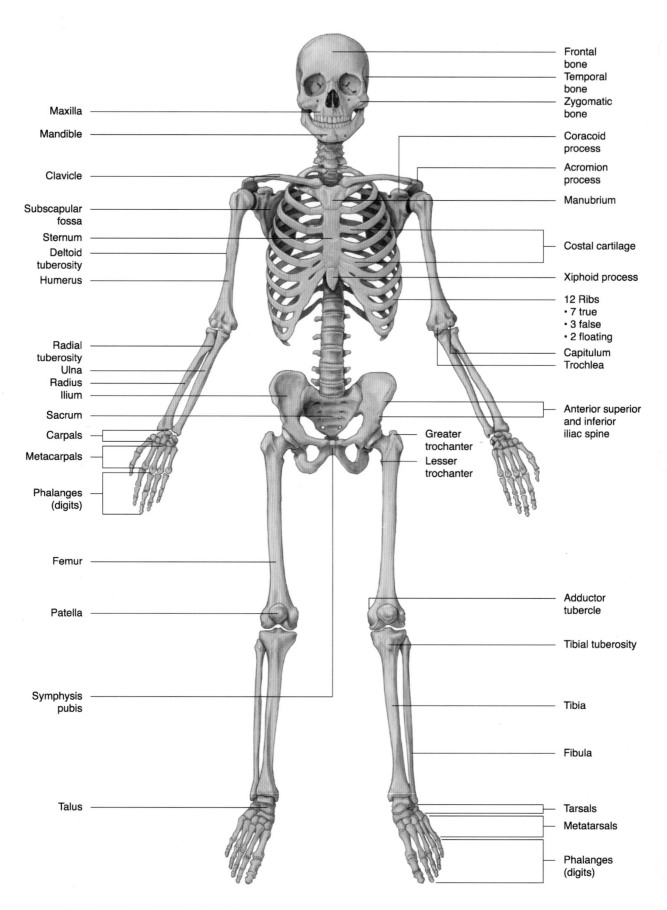

Frontal
bone

Temporal
bone

Zygomatic
bone

Maxilla

Mandible

Coracoid
process

Clavicle

Acromion
process

Subscapular
fossa

Manubrium

Sternum

Deltoid
tuberosity

Costal cartilage

Humerus

Xiphoid process

12 Ribs
• 7 true
• 3 false
• 2 floating

Radial
tuberosity

Capitulum

Ulna

Trochlea

Radius

Ilium

Sacrum

Carpals

Anterior superior
and inferior
iliac spine

Metacarpals

Greater
trochanter

Lesser
trochanter

Phalanges
(digits)

Femur

Adductor
tubercle

Patella

Tibial tuberosity

Symphysis
pubis

Tibia

Fibula

Talus

Tarsals

Metatarsals

Phalanges
(digits)

◆ The Human Skeleton — Anterior View

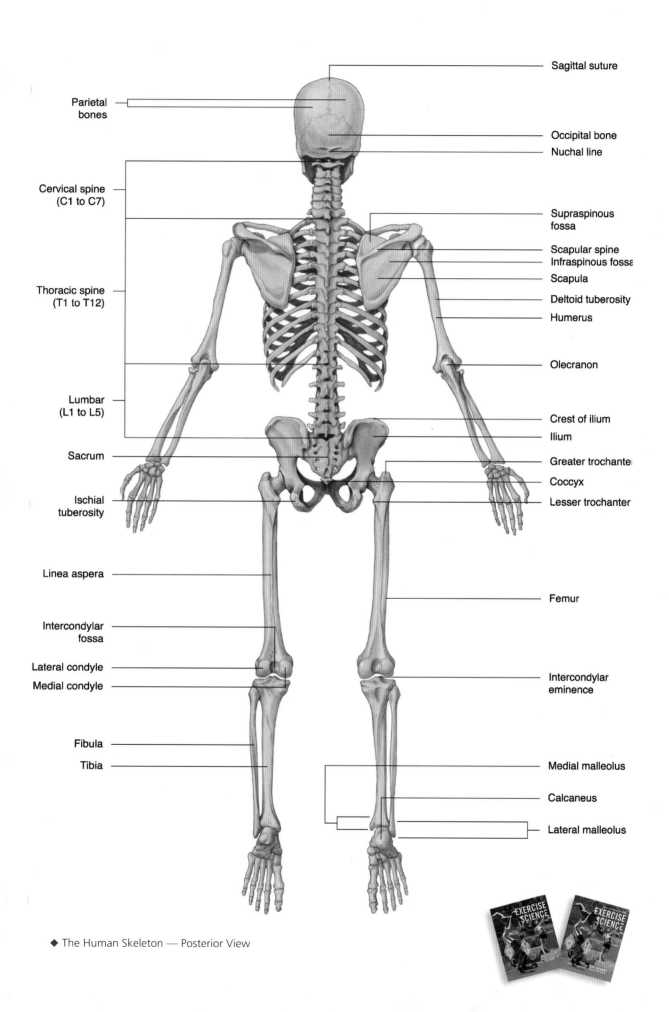

Sagittal suture

Parietal bones

Occipital bone

Nuchal line

Cervical spine (C1 to C7)

Supraspinous fossa

Scapular spine

Infraspinous fossa

Scapula

Thoracic spine (T1 to T12)

Deltoid tuberosity

Humerus

Olecranon

Lumbar (L1 to L5)

Crest of ilium

Ilium

Sacrum

Greater trochanter

Coccyx

Ischial tuberosity

Lesser trochanter

Linea aspera

Femur

Intercondylar fossa

Lateral condyle

Medial condyle

Intercondylar eminence

Fibula

Tibia

Medial malleolus

Calcaneus

Lateral malleolus

◆ The Human Skeleton — Posterior View

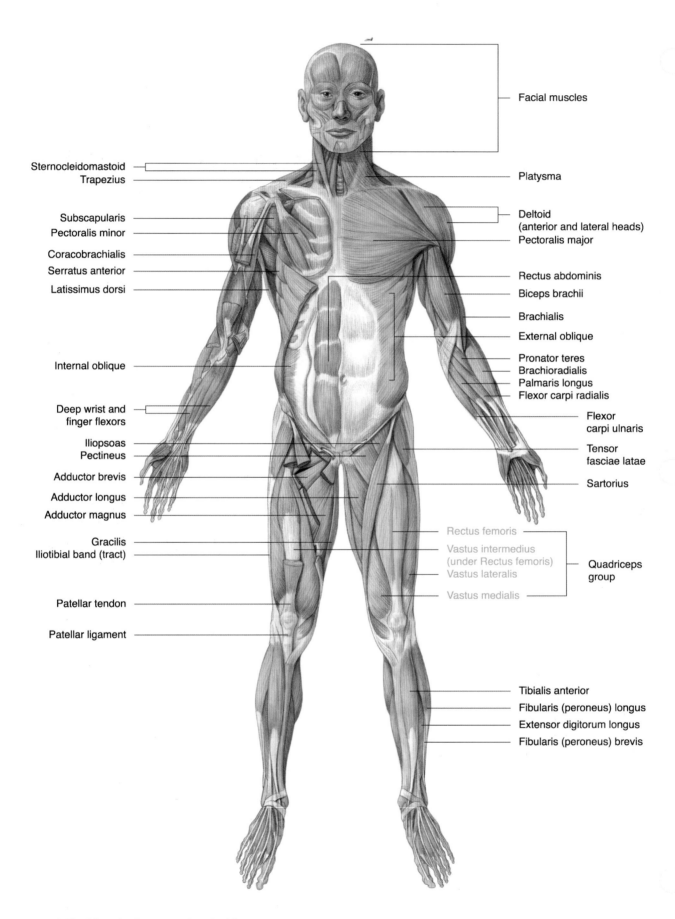

Sternocleidomastoid

Trapezius

Subscapularis

Pectoralis minor

Coracobrachialis

Serratus anterior

Latissimus dorsi

Internal oblique

Deep wrist and
finger flexors

Iliopsoas

Pectineus

Adductor brevis

Adductor longus

Adductor magnus

Gracilis

Iliotibial band (tract)

Patellar tendon

Patellar ligament

Facial muscles

Platysma

Deltoid
(anterior and lateral heads)

Pectoralis major

Rectus abdominis

Biceps brachii

Brachialis

External oblique

Pronator teres

Brachioradialis

Palmaris longus

Flexor carpi radialis

Flexor
carpi ulnaris

Tensor
fasciae latae

Sartorius

Rectus femoris

Vastus intermedius
(under Rectus femoris)

Vastus lateralis

Vastus medialis

Quadriceps
group

Tibialis anterior

Fibularis (peroneus) longus

Extensor digitorum longus

Fibularis (peroneus) brevis

◆ The Muscular System — Anterior View

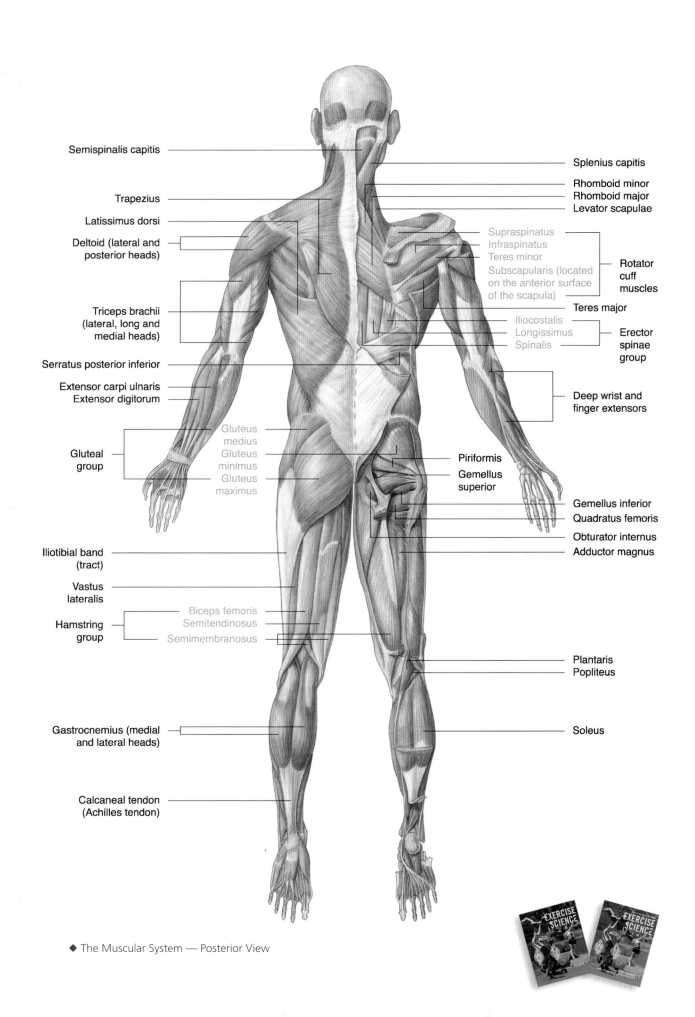

Semispinalis capitis

Trapezius

Latissimus dorsi

Deltoid (lateral and posterior heads)

Triceps brachii (lateral, long and medial heads)

Serratus posterior inferior

Extensor carpi ulnaris
Extensor digitorum

Gluteal group

Gluteus medius
Gluteus minimus
Gluteus maximus

Iliotibial band (tract)

Vastus lateralis

Hamstring group

Biceps femoris
Semitendinosus
Semimembranosus

Gastrocnemius (medial and lateral heads)

Calcaneal tendon (Achilles tendon)

Splenius capitis

Rhomboid minor
Rhomboid major
Levator scapulae

Supraspinatus
Infraspinatus
Teres minor
Subscapularis (located on the anterior surface of the scapula)

Rotator cuff muscles

Teres major

Iliocostalis
Longissimus
Spinalis

Erector spinae group

Deep wrist and finger extensors

Piriformis
Gemellus superior

Gemellus inferior
Quadratus femoris

Obturator internus

Adductor magnus

Plantaris
Popliteus

Soleus

◆ The Muscular System — Posterior View

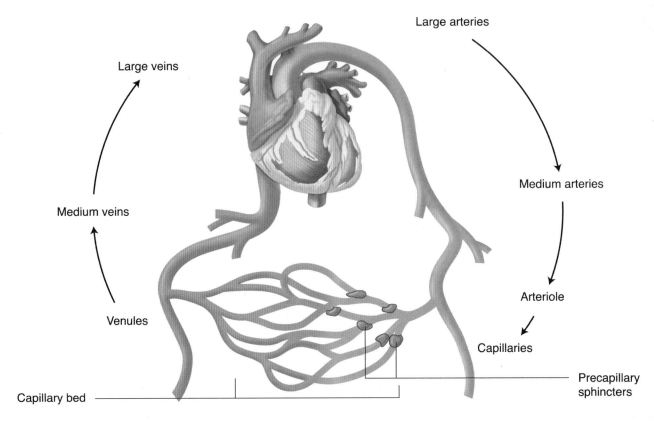

Large veins

Medium veins

Venules

Capillary bed

Large arteries

Medium arteries

Arteriole

Capillaries

Precapillary
sphincters

◆ The Vascular System (Summary)

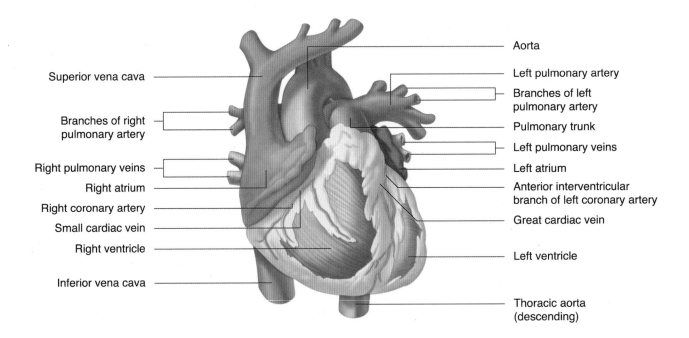

Superior vena cava

Branches of right
pulmonary artery

Right pulmonary veins

Right atrium

Right coronary artery

Small cardiac vein

Right ventricle

Inferior vena cava

Aorta

Left pulmonary artery

Branches of left
pulmonary artery

Pulmonary trunk

Left pulmonary veins

Left atrium

Anterior interventricular
branch of left coronary artery

Great cardiac vein

Left ventricle

Thoracic aorta
(descending)

◆ Coronary Vessels and Other Major Structures (Anterior View)

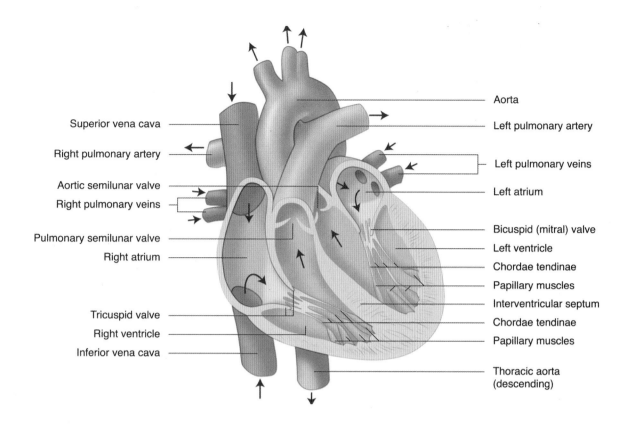

Superior vena cava

Right pulmonary artery

Aortic semilunar valve

Right pulmonary veins

Pulmonary semilunar valve

Right atrium

Tricuspid valve

Right ventricle

Inferior vena cava

Aorta

Left pulmonary artery

Left pulmonary veins

Left atrium

Bicuspid (mitral) valve

Left ventricle

Chordae tendinae

Papillary muscles

Interventricular septum

Chordae tendinae

Papillary muscles

Thoracic aorta
(descending)

◆ Anatomy of the Heart Showing the Flow of Blood

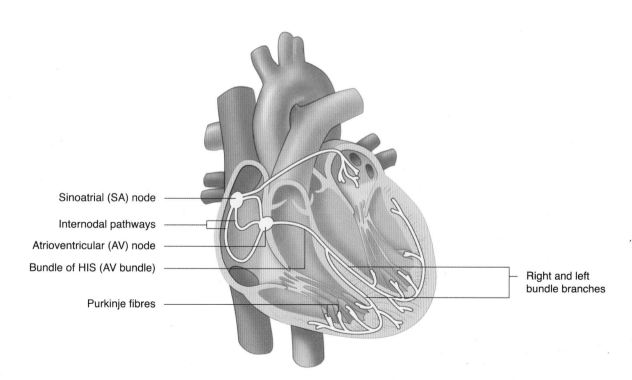

Sinoatrial (SA) node

Internodal pathways

Atrioventricular (AV) node

Bundle of HIS (AV bundle)

Purkinje fibres

Right and left
bundle branches

◆ Electrical Conduction System of the Heart

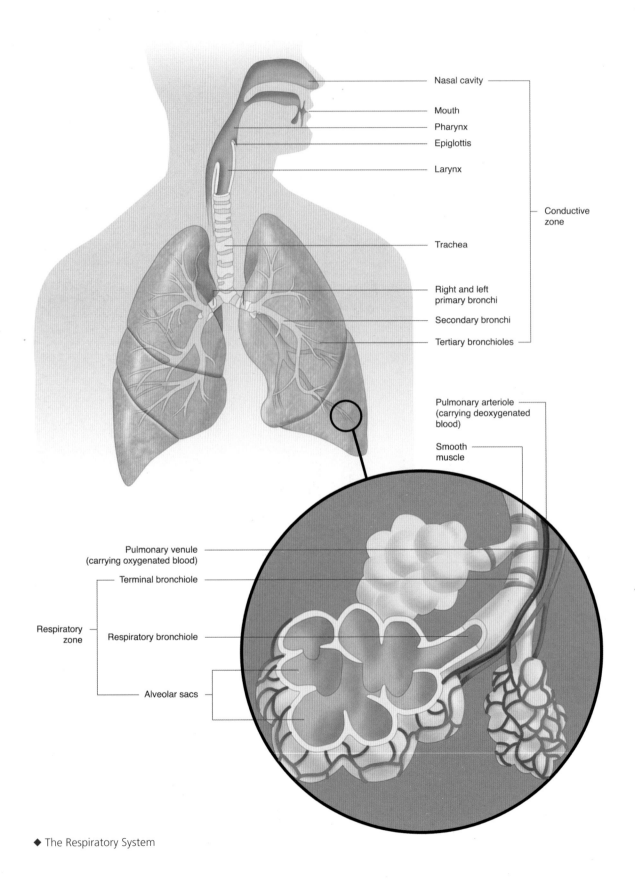

Nasal cavity

Mouth

Pharynx

Epiglottis

Larynx

Trachea

Right and left
primary bronchi

Secondary bronchi

Tertiary bronchioles

Conductive
zone

Pulmonary arteriole
(carrying deoxygenated
blood)

Smooth
muscle

Pulmonary venule
(carrying oxygenated blood)

Terminal bronchiole

Respiratory bronchiole

Respiratory
zone

Alveolar sacs

◆ The Respiratory System